Living on Little

Praise for this book

'*Living on Little* is a rich exploration of ordinary Kenyans' money lives, painting a detailed picture of the painful tradeoffs poverty forces and the incredible investments people are making to build better lives. It is a powerful reminder to keep our eyes open to the systemic barriers that hold ordinary people—and especially women—back from achieving their full potential.'

Rodger Voorhies, President, Global Growth and Opportunity,
Bill & Melinda Gates Foundation

'This book gives insights on the resilience of low-income Kenyans, how the unbankable became bankable through innovative solutions such as M-Shwari, which was launched seven years ago. *Living on Little* is about empowerment and financial inclusion.'

Isaac Awuondo, Chairman, NCBA Bank Kenya PLC

'Julie has provided us with a valuable window into the complex lives of low-income people in Kenya, through the lens of how they earn and manage their money. The stories told go far beyond dry financial details and illustrate the difficult trade-offs made every day by those who simply do not earn enough. They also tell us much about the social dynamics in households and society, as control over scarce resources is often central to both. This is a must-read for anyone working in development, whether in financial services or any other field. It is a compelling story about people who must do so much with so little.'

Greta Bull, CEO of CGAP

'The Financial Diaries are an outstanding resource that document what it means for people to be financially empowered with relevant technologies such as M-PESA. As different Kenyans narrate their lived experiences, we get to appreciate how innovation is useful and the need to support and encourage it.'

Sitoyo Lopokoiyit, Chief Financial Services Officer, Safaricom

'A compelling reading on aspirations and financial strategies of Kenyans who live on little, but maintain focus on advancing their livelihoods for development. The book seamlessly uses money lens to unearth the several income streams that enable a significant Kenya population to have an agency and plan their own future, despite continually being undermined by structural realities of governance.'

Winnie V. Mitullah, Professor of Development Studies,
Institute for Development Studies, University of Nairobi

Living on Little

Navigating financial scarcity in modern Kenya

Julie Zollmann

Practical
ACTION
PUBLISHING

Practical Action Publishing Ltd
27a Albert Street, Rugby, Warwickshire, CV21 2SG, UK

www.practicalactionpublishing.com

A catalogue record for this book is available from the British Library.

A catalogue record for this book has been requested from the Library of Congress.

ISBN 9781-7-8853-1-177 Paperback
ISBN 9781-7-8853-1-184 Hardback
ISBN 9781-7-8853-1-191 Epub
ISBN 9781-7-8853-1-207 PDF

Citation: Zollmann, J. (2020) *Living on Little: Navigating financial scarcity in modern Kenya*, Practical Action Publishing, Rugby <http://dx.doi.org/10.3362/9781788531207>.

Since 1974, Practical Action Publishing has published and disseminated books and information in support of international development work throughout the world. Practical Action Publishing is a trading name of Practical Action Publishing Ltd (Company Reg. No. 1159018), the wholly owned publishing company of Practical Action. Practical Action Publishing trades only in support of its parent charity objectives and any profits are covenanted back to Practical Action (Charity Reg. No. 247257, Group VAT Registration No. 880 9924 76).

Cover photos by Abraham Ali for FSD Kenya.
Cover design by RCO.design
Printed on demand

Contents

Pseudonym index   vii
Acknowledgements   xv
Preface   xvii

1. Introduction: Listening to Kenyans through Financial Diaries   1

2. Looking for money: Generating income from a variety of sources   15

3. Managing money: Meeting daily needs and investing for the future   39

4. Growing up: The challenges of low income for children and young people   69

5. Being a woman: How social norms affect women's lives and livelihoods   91

6. Staying alive: The difficulty in financing healthcare   123

7. Being a citizen: Interactions between low-income people and government   145

8. Living the dream: Hopeful stories of achievement and aspiration   175

Appendix: Methodological note   185
Index   195

http://dx.doi.org/10.3362/9781788531207.000

Pseudonym index

Throughout this book you will meet many of the participants in the Kenya Financial Diaries. Participants' personal information is meant to be confidential, so we have given all respondents pseudonyms and changed identifying details of their stories to protect that privacy. Some respondents will appear in the book more than once. References to specific individuals are provided below.

Pseudonym	Region	Chapter	Notes
Jeremiah and Lenah	Eldoret	Preface	HIV-positive parents lacking money to take a sick child to hospital
Alice	Vihiga	2 Looking for money	Starts a business because of irregularity of remittances
Christopher	Eldoret	2 Looking for money	Runs a spice business and layers different types of businesses on top because of market saturation (also in Chapter 8, 'Living the dream')
Ellen	Eldoret	2 Looking for money	Son with prolonged abdominal problem for which she must save up over several years (also in Chapter 6, 'Staying alive')
Emmah	Vihiga	2 Looking for money	Suffers the loss of entire flock of chickens (also in Chapter 6, 'Staying alive')
Jennifer	Nairobi	2 Looking for money	Demonstration of a constellation of livelihood activities (also in Chapter 3, 'Managing money'; Chapter 4, 'Growing up')
Karen	Mombasa	2 Looking for money	Grows her *mandazi* business until reaches limits of both the market and her time
Leonita	Makueni	2 Looking for money	Prototypical remittance experience
Maggie	Nairobi	2 Looking for money	Grandmother (of Franklin) who has taken in three grandchildren even though she has little financial ability to care for them (also in Chapter 4, 'Growing up')
Patricia	Eldoret	2 Looking for money	Extreme poverty, no social network, stops ARV treatment
Phillip	Eldoret	2 Looking for money	Starts a butchery business with dowry received when daughter marries

Pseudonym	Region	Chapter	Notes
Samuel	Nairobi	2 Looking for money	Successful businessman in Nairobi, who sees his livelihood as a partnership with his wife
Auntie	Nairobi	3 Managing money	Demonstrates the complexity of managing short- and long-term savings needs in the face of very volatile earnings
Candy	Eldoret	3 Managing money	Unable to come up with small amount of money for malaria treatment (also in Chapter 6, 'Staying alive')
Faith	Makueni	3 Managing money	Example of trade-offs between food and education expenses
Jennifer	Nairobi	3 Managing money	Income volatile from month to month (also in Chapter 2, 'Looking for money'; Chapter 4, 'Growing up')
Patrick	Nairobi	3 Managing money	Demonstrates the use of a complex financial portfolio to meet long- and short-term needs (also in Chapter 4, 'Growing up'; Chapter 5, 'Being a woman'; Chapter 7, 'Being a citizen')
Rachel	Vihiga	3 Managing money	Groundnuts salesperson whose daily cash flows show the need for constant, daily money management
Valerie	Vihiga	3 Managing money	Talks about buying her goods daily from different vendors in order to secure credit access
Alice	Mombasa	4 Growing up	Worried about a son (Brian) who has dropped out of school to drive motorbikes (also in Chapter 6, 'Staying alive')
Anna	Vihiga	4 Growing up	Alcoholic son and grandson interfere with farming livelihood
Bendetta	Vihiga	4 Growing up	Alcoholic stepson (Clemence) makes her life very difficult, causes fear, and family unable to intervene
Brian	Mombasa	4 Growing up	Alice's son who dropped out of school to drive motorbikes
Christine	Nairobi	4 Growing up	Sex worker in Nairobi, worried that her daughter (Wambui) will not have a better life
Clemence	Vihiga	4 Growing up	Stepson of Bendetta, an alcoholic who seems to intentionally make his stepmother's life difficult, trying to force her off the family property

Pseudonym	Region	Chapter	Notes
Daniel	Vihiga	4 Growing up	Very promising student (son of Violet) forced to move to a cheaper, low-quality school where he loses motivation
Franklin	Nairobi	4 Growing up	Maggie's grandson with no surviving parent; has repeated pre-school three times because his grandmother cannot afford primary school fees
Geoffrey	Nairobi	4 Growing up	Starts a kiosk at a young age and builds it into a layered business
Jennifer	Nairobi	4 Growing up	Raised by relatives, leaves school early, and marries a 'thug' (also in Chapter 2, 'Looking for money'; Chapter 3, 'Managing money')
John	Nairobi	4 Growing up	After very promising start, drifts into gun making and robbery before repurposing metalworking skills
Leah	Nairobi	4 Growing up	Gets an exciting and lucky break with a modelling job
Lilyan	Vihiga	4 Growing up	Postpones marriage to try to get a job or education of her own
Maggie	Nairobi	4 Growing up	Grandmother (of Franklin) who has taken in three grandchildren even though she has little financial ability to care for them (also in Chapter 2, 'Looking for money')
Marie	Nairobi	4 Growing up	Matthew's wife, left behind at his rural home while he builds a career and looks for a new wife
Martha	Vihiga	4 Growing up	Education of her kids most important accomplishment of her life
Matthew	Nairobi	4 Growing up	After getting a higher level of education and a new job, he is no longer satisfied with the wife (Marie) he married young
Patrick	Nairobi	4 Growing up	Son wants to work in construction against father's wishes (also in Chapter 5, 'Being a woman'; Chapter 7, 'Being a citizen')
Sarah	Vihiga	4 Growing up	Able to send only one of four daughters to college
Tim	Vihiga	4 Growing up	Young man with mental health challenges, even turns down an opportunity to go to university

Pseudonym	Region	Chapter	Notes
Violet	Vihiga	4 Growing up	Mother (of Dennis) who was forced to move her son to a cheaper, low-quality school
Wambui	Nairobi	4 Growing up	Young woman (daughter of Christine) in Nairobi in an abusive relationship and engaged in sex work
Amos	Mombasa	5 Being a woman	His wife (Carol) buys their house without his knowledge
Beauty	Vihiga	5 Being a woman	Shows us the struggle of ending up as a second wife (to Keith)
Bernadine	Eldoret	5 Being a woman	Endures domestic violence for many years before finding a way to leave
Calvin	Eldoret	5 Being a woman	After his family convinces him to give up an extramarital affair, he tries to dig his wife's (Milly's) birth control implant out of her arm
Carol	Mombasa	5 Being a woman	Buys her house in informal settlement but disagrees on priorities with husband (Amos)
Cassandra	Vihiga	5 Being a woman	Has many children, but husband (Victor) sends little and remarries
Collins	Nairobi	5 Being a woman	Talks about his experiences as an unfaithful husband
Dennis	Vihiga	5 Being a woman	Explains his expectations of a good wife
Diana	Mombasa	5 Being a woman	Her husband (Kenneth) withholds and even steals resources from his large family
Ella	Nairobi	5 Being a woman	Discusses the pain of infidelity
Ellen	Nairobi	5 Being a woman	Fundraises for her childbirth in case her husband falls short
Esther	Vihiga	5 Being a woman	Tells us the importance of persevering in marriage
Fiona	Nairobi	5 Being a woman	Helps husband (Mark) invest to claim dignity within the family
Gloria	Eldoret	5 Being a woman	Kicked out of family house after husband's death; loses her daughter
Jackton	Vihiga	5 Being a woman	Arrested for his wife's (Ruth's) brewing business
Keith	Vihiga	5 Being a woman	Husband (of Beauty) with multiple wives
Kenneth	Mombasa	5 Being a woman	Unfaithful husband (to Diana); the family is unable to convince him to change

Pseudonym	Region	Chapter	Notes
Leah	Vihiga	5 Being a woman	Afraid of offending husband by working until later in life
Mark	Nairobi	5 Being a woman	Newspaper seller working to prove himself to his wife's (Fiona's) family
Millicent	Eldoret	5 Being a woman	Learning to relate to and trust a spouse through the church
Milly	Eldoret	5 Being a woman	Husband (Calvin) attempts to dig out her birth control implant
Pamela	Vihiga	5 Being a woman	Her ongoing fertility problems are a huge source of worry
Patrick	Nairobi	5 Being a woman	Rare level of cooperation with spouse and concern that his children see that model (also in Chapter 4, 'Growing up'; Chapter 7, 'Being a citizen')
Rebecca	Vihiga	5 Being a woman	Chased off family land after husband's suicide but refused to leave
Ruth	Vihiga	5 Being a woman	Negotiates fundraising relationships with relatives on husband's (Jackton's) behalf (also in Chapter 6, 'Staying alive'; Chapter 7, 'Being a citizen')
Sally	Eldoret	5 Being a woman	Kicked out of house for complaining about infidelity
Victor	Vihiga	5 Being a woman	Cassandra's husband; took little responsibility for his large family at home
Zainabu	Mombasa	5 Being a woman	Copes with a miscarriage without much support
Alice	Mombasa	6 Staying alive	Requires free antiretroviral therapy (also in Chapter 4, 'Growing up')
Calvin	Vihiga	6 Staying alive	Suffers with incontinence problem after an injury (child of Douglas and Judith)
Candy	Eldoret	6 Staying alive	Has a child with malaria and can't pay for care
Christine	Makueni	6 Staying alive	Child falls from tree and, afraid of the expense of care, delays telling her
Douglas	Vihiga	6 Staying alive	Father of Calvin, who suffers with incontinence problem
Ellen	Eldoret	6 Staying alive	Son with prolonged abdominal problem for which she must save up over several years (also in Chapter 2, 'Looking for money')
Emmah	Vihiga	6 Staying alive	Gets partial treatment for brucellosis (also in Chapter 2, 'Looking for money')
Felisters	Eldoret	6 Staying alive	Son dies during nursing strike (also in Chapter 7, 'Being a citizen')

Pseudonym	Region	Chapter	Notes
George	Vihiga	6 Staying alive	Registration for NHIF after his wife's death
Gloria	Mombasa	6 Staying alive	Teacher in Mombasa needs to suddenly fund a C-section during a doctors' strike
Isaac	Mombasa	6 Staying alive	Compounded costs of care; wife (Monicah) dies waiting for treatment
Jessica	Nairobi	6 Staying alive	Helping stepdaughter through protracted illness causes a setback to her business
Judith	Vihiga	6 Staying alive	Struggles to finance care for a son with an incontinence problem (wife of Douglas, mother of Calvin)
Lydiah	Eldoret	6 Staying alive	Poorly treated illness results in a young mother's death (Peter's wife)
Matthew	Eldoret	6 Staying alive	Mother-in-law hospitalized; bank collected guaranteed loan
Monicah	Mombasa	6 Staying alive	Dies waiting for treatment costs after long period to get diagnosis (wife of Isaac)
Peter	Eldoret	6 Staying alive	Wife (Lydiah) dies after TB goes undiagnosed after many clinic and hospital visits
Rosemary	Makueni	6 Staying alive	Asked for a bribe to use NHIF for husband's stroke treatment (also in Chapter 7, 'Being a citizen')
Roxanne	Vihiga	6 Staying alive	Turns to traditional healers when unable to afford ultrasound
Ruth	Vihiga	6 Staying alive	Copes with son's broken jaw (also in Chapter 5, 'Being a woman'; Chapter 7, 'Being a citizen')
Sandra	Eldoret	6 Staying alive	Suffers through late-term miscarriage because of financial trade-offs (wife of Tim)
Tim	Eldoret	6 Staying alive	Did not see a blood transfusion for his wife (Sandra) as an urgent need; she later miscarried
Alex	Nairobi	7 Being a citizen	Kidnapped from his shop by men dressed as police
Annette	Vihiga	7 Being a citizen	Supplies molasses to local brewers in her region
Beauty	Vihiga	7 Being a citizen	Struggling to sell clothing after the *changaa* crackdown in her area (also in Chapter 5, 'Being a woman')

Pseudonym	Region	Chapter	Notes
Charlie	Nairobi	7 Being a citizen	Arrested for attempting to sell stolen chemicals to al-Shabaab
Cindy	Mombasa	7 Being a citizen	Stands up to police when they try to arrest and extort her husband (Rafa)
Clementine	Vihiga	7 Being a citizen	Discusses brewing as a widow's lifeline
David	Eldoret	7 Being a citizen	Nephew arrested for assaulting a small child, in an apparent attempt to extort David
Duncan	Vihiga	7 Being a citizen	Savings stolen by police during a *changaa* raid (husband of Stella)
Elijah	Mombasa	7 Being a citizen	Discusses the ways in which the *changaa* crackdown shifted but didn't kill his business
Fatima	Mombasa	7 Being a citizen	Placed under house arrest because she cannot afford to bribe police after an arrest transporting brew
Felisters	Eldoret	7 Being a citizen	Loses her investment in land to fraud (also in Chapter 6, 'Staying alive')
Greta	Nairobi	7 Being a citizen	Pays bribe to replace a lost ID
Harriet	Eldoret	7 Being a citizen	Opening story of how much and how little Kenya has changed since independence
Kathleen	Mombasa	7 Being a citizen	Forced to pay bribe for birth certificate
Kevin	Nairobi	7 Being a citizen	Gang member who pays bribe to leave hospital without paying bill
Kombo	Makueni	7 Being a citizen	A family land dispute spans generations
Magdalene	Makueni	7 Being a citizen	Police release her addicted son in the hope he can enter a rehab programme
Nancy	Vihiga	7 Being a citizen	Talks through the implications of the *changaa* crackdown (also in Chapter 8, 'Living the dream')
Nina	Nairobi	7 Being a citizen	Single mother conned in land purchase
Patrick	Nairobi	7 Being a citizen	Impacted by a protracted court case that is quite expensive to resolve (also in Chapter 3, 'Managing money'; Chapter 5, 'Being a woman')
Rachel	Makueni	7 Being a citizen	Frequent trips to town to follow up on birth certificate

Pseudonym	Region	Chapter	Notes
Rafa	Mombasa	7 Being a citizen	Wife (Cindy) stands up for him after an arbitrary arrest
Rebecca	Vihiga	7 Being a citizen	Brewing as an important income source after husband's death (also in Chapter 5, 'Being a woman')
Rosemary	Makueni	7 Being a citizen	Refuses to pay a bribe to get an electricity connection (also in Chapter 6, 'Staying alive')
Ruth	Vihiga	7 Being a citizen	Navigates police bribery for brewing (also in Chapter 5, 'Being a woman'; Chapter 6, 'Staying alive')
Stella	Vihiga	7 Being a citizen	Savings stolen by police during a *changaa* raid (wife of Duncan)
Christopher	Eldoret	8 Living the dream	Works his way out of poverty by layering businesses over time (also in Chapter 2, 'Looking for money')
Nancy	Vihiga	8 Living the dream	Perseveres through challenges with humour (also in Chapter 7, 'Being a citizen')

A note on exchange rates

We cite monetary figures in both Kenya shillings (KES) and US dollars ($) throughout the book. For figures from the 2002–03 study, we use an exchange rate of KES 85 to $1. For the 2015–16 period, the Kenyan currency depreciated, and the average exchange rate was KES 100 to $1.

Acknowledgements

This project has been long in the making, not just the writing, but the planning, the observing, the slow process of learning and trying to make sense of some of the richest data I have ever had the chance to use. Being able to conduct the research that informs this book was a professional dream come true. As a master's student, I was inspired by the work of Stuart Rutherford, Daryl Collins, Jonathan Morduch, Orlanda Ruthven, Parker Shipton, Marguerite Robinson, and Bill Maurer. I am deeply grateful for having had the opportunity to follow in their footsteps.

At the start of this journey, I did not know just how much I would learn or how much joy I would get seeing some insight from this research put to use in thinking through real-world problems. It is truly a gift to be a part of something like this. I am deeply indebted to many people who contributed directly and indirectly to this project.

First, I would like to thank all of the participants in this research. Our participants trusted us with the details of their lives, their money secrets, their hopes and embarrassments. They continue to take our calls and answer our *maswali mingi* (many questions). Thank you for your collaboration and friendship. It is my greatest hope that I have told your stories well.

I would like to thank the project's funders who made this entire endeavour possible. They allowed our team the resources and the freedom to do our best work, helped us troubleshoot problems, and helped us get as much mileage as possible from the data our team collected. They provided thoughtful and energetic collaboration from the initial planning all the way through multiple publications and applications of project insights.

I would particularly like to thank David Ferrand, Amrik Heyer, Edoardo Totolo, Joyce Omondi, Nancy Atello, Rebecca Etuku, and the late Ravi Ramrattan from FSD Kenya. Paul Gubbins was an exceptional source of support, cheerfully helping us put the Diaries data into publicly accessible formats, reviewing dozens of presentations, reports, and book chapters, and making important connections between Diaries insights and academic literature in economics and public health. Tamara Cook was an outspoken champion of the project from its inception. Her encouragement is the reason why this book exists. Thank you.

Evelyn Stark, Janine Firpo, Wendy Chamberlain, Liz Kellison, and Dave Kim all made very helpful contributions from their positions at the Bill & Melinda Gates Foundation. Tillman Ehrbeck at the Omidyar Foundation provided our team additional funding to write up and share our insights around gender issues and to use that to start helpful dialogues with private-sector players.

I thank David Porteous and Daryl Collins of Bankable Frontier Associates (BFA) for giving me the opportunity to lead the Kenya Financial Diaries and to Digital Divide Data for giving the project a home in Nairobi. Amolo Ng'weno has been a champion of this work from the very beginning, helping solve both intellectual and practical research problems, providing mentorship to project staff, sharing project findings, finding new ways to bring those findings to life, and indefatigably reviewing countless papers and versions of chapters. I would also like to thank Alexey Ossikine who went to great lengths to help us build a tablet application and database that made data collection much smoother than it might have been otherwise. Other colleagues at BFA have also been tremendously helpful. Thank you especially to Caitlin Sanford, Laura Cojocaru, Ahmed Dermish, Jeff Abrams, and Clement Sukura.

I've also benefited enormously from the mentorship, feedback, and friendship of several inspiring researchers and colleagues, including, Jenny Aker, Susan Johnson, Billy Jack, Ignacio Mas, Julie Schaffner, Karen Jacobsen, Alex de Waal, Caroline Elkins, Dorothy McCormick, Victoria Baker, Mary Meyer McAleese, and Radha Upadhyaya. I owe a particular debt to Kim Wilson, my mentor and dear friend. Kim taught me how to do rigorous research that takes participants' dignity seriously and even at times has the potential for delight.

I would also like to thank those who generously reviewed and commented on early drafts of this book, many of whom are already mentioned above, but also including Kate Lauer, Ory Okolloh, and Edwin Wachiye. Candace Nelson provided helpful, patient editing.

The research you will read about in this book was difficult to do. The fieldwork was physically and emotionally exhausting, and the interviews themselves were exacting and sometimes tedious. I have been awed by the energy, commitment, and thoughtfulness of the members of our research team throughout 18 months of initial fieldwork and beyond. Many of the insights in this book started with observations raised by team members or debated in our weekly calls or quarterly retreats. Others derive from their careful recording of the details of participants' lives. Thank you Perez Otonde, Catherine Muniu, Victor Mirori, Philemon Bidi, Harrison Kirui, Hildah Ogeto, Naomi Kiiru, Hildah Chao, Norman Manthi, Emmanuel Muasya, Abigail Beja, Nekesa Wekesa, Pauline Munga, Duncan Washington, Michelle Hassan, Daniel Mwero, Peter Njomo, and Anne Gachoka. A special thank you goes to Catherine Wanjala, who not only served as an excellent researcher, but also helped me organize and factcheck this book. The families of our research team also deserve a huge amount of gratitude. Thanks to all of you for your encouragement, and your flexibility with our ever-shifting schedules and sometimes long periods away from home.

Finally, I would like to thank my own great big family, for their abounding encouragement and for teaching me curiosity. I dedicate this book to my grandfather, Bill Siemer, who taught me that there is only one thing we know for sure; the rest we must investigate.

Preface

I first learned about the Financial Diaries as a graduate student reading Stuart Rutherford's essay *The Poor and their Money*.[1] His piece was eye opening. What if we tried to understand more about how ordinary people navigate scarcity inductively, by observing closely what they already do? It wasn't that descriptive work was new per se, but rather that Rutherford watched even more closely, both at short intervals and over a relatively long period, and, in doing so, new insights into economic behaviour emerged. There were so many realities we just hadn't seen before. Rutherford later collaborated with Daryl Collins, Jonathan Morduch, and Orlanda Ruthven on the influential book *Portfolios of the Poor* (2009), introducing a whole new intuition about how low-income people manage money. They demonstrated that low-income people were not living hand to mouth but were instead active and thoughtful money managers. They even amassed significant savings in ways that were often overlooked and disregarded by mainstream financial service providers. I was captivated by the richness and texture of their approach and the ways in which insights from their work could be applied to solving real-world problems.

So I was thrilled when Daryl Collins offered me the opportunity to work alongside her in 2010 and to lead a large Financial Diaries project in Kenya in 2012. The project was run by the consulting firm Bankable Frontier Associates (BFA), with the financial support of Financial Sector Deepening (FSD) Kenya, and the Bill & Melinda Gates Foundation. At that time in Kenya, the mobile money service M-Pesa had exploded onto the financial services scene. The entire financial industry was eager to understand how people were using this novel product, how new services and more traditional informal financial services were interacting, and what the next generation of financial services might look like.

To manage the research, I was seconded to a local firm, Digital Divide Data (DDD) Kenya, where I put together a full-time research team. Our field researchers lived in the communities where they were working, spread over five areas of the country. Each researcher was responsible for covering 30 to 35 households for the entire duration of the roughly 18 months of fieldwork.

Our team visited the same households every two weeks for long, often boring interviews, in which, apart from talking about general happenings in their lives, we would also go through an arduous recounting of all household cash flows, including all income, expenses, and intermediation, with our team recording the size, date, mode, and often other details of every single transaction. We ended up with more than 500,000 of these cash flows at the end of the study. The researcher needed to reconcile sources and uses of money in each interview and often needed to talk separately with both spouses in the household to complete the picture. On occasion, we introduced new sets of qualitative questions, trying to understand aspects of respondents' financial lives and decision making that were not clear from the cash flow-focused questions we asked every two weeks.

We took a lot of our respondents' time. Maintaining respondents' interest and getting accurate data meant building strong relationships between respondents and researchers. As these relationships built over time, we began seeing deeper and deeper into respondents' lives. It was not long before I realized that what respondents were choosing to share with us was going to be meaningful well beyond the financial inclusion world, the sector whose interests had motivated the study. And I saw that if we really wanted to understand what was happening, we would need to do more than just record transactions; we would also need to carefully capture stories.

We were given a very privileged view into the intimacies of people's lives. As a team, we talked early and often about how to be sure that the time and information our respondents shared would be worth it.

One couple gave us reason to think deeply about the ethics of our project. During enrolment into the study, Lenah and Jeremiah were bold enough to tell us that they were both HIV-positive. The couple had been married for five years. Jeremiah told us that meeting Lenah had been the highlight of his life. Although they lived in a one-room house and had very few assets, Jeremiah was hopeful about the future they were building together.

When we met them, Lenah was still breastfeeding their youngest child. Their baby was sick with an unknown illness. Both Jeremiah and Lenah earned their income from casual work, which was hit or miss in their peri-urban settlement. When the baby's health failed to improve, our researcher, Victor, wanted to help. Just a gift of even $3–$5 might be enough for the child to go and see a doctor. Plus, giving is what friends in Kenya do; those who *can* give money, *do* give money to help. But the very purpose of our study was to understand how families cope with these gut-wrenching choices. We gave our respondents small cash (actually, mostly M-Pesa) gifts to thank them for their participation, but these were given at surprise intervals and in surprise amounts to avoid affecting families' financial planning.

Not long into the study, Victor wrote this after an interview with Lenah and Jeremiah:

> This interview was not very conclusive since it was done on a hospital bed. Lenah is the member admitted, suffering from acute tuberculosis. Jeremiah has been instructed by the medics to be by her bedside throughout since she has grown very weak and cannot do anything by herself. [The children] are under the care of Lenah's sister temporarily though it's a task she has assumed rather grudgingly evidenced by

the fact that she had reported Jeremiah to the police station for child neglect. The police boss however ruled in Jeremiah's favour on humanitarian grounds. The family has largely relied on well-wishers within this period since Jeremiah does not have time to engage in *kibarua* [casual work].

Lenah and Jeremiah, like so many of our respondents, were giving our team not just their time but an invitation to witness and record the intimate details of their lives, even in their very worst moments. We were not even helping make sure they could keep their youngest child alive.[2] There were about 350 families in our study at the beginning. The ethical dilemmas we felt in our relationship with Lenah and Jeremiah were not unique.

Reflecting on the ethics of our research as a team at our first retreat, we decided on a few things. First, we would be human. We would listen carefully and faithfully record people's stories. They spoke to us to be heard and so we would listen. Second, we would – as friends would – give very small token gifts to respondents at the worst moments in their lives: during a hospitalization or following the death of a household member. These gifts, like all cash flows, would be recorded. To ensure that this did not place even greater expectations on individual researchers, all gifts would come via the research company, from our business M-Pesa account, or through a supervisor. Third, we would make sure that our respondents knew what happened to the data we collected from them. We would come back to see them to share our project report and a personalized report on their household after the study was over.

Finally, we would do the best we could to make our respondents' contributions matter. We would wring out every drop of insight we could from our data. We would share those insights to the best of our ability with as many stakeholders and partners as possible. Many of our field researchers brushed up on their writing skills, several penning their very first blog posts and giving their first professional presentations through this project. This commitment is the main reason why this book exists. We would not let our respondents' stories – even those that extended beyond the financial inclusion world – go to waste.

And what a waste it would be!

So often, research in development has a narrow focus, often answering one specific, empirical question, narrowly defined. But there is a danger that without a fuller understanding of research subjects' human experience, the microscope of an empirical study can be focused on the wrong part of the slide. I hope that this book complements that work. It points out some obvious realities we, as development practitioners and researchers, often take for granted. It develops new hypotheses, which might be fertile for deeper exploration. It reflects years of deep, systematic listening, something that very few academics and practitioners will ever have a chance to do on their own.

As I listened to respondents directly and as I read transcripts from qualitative interviews and the notes of our team members, I began to see things differently. When we are forced to turn people into abstractions, into 'the poor', their poverty, not their humanity, begins to define them. These stories show something else. We see agents, not victims. We see people living full lives, celebrating key moments, telling jokes, making plans, fighting with their spouses, being awed by and worried about their children. We heard about and witnessed their achievements. We talked about the things that made them proud. Sometimes those were huge transformations; sometimes they were less visible victories, like learning how to make a marriage work. We used the lens of money, but then saw life unfold. The chapters in this book reflect some of those realms of living, those realms where I thought our respondents' stories (and in some cases our quantitative data) gave us something important to say.

When I listened to the stories of our respondents and started to hear themes across families, I was constantly reoriented. My mind was flooded with new hypotheses about how things might really work, new ways of thinking about causal pathways for household welfare outcomes. The data we collected helped me see things I didn't know were there before, things we were not even trying to find. I hope that readers will feel some of that sense of curiosity and inspiration in the remainder of these pages.

Endnotes

1. This essay was later converted to a book with Sukhinder Singh Arora (Rutherford and Arora, 2009).
2. Lenah and Jeremiah's baby eventually improved over several months. Lenah also recovered, but wasn't able to work for several months. Towards the end of the study, the couple separated. Lenah had used some of the money Jeremiah left for food to buy alcohol. Jeremiah was frustrated that she would waste resources and not take care of herself. He thought that if she was now well enough to drink, she should be trying harder to get work. Lenah went to stay with her parents in another town. During the update, Jeremiah and Lenah were one of the few families we were unable to find.

References

Collins, D. et al. (2009) *Portfolios of the Poor: How the World's Poor Live on $2 a Day*, Princeton University Press, Princeton NJ.

Rutherford, S. and Arora, S.S. (2009) *The Poor and their Money*, Practical Action Publishing, Rugby. Available from: <https://sites.google.com/site/thepoorandtheirmoney/the-book> (accessed 26 August 2017).

Chapter 1
Introduction: Listening to Kenyans through Financial Diaries

Abstract

Rapid economic growth and tech innovation are not necessarily improving the welfare of ordinary people in Kenya, the Silicon Savannah. This chapter provides background information on Kenya's development and the Financial Diaries study that informs this book. By listening deeply to ordinary people through Financial Diaries we develop new research questions and hypotheses about how development works. We see old and obvious realities in new ways and gain a new kind of peripheral vision that helps us better understand the ways in which structural issues affect micro-level decision making.

Keywords: Kenyan economy, Financial Diaries, poverty reduction, qualitative research, economic divergence

One of the most iconic images of Nairobi comes from Nairobi National Park, looking northward to the city. An emerald city of sorts appears to rise proudly out from tall, golden grasses, a lean giraffe foregrounding a horizon of glass and steel skyscrapers. Silicon Savannah. Wild. Modern. On the move. Kenya's economy is growing, averaging annual GDP growth around 6 per cent since 2009 (World Bank, 2017). New highways are popping up, feeding into new shopping malls. Until the 2017 elections, the march of democratic progress appeared to be in full swing; a new, progressive constitution had taken hold and the country underwent a peaceful transition of executive power in 2013. Kenya's innovative mobile money system, M-Pesa, has become the poster child for a blossoming tech sector, the Silicon Savannah.

As a narrative, this story of growth and development is exciting and seductive. It is all true, just incomplete. Amid high rates of growth and such widespread, visible change, it is deceptively easy to assume that life for everyone is generally improving. Headline figures tell us that poverty is falling – down from 46.6 per cent in 2005–06 to 36.1 per cent in 2015–16, according to the Kenya National Bureau of Statistics (KNBS, 2018). Problems must be being solved. Surely maternal mortality must be falling. Education must be improving. AIDS is surely – by now – under control. Women must be becoming increasingly 'empowered'. Such is the inevitable march of progress. Except that it is not. Poverty today is primarily a problem of middle-income countries, Kenya being one (Chandy and Gertz, 2011; Sumner and Kanbur, 2011).

http://dx.doi.org/10.3362/9781788531207.001

It is difficult to reconcile the dissonance between the narrative of the urban elite and of the ordinary *wananchi* (citizens), the low-income majority, corralled into Nairobi's slums and spread mostly across a narrow belt of cultivable land running east to west along the southern third of the country. How can it be that 'free' healthcare is anything but? How can it be that a country with nearly full coverage of mobile money and fibre-optic cables is making almost no progress in reducing maternal mortality?[1] How can one part of the country suffer from crisis levels of HIV infection – up to 26 per cent in Homa Bay – completely out of the gaze of the media and with very little national attention (National AIDS Control Council, 2016)? How is it possible that the informal economy – now accounting for an estimated 83 per cent of employment – is actually growing faster than the formal sector (KNBS, 2017a)?

This is a story of inequalities that go well beyond income alone. While the National Bureau of Statistics claimed that the Gini coefficient was falling in Kenya, World Bank figures suggest a slight increase from 2005–06 (World Bank, 2015; KNBS, 2017b, 2018). Apart from that measure, the 2015–16 Household Budget Survey showed that the top 20 per cent of the Kenyan population controlled 56 per cent of overall purchasing power in the country; concentration was even higher in urban areas, where the top 40 per cent of spenders accounted for 90 per cent of all consumption (KNBS, 2018).

Kenya is a country of complicated progress, a country of rapid change, and stubborn stasis. This is as true at the national level as it is within individual families, many of whom are advancing and struggling with the linked domains of their lives – work, finances, relationships, and mental and physical health – simultaneously. This is a book of those stories, a view of Kenya's complicated progress from below, through the lives of the ordinary people trying to build full lives in difficult – but often hopeful – circumstances. These stories – captured systematically over the span of four years – help us understand the nature of the development challenges still facing Kenya's low-income people, and they help us practitioners and scholars to think more creatively and realistically about addressing them.

Why Financial Diaries?

Want to understand a major corruption scandal? Follow the money. Want to know who has a politician's ear? Follow the money. Want to know what a government cares about? Follow the money. Want to really understand how low-income people navigate their lives? Also, follow the money!

Tracing money tells a revealing story about what really happened in any given event. It tells us how resources were collected and deployed. It sheds lights on the wheres and whens of how decisions were made. It shows how people were connected and how they did – or did not – collaborate. It reveals signs of struggle, moments of success, how difficult trade-offs are made, and how spending is prioritized.

With such depth of information, it is no wonder that the research equivalent of following the money – Financial Diaries – has become a popular approach to help us understand low-income people's finances. In Financial Diaries, researchers systematically record household cash flows – all the income, all the expenses, all the borrowing, saving, and investing – over quite a long period of time, using that data as a window into people's experiences and as a way to understand what kinds of financial tools might better fit their lives, and might better solve their financial problems.

In 2012, we set out to do just this in Kenya. Our project funders – Financial Sector Deepening (FSD) Kenya and the Bill & Melinda Gates Foundation – were particularly interested in understanding how new digital financial services, such as the mobile money system M-Pesa and agent banking, were integrated into the financial lives of ordinary Kenyans. They were interested in how these new forms of infrastructure might be leveraged for a new generation of helpful financial services.

We worked in five areas of the country where we believed we would capture key livelihoods and demographic patterns. In those five areas, we selected 14 communities in which to work and, after a screening process, we built up an initial sample of 350 households (we expected attrition to bring this figure down to 300). This sample broadly reflected key national-level attributes, such as education and rural–urban distributions. After a series of enrolment interviews, researchers would visit every household every two weeks and use recall and some paper notes that respondents kept to try to document all the cash flows in the household in the intervening period: every bit of income, every payment and purchase, every deposit and withdrawal from every savings device, and so on. The goal was to capture everything, to match all sources of money to their uses for an entire 12-month period. We ended up with more than 500,000 of these cash flows at the end of the study.

Alongside these cash flows we checked in on families' well-being, looked at key events, and documented qualitative notes about what was happening in the household. These data were supplemented with occasional qualitative modules and a follow-up study in 2015. (The methodological note in the appendix to this book provides more detail.) The result is a rich multi-method data set that sits somewhere between a large, one-off survey and the kinds of intimate ethnographic insights we get from anthropology.

This provides us a unique, privileged view into people's lives, one that offers us – more than anything else – new ways of seeing, as this book will show. I am a development practitioner myself and had already spent several years living and working in developing countries before starting this project, including two years in a rural community in Swaziland as a Peace Corps volunteer. I thought I understood the realities of making decisions on very little money. Still, I found myself constantly reoriented by the data we were collecting.

This kind of a close look at people's lives through the lens of money does three things. First, it offers up new observations, little flashes of insight, that change the way we look at an issue. One example you will read about in

Chapter 3, 'Managing money', is the idea that money should be working. Hearing respondents talk about their savings preferences helped us realize that respondents viewed liquid savings as wasteful. It gave us a new way to categorize savings choices and look at trends. It was a tantalizing hint as to why people choose to keep so little cash savings on hand and face frequent cash flow shortfalls for even relatively small sums. A survey that looked only at savings balances couldn't provide us with that insight.

Throughout the project our team was inundated with new hypotheses about how things might really work, new ways of thinking about causal pathways for household welfare outcomes. The data we collected helped us see things we didn't know were there before, things we were not even trying to find. One example, which you will read about in Chapter 2, 'Looking for money', is about preferences for full-time, formal work. A few women in our study were quite annoyed by their husbands getting formal jobs because of what that meant for the shift in power over long-term financial decision making. This may be the case in a few isolated cases, or perhaps it is a larger issue. Our study was not designed to measure such phenomena through a representative sample at scale. But the issue is not something that would have occurred to me unless we heard it from our respondents first.

The second thing this type of research helps us do is to see obvious realities in new ways, to understand their implications at a deeper level. For example, most development practitioners understand that poverty is quite literally the state of having insufficient money to meet basic needs. Still, we talk about things like 'affordable' healthcare, mobile phones, and insurance, often without acknowledging that even small expenditures require trade-offs, often among other equally 'good' alternatives. Observing those trade-offs in people's real lives helps us think more concretely about what some of these obvious realities mean in the context of our work.

Along similar lines, this research constantly reminded me of something development practitioners sometimes lose sight of: that poverty is a human problem, not just a technical one. When we are forced to turn people into abstractions, into 'the poor', their poverty begins to define them, not their humanity. These stories show something else. We see agents, not victims. We see people *living* full lives, celebrating key moments, telling jokes, making plans, fighting with their spouses, being awed by and worried about their children. We heard about and witnessed their achievements. We talked about the things that made them proud. Sometimes these were huge transformations; sometimes they were less visible victories, such as learning how to make a marriage work. We used the lens of money, but then saw life unfold. The chapters in this book reflect some of those realms of living in which I thought our respondents' stories (and in some cases our quantitative data) gave us something important to say.

Finally, this kind of research offers a sense of the big picture of what's happening in people's lives. So often, those who work in public health are narrowly focused on healthcare or on water and sanitation. Those who work in financial inclusion focus on account access and usage. That focus on the issue at hand is important for developing key technical expertise and making smart programming decisions. However, treating development challenges as purely technical in this way can obscure the bigger story, which often involves structural phenomena that are difficult to address, things like governance and long-standing gender norms. These problems of power cannot be fixed by technical solutions alone. Smart development work demands that we see these issues of context and examine our work carefully through that lens. The kind of research that underpins this book offers a chance to develop some of that peripheral vision, to see the proverbial forest of individuals' lives rather than only the trees of individual decisions in isolated domains.

The topics in this book are big and complex, but our aim is modest. This book has succeeded if it gives you a taste of the experience of discovery our team felt while collecting and analysing the data. It will have succeeded if it helps you think in a more grounded way about how some areas of development work and what it means for ordinary people. For students and practitioners of development, I hope it sparks some ideas about where to focus, how to effect change, and how to design research that helps us know better – and listen better to – the people whose lives we hope to improve.

The setting

This book takes place entirely in Kenya, a diverse country of nearly 50 million people in East Africa stretching from the Indian Ocean coast in the east to Lake Victoria in the west. The contours of the modern Kenyan state are largely a product of the colonial experience, with British colonization creating borders, tribal identities, and even the geographies of the country's main cities (Young, 2002; Elkins, 2005; Anyamba, 2011; Parsons, 2012). Initially a waypoint for the East African railway, Kenya became a British settler colony, with the British actively encouraging European settlement. Significant numbers of British colonists were granted prime land around Nairobi and in the highly productive central highlands (the so-called 'White Highlands') to grow tea and coffee. Displaced tribes in these areas were pushed to the capital, Nairobi, searching for livelihoods, and they became Kenya's business or trading class, an ethnic identity that persists today (Hake, 1977; Obudho, 1997).

The colonial era came to an end in significant part due to the armed rebellion of Mau fighters waging resistance against the British Empire, which finally handed over power to their own chosen leader of independent Kenya, Jomo Kenyatta. Kenyatta used his office and significant resources for buying back settler land for redistribution to dramatically expand his family's own personal landholdings and to distribute wealth to key supporters. His death handed power to a successor, Daniel arap Moi, who was renowned for his authoritarian repression of dissent and of the free press. Moi solidified a pattern initiated by Kenyatta of rewarding loyal supporters with patronage in the form of land, jobs, cash, and public investment in their home areas, leading voters to believe that development would only come to their areas when 'their man' was in office.

Moi was forced from office in 2003, ushering in a period of rocky democratization. That process reached a crisis point in 2007 after Mwai Kibaki had himself sworn into office late in the evening in the midst of a disputed election, sparking widespread ethnic violence around the country and forcing a power-sharing agreement between Kibaki and the opposition leader, Raila Odinga. That process helped usher in a new, progressive constitution in 2010, which, notably, introduced a process of decentralization of many key government functions to 47 counties, each headed by an elected governor.

By the time the 2013 elections rolled around, the leaders of the two major factions that had been engulfed in violence in 2007–08, Uhuru Kenyatta and William Ruto, had been indicted by the International Criminal Court (ICC). Kenyatta and Ruto joined forces politically on a nationalist campaign based on resisting the imperial power of the Western world as embodied by the ICC and on securing their freedom by being elected on a joint ballot. It worked: the two were elected in 2013 and again in 2017 after the opposition boycotted the second round of an election annulled by the Supreme Court after the first round.

The 2013 elections took place during this Financial Diaries study. Throughout our research, we heard about respondents' hopes for what the new constitution would bring, their cynicism as sporadic ethnic violence emerged in some of their neighbourhoods, and their frustration when election-related tension slowed their businesses and drove up food prices.

The current government routinely makes overtures towards development for ordinary Kenyans – as in the current 'Big Four' agenda, setting a government focus on food security, affordable housing, universal healthcare, and manufacturing. The sincerity of such commitments is routinely questioned by civil society, however, as the country makes budget cuts in priority areas, such as healthcare, and new corruption scandals come to light. MPs continue to increase their own salaries and allowances, which are already some of the highest relative to national income in the world. Donor government pressure to hold government officials to account is tempered by Kenya's strategic importance in the 'War on Terror' and Western governments' fears of the rising influence of China in the region.

Despite its troubling politics, Kenya's macro-economy is one of the strongest in the region. It is a large economy and is quite diversified, providing some insulation from the vagaries of global commodity prices and exchange-rate fluctuations. Many believe that the country's strong private sector prevents political disputes from escalating into more frequent or broader episodes of violence.

While perhaps some of us would hope for even stronger performance, the country has succeeded in reducing poverty over time, with the percentage of individuals below the official poverty line falling from 46.8 per cent in 2005 to 36.1 per cent in 2015. Poverty reduction has just recently overtaken the pace of population growth, resulting in a small recent decline in the number of Kenyans counted as 'poor'. Average consumption levels are still staggeringly low, however, with median per capita consumption expenditure at 5,830 Kenyan shillings (KES) ($58) per month in 2015. Inequality is also quite high, with a Gini coefficient of 39.1, estimated from the 2015–16 Kenya Integrated Household Budget and Expenditure Survey (KNBS, 2018). However, it is important to remember that this survey excludes Kenya's highest-income earners. Oxfam estimates that just 8,300 people – 0.1% of the population – own more wealth than the bottom 99.9% (Oxfam, 2019).

Kenya is diverse in many ways. It is home to a large number of ethnic groups, often popularly referred to as '42 recognized tribes', although the list of recognized ethnicities in the national census is constantly in flux (Balaton-Chrimes, 2011, 2017). Its landscape and livelihoods are also incredibly varied, from semi-arid zones in the country's far north, through hot and humid coastal zones with sandy soils and frequent droughts, to the highly productive and cool highlands and a fertile belt of productive farmland stretching from around Nairobi to Lake Victoria. Farms on the dry plains extending from Nairobi towards the coast can be quite large, but they suffer from frequent droughts and low productivity, while the rural areas towards the west are densely populated, typically with small farms but higher food security.

The sample

This diversity posed sampling challenges for us in this research project. We had to determine specific geographies in which to focus our work due to the need to conduct repeat, in-person interviews over time. The project advisory group helped us with these decisions; we aimed to cover as much of this diversity as possible, particularly focusing on the livelihood zones where the majority of Kenyans lived. We decided to work in the following five areas of the country:

- Nairobi: Kenya's capital city was home to 4 million Kenyans at the time of the study. Many of its low-income residents live in informal settlements with little public infrastructure. We chose to focus on a string of these settlements in the north-east part of the city. The neighbourhoods we selected represented somewhat varying income levels and ethnic compositions.
- Mombasa: This large coastal city offered us another view into urban life, outside the capital in an area dominated by international trade and tourism. We were able to sample both migrant urban households and local urban households in the city. We also selected some neighbourhoods in rural areas surrounding Mombasa, where poverty levels are persistently high and education levels are below the national average.
- Makueni: This rural county experiences frequent drought-related food insecurity. It is home to the ethnic Kamba people. Its relative proximity to Nairobi (about three hours' drive) means that many families here are

divided, with male income earners living in the city while their wives live in the rural area, tending the farms and caring for children with the help of remittances, supplemented with their own livelihood activities.

- Eldoret: This is another large, important town in Kenya, but its economy is driven in large part by agricultural trade from the surrounding, highly productive farming communities in the region. We drew a small sample from the town itself, a small sample from a peri-urban area about an hour outside the city, and a sample from a rural area reaching up into the Nandi Hills.
- Vihiga: This area was selected to give us a view of the lives and livelihoods of the many Kenyans who live in densely settled Western Kenya and who work mainly as subsistence farmers. This area is about an hour and a half north of Kisumu. Most of our respondents in the rural communities we studied here lived on small, family-owned farms, where they produced maize and beans, and sometimes eggs and milk, and where many were also connected to the illicit brewing industry.

While these sites cover a lot of ground in Kenya, they notably exclude pastoralist livelihoods in the north of the country and a number of other livelihood zones and communities. We also excluded higher-income Kenyans, representing many of Kenya's highly educated and politically influential people.

We built our sample by targeting neighbourhoods in these key geographies noted above, introducing ourselves through local leaders, and screening participants for their willingness to participate and a range of background characteristics. Based on screening data, we pieced together a sample that attempted to reflect the diversity of Kenya's population and invited people to participate in the study.

The sample we ended up with is not statistically representative of the Kenyan population but we tried as much as possible to reflect the rural–urban distribution, livelihood patterns, household structures, and education levels of Kenya's low-income people. We intentionally focused on low-income households, meaning that median per capita consumption was lower in our sample than the national average. Our study households also tended to be slightly bigger on average, partly because we captured a larger share of the poor and partly because we included individuals who joined a household over the course of the study year. Table 1.1 compares the Financial Diaries sample with other large, nationally representative surveys.

While median per capita consumption expenditure was just KES 4,157 ($42) for our urban respondents and KES 2,084 ($21) for our rural ones, incomes and consumption levels varied considerably within the sample, reflecting an array of experiences. The lowest-income household in the study had an average monthly income of KES 627 ($6–$7) during the Diaries, and the highest earned about KES 195,798 ($1,957) per month. In addition to measuring such figures in absolute terms, we also asked each family in the Diaries to estimate how much they would need to earn per month to be comfortable. The median

Table 1.1 Kenya Financial Diaries sample compared with nationally representative surveys

	Kenya Financial Diaries (KFD) 2013, 2015	Kenya Integrated Household Budget Survey (KIHBS) 2015–16	National Census 2009	Demographic and Health Survey (DHS) 2014	FinAccess 2016
Urban	31%	43.6%	32%	40.8% women 43.9% men	37%
Rural	69%	56.4%	68%	59.2% women 56.1% men	63%
Household size	5.2 (Diaries) 5.0 (update)	4.0	4.4	3.9	4.2
Male-headed households	54.7%	67.6%	68%	67.8%	74%
Cook primarily with firewood	62%	55%	65%	56%	63%
Main dwelling has an earth floor	52%	30%	57%	47%	57% (2009[4])
Age of household heads	47.7	44.6			
Years of education of household heads[1]	8.3	8.1			
Household heads with no education	5%	13.7%			
Per capita monthly consumption (KES)	3,595 (mean) 2,673 (median)[2]	7,811 (mean) 5,830 (median)[3]			
Share of consumption on food items	56.8%	54.3%			
Sample	298 households	21,773 households	38 million individuals / 8.78 million households	40,300 households	8,665 adults

Notes

[1] This was calculated using a shared methodology across the two surveys, based on raw data.

[2] This consumption figure includes consumer durables in order to equate with KIHBS' measure. It inflates 2013 figures up to 2015 using the consumer price index to adjust for inflation.

[3] The KIHBS consumption aggregate is based on different methodology, extrapolating from recall over seven days for food, 30 for non-food, and 365 for durables. KIHBS also equalizes prices across locations. The Diaries use respondent-reported expenditure figures and estimated values of food consumed from household production, taking the household average over the course of the study.

[4] There was a problem in the coding of this variable in the 2016 and 2013 FinAccess surveys, hence the use of 2009 data.

household said that this figure would be KES 10,000 in rural areas and KES 20,000 in urban areas. As of the 2015 update, 43 per cent of respondent households were earning more than their stated comfort threshold. The median household living above its stated comfort level was making about KES 18,864 ($188) in 2015, but this 'comfortable' level of income went as low as KES 1,542 ($15) for one household.

As we proceed through the rest of the book, it is helpful to keep this background in mind. Yes, we are talking about low-income people, but there is still wide variation in just how poor respondent households really are and how much their low incomes define their experiences and their feelings of hardship.

Organization of the book

This book is organized into chapters around topical themes. While the themes are all related, chapters are designed to stand alone, so it is easier to revisit individual themes independently. We begin with two chapters on money, the entry point for the Kenya Financial Diaries. In Chapter 2, 'Looking for money', we examine the livelihoods of respondent households, including how they pieced together income in complex and shifting tapestries of work in the face of severely limited opportunities. We look at the realities of returns on agricultural investments and consider the key role of remittances in making poor people's lives more liveable. We pay attention to how respondents start and sustain their enterprises, observing that small business plays an outsized role in propelling low-income Kenyans to higher income levels and living standards.

In Chapter 3, 'Managing money', we present key insights around money management strategies of the households and individuals in our study. We see that low-income families are constantly making trade-offs in what they spend, but also in how they save and invest, and we look at how those trade-offs leave them vulnerable in a country like Kenya, where public health, education, and financial safety nets are limited.

The following chapters allow us to explore what these financial realities mean in topical domains of Kenyans' lives. Chapter 4, 'Growing up', explores the ways in which childhood experiences set the stage for adult outcomes. Economic realities often require children to live with grandparents and other relatives; for some, this has a lasting impact into adulthood. Families struggle to pay steep fees for their children's education, limiting upward mobility for all but the luckiest of low-income children. Young people living in poor families – especially once they are forced to end their education – face the same temptations and challenges as young people anywhere, although after a childhood of deprivation, it can be particularly difficult to avoid them. And often, low-income young people simply do not have the resources to buy second chances.

Chapter 5, 'Being a woman', explores the ways in which gender norms shape the lives of Kenyan women, particularly in the context of marriage, where women's agency and behaviour are tightly circumscribed by thick webs of norm enforcement. We argue that getting more resources into the hands of women and helping couples learn to cooperate on finances are keys to better welfare outcomes for women, men, and families.

We then move to the world of health in Chapter 6, 'Staying alive'. In this chapter we observe respondent households' struggles to achieve good health, primarily by financing the healthcare they need. While there are some bright spots where access to care has been improving (as with HIV), poverty and liquidity problems often prevent people from getting care, and the results are devastating – physically, financially, and emotionally. We see that simply lowering costs for primary care treatment – without addressing care quality – may not reduce the burden of healthcare expenditure on the poor.

Chapter 7, 'Being a citizen', turns to respondents' experiences with their own government. We see that living in a clientelist state often means that ordinary people suffer the most from shortcomings in governance, most especially through several forms of corruption. Our research cannot measure the full impact of high-level government theft on low-income people, but it can show the many ways in which low-income people try to navigate a broken system to their own advantage. The chapter recalls respondents' interactions with government in the enforcement of a ban on illicit brewing, as victims and perpetrators of electoral violence, and through attempts to access government services, protection, and justice.

The final chapter, Chapter 8, 'Living the dream', delves into respondents' aspirations and priorities, financial and non-financial. We look especially at building homes, educating children, affirming social status, having fun, and staying sane. We look at the relationship between material well-being and emotional well-being through respondents' narratives of achievement and aspiration and consider the pathways that seem to be working in bringing our respondents closer to their own life goals. The chapter shows how far people can push themselves and imagines how much change could be possible if the government and development community were better partners.

As a privileged outsider, I recognize that my own presentation of these insights is biased and incomplete. It is an uncomfortable role to speak on behalf of others. To the best of my ability, I have drawn on the stories of respondents themselves – often their own words – along with the detailed notes and guidance of my spectacular field team as well as advice from a wide collection of content and context experts. Throughout this text, I use the pronoun 'we' rather than 'I', reflecting the views of the broader research team that shaped this work.

There is a substantial body of academic literature on each topic covered in this book. We cannot hope to do justice to that body of work here. Instead, this account is meant to complement scholarly literature with a more personal, on-the-ground view, dedicating the lion's share of the space on these pages to respondents' stories and voices.

Still, for each theme, we bring in some larger global and Kenya-specific data that help contextualize these stories and our own observations. After all, this is not *just* a collection of stories. One of the challenges that comes along with the richness and depth of our Kenya Financial Diaries data – quantitative and qualitative – is that we are immersed in the diversity of experiences, the uniqueness of the lives of each respondent. But the aim of the researcher is to see from that richness some general, helpful truths. This book is my attempt to do that: to weave nuances into themes through the authentic experiences of 298 low-income families.

Endnote

1. See Murumba (2017). Kenya was making very slow progress against maternal mortality until this spike in 2017, which caused a major setback.

References

Anyamba, T. (2011) 'Informal urbanism in Nairobi', *Built Environment (1978–)* 37 (1): 57–77.

Balaton-Chrimes, S. (2011) 'Counting as citizens: recognition of the Nubians in the 2009 Kenyan census', *Ethnopolitics* 10 (2): 205–18 <https://doi.org/1 0.1080/17449057.2011.570983>.

Balaton-Chrimes, S. (2017) 'Recognition, coloniality and international development: a case study of the Nubians and the Kenya Slum Upgrading Project', *Postcolonial Studies* 20 (1): 51–67 <https://doi.org/10.1080/13688 790.2017.1355878>.

Chandy, L. and Gertz, G. (2011) *Poverty in Numbers: The Changing State of Global Poverty from 2005 to 2015*, Brookings Institution, Washington DC. Available from: <https://www.brookings.edu/research/poverty-in-numbers-the-changing-state-of-global-poverty-from-2005-to-2015/> (accessed 27 December 2017).

Elkins, C. (2005) *Imperial Reckoning: The Untold Story of Britain's Gulag in Kenya*, reprint edition, Holt Paperbacks, London.

Hake, A. (1977) *African Metropolis*, Palgrave Macmillan, New York.

KNBS (2017a) *Economic Survey 2017*, Kenya National Bureau of Statistics (KNBS), Nairobi. Available from: <https://www.ke.undp.org/content/dam/kenya/docs/IEG/Economic%20Survey%202016.pdf> (accessed 4 February 2020).

KNBS (2017b) *Basic Report on Well-being in Kenya Based on Kenya Integrated Household Budget Survey 2005/06*, Kenya National Bureau of Statistics (KNBS), Nairobi.

KNBS (2018) *Basic Report on Well-being in Kenya Based on the 2015/16 Kenya Integrated Household Budget Survey (KIHBS)*, Kenya National Bureau of Statistics (KNBS), Nairobi.

Murumba, S. (2017) 'Maternal deaths double in six months', *Daily Nation*, 17 October. Available from: <http://www.nation.co.ke/news/Maternal-deaths-double-in-six-months/1056-4144270-138tikb/index.html> (accessed 5 November 2017).

National AIDS Control Council (2016) *Kenya HIV County Profiles*, National AIDS Control Council, Nairobi. Available from: <http://nacc.or.ke/wp-content/

uploads/2016/12/Kenya-HIV-County-Profiles-2016.pdf> (accessed 27 December 2017).

Obudho, R. (1997) 'Nairobi: national capital and regional hub', in C. Rakodi (ed.), *The Urban Challenge in Africa: Growth and Management of its Large Cities*, United Nations University Press, Tokyo.

Oxfam (2019) *Kenya: Extreme Inequality in Numbers*, Oxfam International, Oxford. Available from: <https://www.oxfam.org/en/kenya-extreme-inequality-numbers> (accessed 11 December 2019).

Parsons, T. (2012) 'Being Kikuyu in Meru: challenging the tribal geography of colonial Kenya', *Journal of African History* 53 (1): 65–86 <https://doi.org/10.1017/S0021853712000023>.

Sumner, A. and Kanbur, R. (2011) 'Why give aid to middle-income countries? Andy Sumner and Ravi Kanbur', *The Guardian*, 23 February. Available from: <http://www.theguardian.com/global-development/poverty-matters/2011/feb/23/aid-to-middle-income-countries> (accessed 27 December 2017).

World Bank (2015) 'GINI index (World Bank estimate)'. Data available from: <https://data.worldbank.org/indicator/SI.POV.GINI?locations=CO> (accessed 3 June 2019).

World Bank (2017) 'Kenya data, NY.GDP.MKTP.KD.ZG'. Data available from: <https://data.worldbank.org/country/kenya> (accessed 27 December 2017).

Young, C. (2002) *Ethnicity and Politics in Africa*, African Studies Center, Boston University, Boston MA.

CHAPTER 2

Looking for money: Generating income from a variety of sources

Abstract

Kenyans piece together livelihoods from multiple income-generating activities by necessity. Their capital and the markets they serve typically do not allow for specialization. Families in our study often overestimated the importance of agriculture and underestimated remittances as a share of total household income. Livelihood strategies seemed to exist on a continuum of preferences, with small enterprise being the most highly prized for its potential to deliver upward mobility.

Keywords: livelihoods, small business, income generation, remittances, agriculture

> What made me work hard? For one, I never wanted to go to my dad to ask for money even though he had property. Going to tell him that my child has not eaten, that was just out of the question. My kid wants clothes, and me and my wife do too. I didn't want to be a laughing stock in the community, with people saying things like, 'This guy got married, and he can't take care of his wife!' So, I must be this side and [my wife] on that side, we both look for money so that we can sustain ourselves and plan for our future. (Samuel, Nairobi)

Rather than using the terms 'working' or 'earning' or 'jobs', the phrase our participants used most to describe their livelihoods was 'looking for money'. This is a telling phrase. Yes, it means earning money, but not *just* through the sweat of labour. There is no formal job implied. 'Looking for money' suggests cleverness, persistence, the discovery of funds that can be shaken loose for some important purpose. What can you make? What can you sell? What service can you provide? What claim can you make and upon whom? And, importantly, how can you stitch enough of that together, first to solve immediate problems and second to build a life?

Most respondents in the Kenya Financial Diaries were looking for money, not 'working' in the ways we think of jobs in advanced economies – they were not even necessarily pursuing a well-defined livelihood. Many, instead, looked a lot like Jennifer. Jennifer's husband abandoned her at the hospital after the birth of her second child. With little family to fall back on, no land or property, and only a third-grade education, she still had to find some way

http://dx.doi.org/10.3362/9781788531207.002

to take care of herself and her kids. 'I don't have anywhere that I am expecting to get money, but I have faith that all will be well, because I'm a hard-working woman,' she told one of our researchers.

She was certainly hard-working. In the 2015 Diaries update, we found her washing clothes and selling coffee to earn a living. But during the Diaries year (2012–13), we observed her earning strategies constantly shifting, based on both desperation and opportunity (Figure 2.1).

As the Diaries began, Jennifer was earning most of her income from selling chapatti, but business slowed in November, and she slowly felt forced to use her capital for food. The business had been a great consolation, providing some stability in cash flows. '*Vibaruas* [casual jobs],' she told us, 'are dangerous, because there are times they don't come for a whole week!' When the business collapsed, she went back to those *vibaruas*, washing clothes when she could pick up jobs. This was not a reliable strategy; she travelled a long distance to a waiting area and sometimes would not be picked by an employer. If she did get work, she typically earned only $1–$2 for the day.

Early in the new year, she caught a lucky break and was offered a temporary, part-time job working in the canteen of a local school. At the weekend she would pick up some washing jobs for extra money. The canteen job did not last, though, and she was on her own again when schools closed for the holidays at the end of the first term. She went looking for work in the community and was soon offered a position as a barmaid. The money was good but she hated the long hours and having to stay up late with drunken men. Still, that money, along with some extra earned in a very brief foray into prostitution, helped her get enough together to get back to her chapatti business, which was again booming at the project's end.

Jennifer's patchwork of constantly shifting income sources resists classification into any neat category. She is not a labourer, not a businesswoman, not an employee, not a remittance recipient, but rather all these things at different times. She had to hustle to find all these various income sources and felt strained by not knowing where the money would come from to pay rent and buy food when one of her strategies was not working. Once, at a particularly low point, she told us that she beat her daughter who lost KES 50 ($0.58) when Jennifer had sent her to the shop to buy food. Jennifer was upset with herself. She did not mean to be so harsh, but that was her last 50 shillings, and she didn't know where the next inflow would come from. At one point she broke down crying and told us how she wished she could go home upcountry, but she knew she was stuck in Nairobi since she had children. They would be too much of a burden to impose on her mother. For her, having many sources of income over the course of a year was not some kind of thoughtful diversification strategy, but rather a result of desperation and necessity. No single source of income was sufficient to support her family (Figure 2.2). None was reliable from week to week or from month to month.

Not all respondents lived as close to the edge as Jennifer, but characteristics of her income earning patterns reverberated throughout our sample

Jennifer's Monthly Household Income (KES)

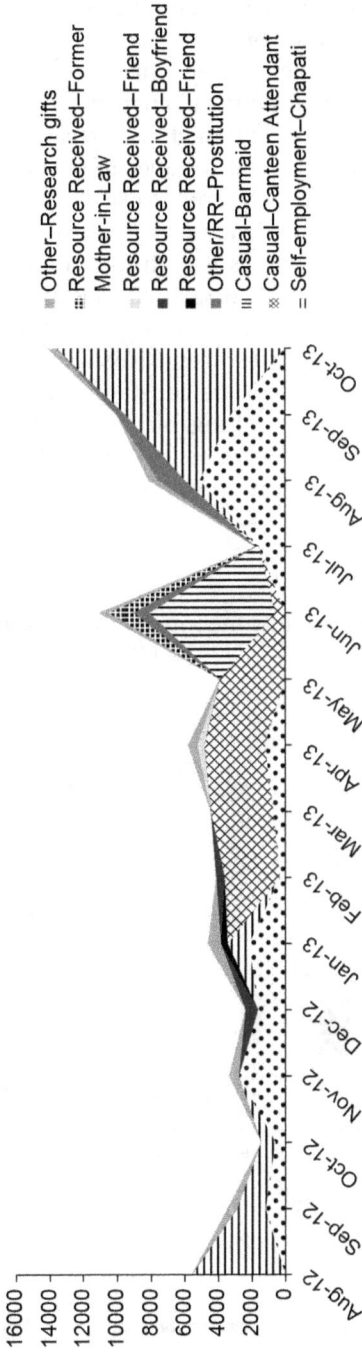

Legend:
- ▦ Other–Research gifts
- ⁝ Resource Received–Former Mother-in-Law
- ░ Resource Received–Friend
- ■ Resource Received–Boyfriend
- ■ Resource Received–Friend
- ▩ Other/RR–Prostitution
- ≡ Casual–Barmaid
- ⊠ Casual–Canteen Attendant
- ⁼ Self-employment–Chapati

Figure 2.1 Jennifer is one household with the median number of income sources in the study. The chart below shows her income structure over the year, revealing a pattern of shifting strategies throughout the year.
Note: Time frames of observations are not exactly the same for every household. In some areas we were able to start Diaries more quickly than in others. Where we started later, we also ended later. However, when we present figures that span across the sample, such as average income levels and consumption, we use a common shared period of months when all households were being studied.

and shake some widely held, implicit assumptions about how low-income people generate liveable incomes. For some time, general understandings of these kinds of livelihoods were defined by what they are not. They are not 'proper jobs', but rather *in*formal, *un*stable, characterized by *un*employment (Ferguson and Li, 2018). New concepts such as 'precarity', 'survivalist', and 'improvised' livelihoods have emerged to label these income-earning strategies according to what they *are* (Ferguson, 2006; du Toit and Neves, 2014; Scully, 2016; Standing, 2016). The benchmark against which these kinds of work are measured is a salaried job, as if such jobs are the norm and these other forms of work the exception. But salaried jobs are exceedingly rare in Kenya and, in fact, throughout Africa. Only 16 per cent of Kenyan workers, about 2.8 million people, earn formal wages (KNBS, 2019).

More often, families like Jennifer's are constantly looking for money, an activity encompassing constantly shifting mixes of labour, enterprise, and redistribution, not by choice, but by necessity (Figure 2.2) (Ferguson, 2006). Such livelihoods are often inherently uncertain and volatile, but they are

Average monthly income by single source ($),
ranked from lowest to highest number of sources in sample

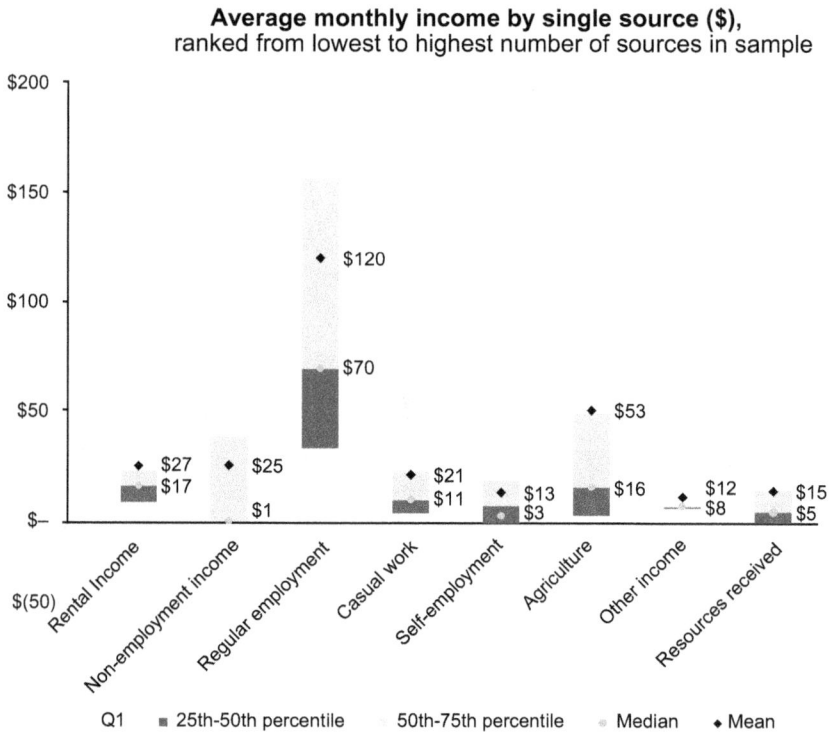

Q1   ■ 25th–50th percentile   50th–75th percentile   ● Median   ◆ Mean

Figure 2.2 The median income from any single source is too small for most families to live on, with the rare exception of those with regular jobs, who still typically need a supplement to achieve household consumption levels above $2 per day.

differentially so. Most individuals and families aim to change their situation not by getting one of the very few formal jobs that are available, but by earning more and earning more regularly through small businesses and productive investments, whether those be in land and cows or in one another.

Economic growth is not changing this reality. Instead, in Kenya, like much of Africa, we observe significant growth in GDP without commensurate growth in formal jobs. In Kenya in 2018, the economy grew at 6.3 per cent, while wage jobs in what the government calls the 'modern' sector grew only 2.8 per cent (KNBS, 2019) An estimated 91 per cent of new 'jobs' (very loosely defined) are being created in the informal sector (KNBS, 2019).

Social scientists have begun to recognize this enduring reality. Development in Kenya simply may not look anything like economists once expected. It is unrealistic to expect Kenya to achieve development through mass employment in manufacturing, as we saw in Asia (Ferguson, 2015; de Melo, 2017; Osei, 2017; Rodrik et al., 2017; Ferguson and Li, 2018). Instead, growth without much formal job creation is likely to continue. This means that, if we hope to see growth accompanied by widely shared improvements in well-being, we need to make better sense of the realities of livelihoods today, understand how they link to economic growth, and reconfigure our understanding of the meaning and roles of labour, ownership, and distribution.

Livelihood patterns in the Kenya Diaries

How might we define these livelihoods? It is clear that they are not composed of singular earning activities. Like most of our respondents, Jennifer had a large number of income sources. Over the course of a year of Financial Diaries observation, our team recorded each income source separately, including each kind of business, each type of casual work, and each sender of remittances or gifts, what we called 'resources received' or 'RR'. By this classification, the median household in the Diaries had 10 separate income sources during the year of observation. The individual sources of RR were the most numerous, but even excluding those, the median household had five separate income sources.

Sometimes, as in Jennifer's case, that was because of shifting earning strategies over the course of the year. But even when income sources persisted over many months, households had a portfolio of income sources rather than a single occupation. This was not necessarily a strategy meant to diversify unstable earnings. Increasing aggregate household income through a single source via specialization was simply not a viable option for many. Specialization can only improve efficiency and net earnings if there is a viable market for *more* of those specialized goods and services. In reality, there are only so many casual work opportunities within an accessible radius. Markets within reach where a person might sell groundnuts or vegetables are limited in size. Farms are often quite small. Earning enough to live on – or, as many hope, to amass some savings – requires earning in many different forms.

This has important implications. If you were to give Jennifer a title based on her occupation, what would it be? In the Diaries sample, the most important income source in the median household accounted for 58 per cent of income. That is certainly significant. But, it is also important to note that, for a quarter of households, the largest income source accounted for less than 41 per cent of household income. This tells us that the realities of income are more complex than a designation by 'main' livelihood – a frequent survey question and segmentation variable – might suggest.

Asking low-income households about their main income source appeared to elicit an identity – or perhaps an expectation or aspiration – rather than the largest source of actual earnings. For only about half of our respondent households did the main income source reported during a screening interview match the largest source of income recorded during the project.[1] Some of that discrepancy is because livelihood strategies – like Jennifer's – are forced to change and adapt to circumstances. But much of it comes from systematically overestimating the importance of farming and underestimating reliance on remittances. In the Diaries, 21 per cent of households reported farming as their main income during screening, but only 8 per cent received the largest share of their income from agriculture. Only 8 per cent of households reported reliance on remittances during screening, when remittances in fact accounted for the largest share of income in 27 per cent of households (Figure 2.3). A larger number of our respondent households relied on direct redistribution in this form than on 'jobs' in the traditional sense. And this covers just direct, monetary distribution; indirect forms of redistribution are even more substantial, as we will explore later in this chapter.

Rather than taking income as a given, Jennifer and many of our other respondents were forced to constantly seek additional earnings in response to expenditure needs. Households that survive so close to the margins, without stable and sufficient income, cannot limit their necessary spending against a fixed budget constraint. 'Living within your means' – a virtue in the middle class – is not an option when there is not enough money to meet basic needs and earning opportunities are never guaranteed. Plus, various unexpected expenses (essential home repairs, medical expenses) are bound to crop up from time to time. In those moments when a lump sum is needed, our respondents again told us that they 'look for money'. Sometimes that means turning to financial devices such as savings and borrowing. But it also means trying to bring new money to the household by picking up any extra work they can, and, quite often, asking their social networks for help.

These resources from the social network not only increase total household incomes, but – at least in rural areas – they dampen some of the income volatility that households would otherwise face. The median household in our study saw its income fluctuate by 55 per cent from month to month during the Diaries year. In rural households, that volatility would be even higher – 64 per cent – if there were no inter-household gifts and remittances coming into the household.

Main source of income reported at screening and measured through Diaries cashflows (%) (n=290, 8 households did not undergo the same screening)

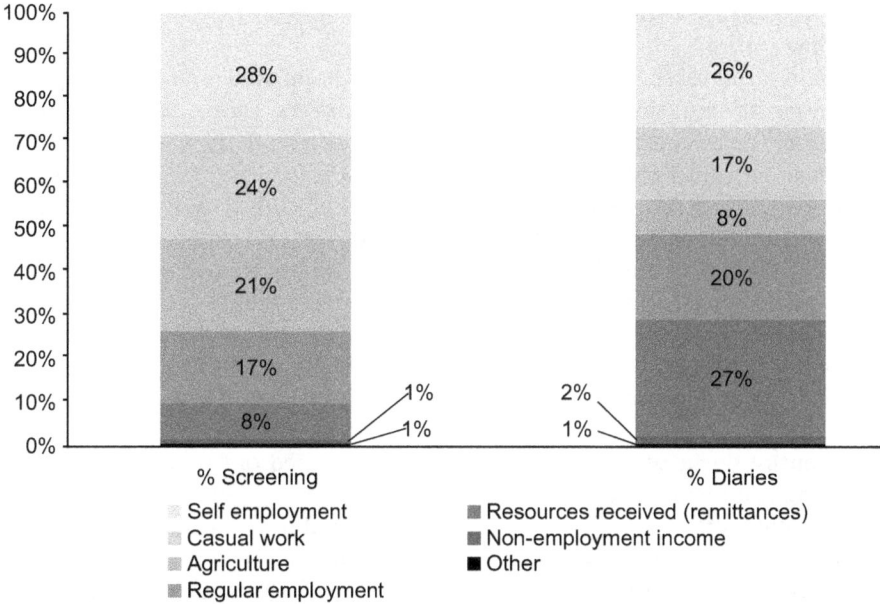

Figure 2.3 text:

Legend:
- Self employment
- Casual work
- Agriculture
- Regular employment
- Resources received (remittances)
- Non-employment income
- Other

% Screening values: 28%, 24%, 21%, 17%, 8%, 1%, 1%

% Diaries values: 26%, 17%, 8%, 20%, 27%, 2%, 1%

Figure 2.3 Households systematically overestimated the importance of agriculture and under-estimated the importance of remittances in their income portfolios.

Planning around low and volatile incomes is not easy, as we will see in Chapter 3, 'Managing money'. Complications are compounded by complexities around negotiating how income is earned and used within the household, for planning against risk, and for the project of *maendeleo*, 'development', the collective goal for respondent households.

So how do these blended earning strategies fit into the *maendeleo* plan? In this chapter, we will take a look at the income categories from Figure 2.3 and unpack the nature and importance of each form of earning in our respondents' lives. Why do people earn the way they earn? Why do they overestimate some strategies and underestimate others? We will close with a particularly close look at small businesses, because these are perhaps the least understood and – in respondents' views – the most important drivers of improved well-being. Under current conditions – according to our 2015 update – business growth is the most viable short- to medium-term route out of poverty. We hope to offer some answers about why and how this is the case, and also to raise some questions about what 'business' really is for ordinary people in Kenya. Do 'businesses' really reflect entrepreneurship or are they merely safety nets in disguise?

The surprising (un?)importance of agriculture

Respondents' overestimation of agricultural income raises important questions. Our sample was 70 per cent rural, and three-quarters of our rural respondents did at least some farming. Why doesn't agriculture matter more as an income source?[2]

First, farms can be quite small in the densely populated rural areas of Kenya. The median farm size in our sample was half an acre. Farm sizes tended to be larger in the drier and sandier areas where soil productivity was poor.

Income from agriculture varied widely by the types of farming in which households were engaged. The most profitable farming activity was cash-crop production, especially tea and fruit trees for those few farmers with sufficient land in the right climactic zones and with the ability to make patient investment in crops that take years to mature. The other highly profitable agricultural goods were vegetables, eggs, and milk. Eggs and milk were particularly desirable because they generated relatively steady income throughout the year and could create income for producers on a daily basis. These could become very important sources of income but were quite vulnerable. Single dairy cows and entire flocks of chickens were sometimes wiped out quickly by disease, causing real income crises.

Emmah, a rural woman in Western Kenya, told us about how difficult this could be. When we asked her about a time in her life when she faced a lot of financial stress, she remembered back to 1999. She was staying at the rural home with her children while her husband was living in town, spending much of his income on alcohol and a mistress. She was getting by by raising chickens, but a disease killed her entire flock – 30 birds – at once. Feeling desperate and suicidal, she took herself to a hospital, where the staff talked her down. She still raises chickens – and even acts as an informal vet in the community – but balances that income with income from remittances and casual work. During the update year, she lost 50 four-week-old chicks, but the blow was much less severe that time around due to her more diversified sources of income.

Although it is not a big income earner, most farming households focus most of their farming attention on maize, the main staple food in Kenya. Eighty-three per cent of our farming households produced at least some maize. These farmers mostly appeared to take a low-risk, low-expectation approach to these food crops. Median maize production investment per acre was just KES 2,170 ($26) in the Diaries year. This approach may be rational, given the difficulty in turning a profit with increased inputs and labour investments alongside rainfall and crop disease risks. Based on five-year recall data from our respondents, we estimated the probability of a rainfall-related crop loss at about 40 per cent every year.

A small number of our respondents took loans for agricultural inputs. While most of them reported increases in yields, only some saw increases in profits after accounting for the cost of the loan and – most importantly – the costs of additional labour they hired to ensure that their investments translated into increased yields. Our sample of borrowing households was quite small, but a randomized control trial with rice farmers in Mali also suggested that increasing input usage may not always be profitable.[3] Tavneet Suri demonstrated that low adoption of fertilizer and hybrid maize seed may in fact be because, while average farmers see gains, there is a significant share of the farmer population that does not realize yield gains or realizes only small gains that may not be profitable (Suri, 2011). Taken together, the evidence suggests that capital for improved inputs may not be the most important productivity constraint for all smallholder farmers.

Net household income gains from increased input usage were also affected by the opportunity cost of household members – mostly women – shifting more of their labour use from paid work on neighbours' farms during the most intensive labour seasons to unpaid labour on the household plot. Household plots generated relatively less cash income, and cash income from farming was often controlled by men.

As an income source, maize farming did not do well for the households in our study. The median farming household in our study achieved no –zero – net monetary revenue per acre during the Diaries year. The mean agricultural revenue in that year rises to KES 14,242 ($167), driven mostly by non-maize production. But maize (along with other products) is an important source of food for many households, and incorporating consumption into cash income sees net income per acre rise to KES 24,752 ($291) for the median farming household (but remember that most do not own a full acre of land).

Producing food does not eliminate the need for cash income – even for food spending. The median rural household still allocated 49 per cent of consumption spending to food. This share was higher than in urban areas, where larger incomes and the need for other kinds of consumption expenditures (such as rent and transportation) meant that a smaller share (43 per cent) of the consumption budget went to food.[4]

What we observed is that households' consumption of food from their own production was not a major source of income, but it was a very important means of dampening consumption volatility. When we incorporate the value of consumption of farm produce into our consumption calculations, median month-to-month volatility in consumption falls from 54 per cent to 45 per cent in rural areas.[5] This leads us to wonder: is staple food production today more a safety net than a source of income?

This observation of agriculture's importance in the household income portfolio is a troubling one. We know that a large share of low-income people engage in farming, and we know that productivity gains in agriculture tend to translate into faster poverty reduction than productivity gains in other sectors (Johnston and Mellor, 1961; Fogel, 1994; Block, 1999; Ligon and Sadoulet, 2007; Thurlow and Wobst, 2014; Klasen and Reimers, 2017). Such evidence has – rightly – made agriculture a priority for many development practitioners and donors. However, we observed among our households that, during this study, agriculture at this micro-scale did not serve as a pathway out of poverty for very many families.

Where are the cash transfers ('non-employment income')?

Cash transfers are becoming an increasingly important policy tool globally for addressing extreme poverty, but at the time of our study, only seven respondent families were receiving funds from a government cash transfer programme, all of them in the Mombasa and Vihiga counties, and all of them through the Orphans and Vulnerable Children programme. Kenya reportedly expanded this programme to 240,000 households in 2016 (World Bank, n.d.) and introduced a transfer for the elderly in 2018 (though implementation progress is unclear). Given how small these programmes were during our study, few expected that they could benefit from them, but they did provide a helpful lifeline to those who received them, even though the timing of payments was often erratic and difficult to plan around. On average, those receiving these payments received KES 4000 ($47) every two months, but often payments were delayed and were dispersed after three or four months. This represented about 19 per cent of the recipients' incomes. Overall institutional transfers were somewhat more widespread than government cash transfers and included occasional payments from NGOs and churches. Although enthusiasm is growing for larger-scale cash transfer programmes in Kenya and around the world, they remained quite limited throughout our study.

Rethinking remittances and gifts ('resources received')

Instead of large-scale institutional transfers, the real social safety net was informal, person to person, based on complex relationships of mutual support and distributive obligations. In fact, the term 'safety net' is probably not the right word to describe the role of remittances in people's lives. These transfers were very important for helping people endure shocks, for catching people as they fall, as the term 'safety net' implies. But they were also the *main* source of basic subsistence for many – for 27 per cent of households in our study – and an important form of supplementary income for many more, even in the absence of shocks. For many people, remittances were 'Plan A'.

Leonita was a typical example. She lived with her elderly in-laws and youngest child on her husband's property in rural Makueni County. She diligently tried to earn an income of her own by plaiting sisal ropes for sale, but, although it occupied much of her time, it earned her very little money, accounting for only about 9 per cent of household income during the Diaries. Most of her income (77 per cent) was from remittances, some from her husband, and much more from her adult daughters, one who worked in Nairobi and another who was married to a soldier stationed in Somalia. Both daughters regularly sent money at the end of each month to help with their mother's general upkeep and school fees for their youngest sibling, who was still in secondary school. In an average month, Leonita's total household income was around KES 3,250 ($38). She was also able to farm to offset some food spending and only very rarely experienced hunger, even on such a meagre income. Remittances kept the entire family afloat.

Anthropologists and economists have documented widely the importance of gift giving, exchange, and egalitarian distribution among kin and sometimes wider social groups in Kenya and throughout much of Africa (Platteau, 1996; Collier and Gunning, 1999). However, narrow frames of analysis have made it difficult to make sense of the general implications of such behaviours on long-term growth and poverty reduction. Anthropologists have tended to recognize the value such cultures place on collective welfare, while also recognizing that such norms are problematic for some individuals and give rise to practices aimed at evading sharing obligations (Ferguson, 1994). Some economists, in contrast, have viewed such extensive redistributive gift giving as a tax on accumulation, arguing that such practices reduce private investment and economic growth. Some have even argued that these practices partially explain why Africa failed to develop (Platteau, 1996; Collier and Gunning, 1999). Many modern development economists, however, recognize the positive attributes of networks, attempting to measure and quantify them as 'social capital' (Glaeser et al., 2002).

In the era of mobile money, the anthropological and economic views have intersected. Extensive remittance networks enabled the rise of Kenya's famous M-Pesa mobile money system (Morawczynski, 2009). M-Pesa in turn brought new efficiencies to existing distributive channels. Research by Billy Jack and Tavneet Suri showed that M-Pesa helped those facing negative shocks receive more remittances from wider networks and reduced poverty over the longer term, with particularly pronounced effects on female-headed households. They show that these remittance efficiencies particularly helped women to increase their business-related income (Jack and Suri, 2014; Suri and Jack, 2016).

Our respondents' experiences provoked two somewhat new questions about the ways in which such networks are understood. First, are extensive remittance networks a response to risk or to prolonged, chronic scarcity? Second, are distributive demands better understood as a tax on accumulation or a dividend on extensive social investment?

Diaries households seemed to show us that chronic scarcity – not just risk – was critically important to the emergence and persistence of distributed networks. The economic literature has tended to place more emphasis on the risk-sharing dimensions of social networks (Collier and Gunning, 1999; Jack and Suri, 2014). These properties were very important for our respondents. Resources from friends and family were not only the most important de facto source of money and in-kind resources during a shock, but also the most important ex ante strategy respondents cited to cope with shocks (Zollmann, 2015). Social networks were also able to mobilize much more money than other coping strategies, such as savings, credit, and asset sales. In the face of the costliest kinds of shocks – particularly hospitalizations or the death of the main income earner – social networks were even more important, with contributions exceeding months' or years' worth of average household incomes.

Even though social network mobilization is the most powerful weapon in the risk-coping arsenal of Kenya's low-income families, it still has many shortcomings. The timing of contributions may not always perfectly match need. For example, we observed multiple occasions in which health financing came too late to save a life when a person needed urgent medical care. Not everyone benefits equally. Those with diminished networks (divorced women, for example) or limited abilities to make claims on others (men as opposed to women) are less able to mobilize giving in times of need. And, yes, helping others in the social network can take a toll on the assets of network members who contribute their savings to bail out a family member instead of making some other kind of investment that may have had higher individual returns.

But we did not observe remittances only in times of acute shocks; instead, we saw heavy month-to-month reliance on them for basic survival. A large share of households had remittances as their most important income source. The median households in the study received 15 per cent of their annual income from remittances. This source of income did not just save lives in the event of a medical crisis but also by meeting basic needs of network members for food and shelter. The transfer patterns we observed did not reflect reciprocal risk-pooling patterns for the most part, but instead distributive ones, from the relatively better off to the relatively worse off, even though many in the relatively better off group were still below the poverty line. Only 23 per cent of our respondent households were net givers of remittances, but still half of those survived on less than $2 per day. While the median net giver household earned only KES 13,162 ($155) per month, they still gave away about 9 per cent of their monthly income to others.

Which brings us to the second question. If distribution is essential for survival in a context with few opportunities for jobs and economic advancement, is the act of distribution more like a tax or more like a dividend paid back to 'investors' whose pooled contributions helped someone achieve their relatively better-off status? Those investors, for example, ensured that a successful child made it through school, had someone to care for her children while she looked for money outside the home village, or helped a network member pay a bribe to land a well-paid job.[6] That is the kind of reasoning that our respondents most seemed to reflect.

Yes, producing dividends for a network of investors can be a burden. But the returns also enable the initial investment to the communal project of *maendeleo*, the idea that a family develops and that they rise and fall together through shared burdens and shared successes. How would households otherwise afford investments in education or cope with the costs of healthcare? In the absence of massive state intervention, what are the alternatives? A peek at those with limited or diminished networks provides some clues about what the world would look like without this form of sharing. It looks like Maggie, whose grandchildren regularly go hungry. She has sent one grandson to kindergarten three times, unable to raise the $20 to get him admitted into first grade. It looks like HIV-positive Patricia, who stopped taking her antiretroviral medications (ARVs) because she eats too little and too infrequently to keep them down. It looks like Ellen, who was forced to save for years to afford treatment for her son's debilitating abdominal illness. In sum, despite their shortcomings, social transfers are enormously important and could be conceived of as a rather capitalist response to extreme scarcity, unlikely to diminish in importance until a much larger share of the population is able to independently earn enough to live well above the poverty line.

'Regular' employment

That kind of future is unlikely to arrive quickly. Only about 16 per cent of Kenyan workers have formal, salaried jobs, and this level has persisted (and has even fallen slightly) since 2012 and for long before that (KNBS, 2017). In our sample, we did not classify jobs as formal or informal. Instead, we considered wage employment, where a job was steady and wages paid on agreed intervals to be 'regular' jobs. In our sample, some of these were formal jobs, especially for teachers, security guards working with large security companies, and a few factory workers. Many others were informal workers, working without contracts as M-Pesa attendants, school watchmen, truck and matatu drivers, shop clerks, and tea pickers. With only about 20 per cent of respondent households getting their main source of income from these kinds of jobs, they are not 'regular' in the sense of being typical, only in the sense of being relatively stable in terms of the interval of wage payments.

It is tempting to assume that such jobs would be an aspirational form of income for many. Labour activists and governments often advocate for the creation of these types of jobs, which are expected to come along with certain labour protections and worker benefits, such as pensions, health insurance, and maternity leave. However, in reality, such jobs are both rare and not as liberating as one might expect. Many such jobs are not particularly secure and do not offer the potential for upward mobility. Many do not provide sufficient incomes for workers' families to live above the poverty line without supplementary income. Such jobs might even bring in less income – through more short-term predictably – than self-employment alternatives. Some wives in our study were disappointed when their husbands took these kinds of jobs, as taking such lower-paying jobs that paid only once a month shifted more day-to-day spending onto them, the wives. Wives also saw their bargaining power for lumpier investments eroded, since men's lumpy incomes were better suited to those kinds of longer-term choices. Both in this study and in other research in Kenya with higher-income groups, we have found that many workers with 'regular' jobs maintain side investments and aspire to become self-employed. Self-employment offers greater possibilities of earning, more freedom, more flexibility over how one spends one's time, and the possibility of an income that lasts into one's old age.

Casual work

Casual work, or *vibarua* (singular *kibarua*), occupied the lowest rung on the income preference ladder. This kind of work is typically highly unpredictable, involving the provision of raw labour for a daily cash exchange. Median daily earnings from a casual job were KES 150 ($1.76) in rural areas and KES 300 ($3.53) in urban ones. To earn most of one's income from *vibarua* – as did almost a quarter of our respondents – signalled vulnerability and a lack of assets that might allow one to graduate to the far preferred livelihood dominated by self-employment. More often, casual work was just one piece of an income patchwork, which included remittances, agriculture, and multiple kinds of casual gigs.

Not all types of casual work were the same, though. Urban construction labourers, for example, could typically work as much as they wanted, earning between KES 300 and 500 per day, which allowed for some financial stability. That was very different from the seasonally available casual work of helping with planting, weeding, and harvesting on other people's farms or the occasional work one might get hauling water or doing laundry for a slightly better-off (or disabled) neighbour. In their economic histories, women often spoke of casual work as a means to tide the family over between the times their husbands sent remittances. Young people talked about picking up casual jobs as a way to help fund their education. Young men would recall periods when they bounced around picking up casual work as part of their growing-up process, trying to accumulate some money to start a business or find some more promising opportunity. Older men talked about the shame of seeing their wives having to take up casual work. For them, this was a humiliating sign of their own failure to provide enough for their families. When we asked people about what it looked like to be financially successful, a common answer was that a person no longer needed to do casual work. That work was hard, unreliable, and often shameful. Casual work was taken out of desperation, as a necessary supplement, or to hold steady while waiting for something else. These kinds of gigs were never the plan.

Biashara ni maisha (business is life)

Real *maendeleo* (development) required investment. Respondents knew that no one would hire them out of poverty (although they hoped that might be possible for their children). No one expected the government to come to the rescue. They told us that to be financially successful, one must be thrifty and clever, planning an array of family projects that allow the unit to move forward together. Some of those investments were in land, dairy cows, and education of children. But business played a central role.

Sixty-one per cent of Diaries households engaged in some kind of business (a term we use interchangeably with 'self-employment') during the Diaries year. These are activities in which the individual or household invested some of their own funds in order to run an enterprise with the intention of making money.[7]

Among those households, income from business typically accounted for about half (mean 48 per cent; median 50 per cent) of all household income. It was the most significant source of income for 27 per cent of households in our study and for 18.4 per cent of adults in the nationally representative FinAccess survey of 2016 (Central Bank of Kenya et al., 2016). Starting a new business or expanding an existing one was the leading reason Diaries respondents reported for improvements in economic well-being between 2013 and 2015.

Phillip was one example. Phillip was one of the larger maize farmers in the study, living on a family farm outside Eldoret with his wife and seven children. In his best year on the farm (2011), he harvested 30 90-kilogramme bags of maize.[8] In terms of cash income, though, his family got by on only about KES 4,000 ($40) per month. When we saw him in 2015, that income had risen dramatically to about KES 26,000 ($260). A big part of the absolute change was the receipt of a dowry payment for one of Phillip's daughters. That money wasn't all consumed: part of it enabled Phillip to start a butchery business, which was bringing in an extra KES 1,000 ($10) per week in profits. It was the business, more than the dowry payment, that gave him peace of mind as he looked to the future of school fee payments.

Entrepreneurship is a hallmark of Kenyan culture and has been embraced by politicians from the time of independence up to today. President Uhuru Kenyatta even told a class of university graduates in 2014 that business and self-employment were viable solutions to low youth employment (Nation Correspondent, 2014). But are the enterprises of ordinary Kenyans the seeds of industry, innovation, and employment creation?

When we take a closer look at Diaries respondents' businesses, we see that they were central to many people's lives but tended not to be the seeds of growing enterprises set to create millions of jobs. Instead, they seem to be something quite different. While often lumped in with micro, small and medium enterprises (MSMEs or SMEs in development lingo), they operated on a very different scale and according to a very different set of logics. So, what were these businesses really like?

Low investment, low revenue

These businesses were very, very small. Of the 369 businesses registered by Diaries households at the start of the main study, the median starting capital was just KES 600 ($7). Twenty per cent of these businesses – often service-based ones such as hair salons – started with no capital at all. Seventy-five per cent of the businesses were started with less than KES 5,000 ($59). Only a few businesses generated enough income to sustain a family independently. The median businesses earned only about KES 1,500 ($18) per month in profit during the months they were active during the Diaries. Only 11.5 per cent of the businesses in our sample produced an average monthly profit of KES 10,000 ($118) or more, the median amount that our respondents reported they would need to live comfortably.

This reality of low profits was not intentional, but rather part of the reality of operating under both credit- and demand-constrained markets. When we look at start-up costs and profitability across rural and urban areas, we see that the capital required to start an enterprise is roughly similar in both places, but that urban businesses tend to be more profitable. This comes as no surprise given that rural business owners have a smaller accessible market, both in the numbers of potential customers and their income levels.

> Like I told you, the market is very small and the people from this side are just peasants, they go for small-small things, but if the market could be big, we could be making a lot of money. (Paul, Vihiga)

Being able to start a moderately profitable – even if very small – business with very little money means that businesses can serve almost like a safety net for people recovering from hardship. We see this in people's life stories, not just in Kenya but in other places with large, informal markets (BFA, 2016). When someone hits rock bottom, they often turn to family and friends, church, or some meagre savings to buy a small amount of stock to trade and start their economic lives over again.

Informal

Few small businesses are formally registered with any government body in Kenya generally, but many – especially those with physical premises or that operate in designated market areas – obtain operating permits or pay a daily fee to local government offices, including town councils. Among the businesses in our sample, only 13 per cent had even that basic kind of operating permit.[9] This is very low. Other studies have attempted to conduct censuses of retail establishments in small towns, and while they included even very small kiosks, registration rates were much higher, in the 80 per cent range.[10]

No records

Only about 24 per cent of the businesses registered during the Diaries reported keeping any kind of written record of business sales and expenses, and we observed that even when this was done, it was rarely consistent or accurate. For the very small businesses, like those selling *mandazi* (fried dough snacks), respondents could recall daily sales and stock purchases easily with mental calculations. Keeping a written record seemed pointless to them; their businesses were small and simple. By necessity, business and household expenditures were all mixed into one budget:

> We don't separate the money for business and for buying food. The most important thing is to make sure that the children are fed, and they are well. (Leah, Nairobi)

Temporary

Many of these businesses were not built to last. Respondents often started them in a moment of need and closed them just as easily when activity slowed down, when capital needed to be diverted to pressing household needs, when a woman business operator was dealing with a sick relative or a new baby, or when the business operator had a chance for some other kind of higher-paying, temporary work. On occasion, businesses sprang up to serve a particular, temporary market – like selling lunch at a construction site – and closed when the opportunity passed. Forty-eight per cent of the businesses that operated at some point during the Diaries were closed by the time of the update interview two years later. The median age of businesses operating during the Diaries was just one year. Only the most established 25 per cent of businesses had passed the five-year mark of at least intermittent operation.[11]

Undifferentiated, for a reason

The businesses run by our respondents provided basic goods and services that were in demand within local communities. Our respondents were selling the same things that other respondents were buying. Many small business operators in the sample did very simple, low-capital trading, most often of foodstuffs and cooking fuels such as firewood and charcoal. This is no surprise, since food consumed about half of our respondent households' budgets. Another big segment of business operators prepared and sold cooked foods, doing some very basic value addition. When it comes to services, the businesses in our sample mostly provided transportation (motorbike taxis and pushcarts), tailoring (the making and repairing of clothing, including school uniforms), and hair plaiting and cutting services – again, the same kinds of services being purchased by respondents in the same communities. The median household in the study did 85 per cent (by value) of its expenditures within 30 minutes' walking distance from home, showing just how local markets are for basic goods and services. Most of the businesses in our sample were limited in their size and scope by the realities of these local markets.

Low tech

The majority of respondents' businesses were based on simple trading. The capital needed to start and grow them often went towards stock rather than fixed capital or technology. The most common machine and equipment investments we saw were things like cooking pots and stoves (for those preparing food or brewing alcohol), motorbikes and carts (for transportation), and sewing machines (for tailoring). A few respondents had been able to make more substantial investments in bore holes (for selling water) and posho mills (for grinding maize) at some point in their lives. Those investments might enable long-term businesses but did not come out of an organic growth trajectory, building up from small trading; rather, they came from lump sum income windfalls. Very, very few businesses run by Diaries respondents have grown or will ever grow large enough to make formality appealing or even to cross the threshold of hiring a single employee. For most, scale is not even the goal.

Born of necessity, not invention

These enterprises were not based on innovation, but rather emerged out of the necessity of earning sufficient income in contexts where employment was scarce.

> I gave birth in June 2000. We didn't have anything. There was no money; the little money we had was for food. We didn't have any capital to start that business, so after some time [my husband] got a menial job and with the money he got, we started a small business, and that is when life started changing a bit. (Florence, Nairobi)

Businesses were particularly important for our female respondents. Kenya's national MSME survey in 2016 found that about 61 per cent of unlicensed businesses were owned by women. In addition to diversifying the household's overall earnings, these businesses allowed women to fill gaps in the household budget, particularly in areas that were priorities for women, and also gave them some independence in financial decision making:

> Before our child started going to school [my husband] was never sending money consistently. We just used to do business to put something on the table. (Alice, Vihiga)

Even those who were employed worried that their wages were not sufficient to meet their families' needs, that their jobs were unstable, that they had little opportunity for wage growth within their jobs, and that they would need some alternative income source in order to slow down in old age.

> You know, when you tell your wife to just sit there and not do anything, you can go and be told there is no work anymore. When this happens, it is never easy getting work elsewhere. That's why I decided to start a business for her, because I wanted security. (Samuel, Nairobi)

Business offers nearly everyone the possibility of earning just a little bit extra, not typically by doing something new or innovative but by offering the goods and services in demand from their own communities, hoping to capture some local market share.

Mostly low growth

While the median business run by a Diaries household brought in only KES 1,500 ($18) per month, a smaller number were more substantial, serving as a real basis for the household livelihood rather than just a supplement. Only a very small number were specialized or growth-oriented, where capital fuelled expansion. Market size and saturation were just as much of a bottleneck as capital for respondents' businesses. Running multiple businesses – rather than expanding an existing business – therefore made much more economic sense.

For example, Karen started small selling *mandazi* (fried dough triangles) in the morning to schoolchildren walking along the road in a densely populated community outside Mombasa. Since she had only a little starting capital, she would often sell out in the early days. She could grow by incrementally adding more stock, and she did this for about a year. Eventually, though, she reached the point where adding more *mandazi* would just mean that her product would go unsold. But her profits from the *mandazi* were not enough to meet her household's needs. She decided to sell fried potatoes in the afternoons, catching the children as they came home from school along the same road.

By the time the Diaries were ending, she had reached the limits of her own time. She would wake at 4am to start cooking the *mandazi*, then go to sell them. By mid-morning she was home preparing potatoes and would finish selling those in the evening. If she wanted to earn more, she would need another product line. To do that, she could hire someone, but that came with only moderate returns, since that person must also be paid. Hiring someone also meant that her income would be hit even more during sales slumps and she would have to deal with the headaches of management. Her other options would be purchasing some equipment that would help her use her own time more efficiently, perhaps then freeing up some time midday to sell lunch to workers in the local godowns (warehouses for packing commodities for export).

Christopher followed a slightly different path. He ran a successful spice business in the local market of a medium-sized town. When he reached his peak in that town, he expanded his market reach, travelling twice a week to markets in smaller towns where he would sell his goods while his wife tended their main stall at home. But when sales from travelling markets also peaked, he realized he needed to add a new kind of business to increase his earnings. He took a loan from the bank to buy a second-hand motorbike and hired a driver to run it as a motorbike taxi. The last time we saw him, he had added a second motorbike to his growing fleet while continuing to run the spice business. He had purchased land where he was planning to build apartments. Expanding his income required him to venture into different kinds of business investments. His market just could not support the expansion of a specialized venture. A patchwork livelihood was the only way to expand one's earning potential.

Fulfilling

The same features of these businesses that make them unlikely to fuel long-term growth in Kenya – their informality and their very small-scale and temporary nature – are the same features that make them so important to low-income families. A low-income person can move in and out of business activities with ease, turning a meaningful profit, even if in nominal terms that profit is small. This allows for an important cushion in otherwise vulnerable circumstances. If Kenya's economy were more formal and respondents faced even lower demand for their small-scale trading enterprises, it is likely we would see signs of much greater hunger and vulnerability.

> Now I am at least better, because when I started I was staying in a grass thatched house, but when I started this business of brewing alcohol, I saved some money and built that house then later moved to this house and improved it. I then realized that my brothers had no place for sleeping and that land was theirs. I moved from that land to this one, which was for my grandparents. After coming here is when I started progressing and I will even build a better house than this one, now I am at least better unlike before. (Michael, Vihiga)

Inefficiency and opportunity

The experience of Diaries households looking for money leads us to view elements of low-income people's livelihoods in some new ways. We see, for example, that individuals' livelihood identities and the share of their incomes coming from various sources often diverge. In the absence of public safety nets, some livelihood strategies serve more effectively as safety nets than as pathways out of poverty, although the two functions are clearly interlinked, with those able to manage risk being in a better position to make investments in businesses that help them grow their incomes. Growing an income most often came from business activities in our sample, but we see that those businesses must overcome both market constraints and capital constraints in order to generate sufficient returns to become sufficient as a sole source of livelihood for a family. Our respondents' experiences also show the ways in which livelihood strategies are gendered. We see, for example, that a family investing more in agricultural inputs may increase women's unpaid labour on the family farm at the expense of labour on other people's farms, which gives her an independent source of cash flow and greater financial decision making in the household. Similarly, when a husband gets a job with regular monthly wages, some women report diminished power in negotiations over 'big' and future-oriented household financial decisions. We will explore some of these intra-household dynamics in greater detail in Chapter 5, 'Being a woman'.

The improvised and patchwork livelihoods described in this chapter may seem precarious. For many they are. But they also present opportunity, the possibility that things could be very different five years from now. This kind of livelihood optimism was widely shared among our respondent households, sentiments we will unpack later in this book. Ironically, the kind of productivity-enhancing growth that we might hope to transform a country like Kenya is likely to simultaneously disrupt the positive attributes of these kinds of livelihoods, particularly when those changes happen in firms targeting the domestic market. The experience of South Africa is telling. Formal, higher productivity businesses make eking out a living in the world of informal business increasingly difficult. There, government has stepped in with a massive system of social transfers, but the space for opportunity, for transformation, is squeezed (James, 2014; Ferguson, 2015; BFA, 2016). As new technology disrupts old business models in Kenya, policymakers and development practitioners face a very real challenge of managing enhancements in productivity and preserving widespread opportunity and possibility for the low-income majority.

Endnotes

1. Farming was the main source of monetary income for 11% of rural households; including the imputed value of consumed production raises that to 24% of rural households.
2. In reality, the low share of income from farming is not a new phenomenon. That farming often constituted less than half of rural households' incomes was documented as early as 1977 in the Kenya Central Bureau of Statistics' Integrated Rural Survey. But it is still a fact that gets obscured in development practitioners' (and politicians') conceptions of rural livelihoods.
3. In this study of rice farmers in Mali, free fertilizer distribution increased fertilizer usage, but not farmer profits (Beaman et al., 2013).
4. While often overlooked in programme design, this is not a new insight; economists have observed similar patterns in survey data (see Banerjee and Duflo, 2007).
5. Median consumption volatility in urban areas was 42% from month to month.
6. Similar thinking has been documented in Johnson and Krijtenburg (2015) and Kusimba et al. (2016).
7. We classified those kinds of activities where only labour and not capital were involved separately. Agriculture – for consumption and profit – was also tracked separately.
8. In 2013, one 90-kilogramme bag could be sold for between KES 1,500 and 3,500 ($18–$41), depending on the time of year of the sale.
9. This is likely an overestimation, since this question was asked for most businesses at the start of our study, when trust levels were low, and respondents may have feared reporting unregistered business activity.
10. Taken from unpublished retail merchant census studies from FSD Kenya.
11. This is consistent with the Global Entrepreneurship Monitor, which finds that rates of business discontinuance are quite high in Africa and other 'factor-driven' economies. High rates of entrepreneurial activity in a market are also correlated with high rates of discontinuance (see Kelley et al., 2016).

References

Banerjee, A.V. and Duflo, E. (2007) 'The economic lives of the poor', *Journal of Economic Perspectives* 21 (1): 141–68 <https://doi.org/10.1257/jep.21.1.141>.

Beaman, L. et al. (2013) 'Profitability of fertilizer: experimental evidence from female rice farmers in Mali', *American Economic Review* 103 (3): 381–6 <https://doi.org/10.1257/aer.103.3.381>.

BFA (2016) *Credit on the Cusp: Strengthening Credit Markets for Upward Mobility in Africa*, FSD Africa, Nairobi. Available from: <http://www.fsdafrica.org/knowledge-hub/documents/credit-on-the-cusp-report/> (accessed 3 December 2017).

Block, S.A. (1999) 'Agriculture and economic growth in Ethiopia: growth multipliers from a four-sector simulation model', *Agricultural Economics* 20 (3): 241–52 <https://doi.org/10.1016/S0169-5150(99)00007-9>.

Central Bank of Kenya, KNBS, and FSD Kenya (2016) *2016 FinAccess Household Survey: February 2016*, Central Bank of Kenya, Kenya National Bureau of Statistics and FSD Kenya, Nairobi. Available from: <https://fsdkenya.org/publication/finaccess2016/> (accessed 6 February 2020).

Collier, P. and Gunning, J.W. (1999) 'Explaining African economic performance', *Journal of Economic Literature* 37 (1): 64–111 <https://doi.org/10.1257/jel.37.1.64>.

de Melo, J. (2017) 'Pathways to structural transformation in Africa', *Brookings*, 30 October. Available from: <https://www.brookings.edu/blog/africa-in-focus/2017/10/30/pathways-to-structural-transformation-in-africa/> (accessed 17 August 2018).

du Toit, A. and Neves, D. (2014) 'The government of poverty and the arts of survival: mobile and recombinant strategies at the margins of the South African economy', *Journal of Peasant Studies* 41 (5): 833–53 <https://doi.org/10.1080/03066150.2014.894910>.

Ferguson, J. (1994) *The Anti-politics Machine: Development, Depoliticization, and Bureaucratic Power in Lesotho*, new edn, University of Minnesota Press, Minneapolis.

Ferguson, J. (2006) *Global Shadows: Africa in the Neoliberal World Order*, Duke University Press, Durham NC.

Ferguson, J. (2015) *Give a Man a Fish: Reflections on the New Politics of Distribution*, Duke University Press, Durham NC and London.

Ferguson, J. and Li, T.M. (2018) 'Beyond the "proper job": political-economic analysis after the century of labouring man', Working Paper 51, Institute for Poverty, Land, and Agrarian Studies, Cape Town. Available from: <http://www.plaas.org.za/plaas-publications/working-paper-51-beyond-%E2%80%9Cproper-job%E2%80%9D-political-economic-analysis-after-century> (accessed 15 May 2018).

Fogel, R.W. (1994) 'Economic growth, population theory, and physiology: the bearing of long-term processes on the making of economic policy', *American Economic Review* 84 (3): 369–95. Available from: <https://www.jstor.org/stable/2118058> (accessed 6 February 2020).

Glaeser, E.L., Laibson, D., and Sacerdote, B. (2002) 'An economic approach to social capital', *Economic Journal* 112 (483): F437–58 <https://doi.org/10.3386/w7728>.

Jack, W. and Suri, T. (2014) 'Risk sharing and transactions costs: evidence from Kenya's mobile money revolution', *American Economic Review* 104 (1): 183–223 <https://doi.org/10.1257/aer.104.1.183>.

James, D. (2014) *Money from Nothing: Indebtedness and Aspiration in South Africa*, Stanford University Press, Palo Alto CA.

Johnson, S. and Krijtenburg, F. (2015) '"Upliftment", friends and finance: everyday concepts and practices of resource exchange underpinning mobile money adaption in Kenya', Working Paper 41, Bath Papers in International Development and Wellbeing Centre for Development Studies, University of Bath, Bath. Available from: <https://www.econstor.eu/handle/10419/128136> (accessed 25 June 2018).

Johnston, B.F. and Mellor, J.W. (1961) 'The role of agriculture in economic development', *American Economic Review* 51 (4): 566–93.

Kelley, D., Singer, S., and Herrington, M. (2016) *2015/16 Global Report*, London: Global Entrepreneurship Monitor. Available from: <https://www.gemconsortium.org/report/gem-2015-2016-global-report> (accessed 6 February 2020).

Klasen, S. and Reimers, M. (2017) 'Looking at pro-poor growth from an agricultural perspective', *World Development* 90: 147–68 <https://doi.org/10.1016/j.worlddev.2016.09.003>.

KNBS (2017) *Kenya Economic Survey 2017*, Kenya National Bureau of Statistics (KNBS), Nairobi.

KNBS (2019) *Economic Survey 2019*, Kenya National Bureau of Statistics (KNBS), Nairobi.

Kusimba, S., Yang, Y., and Chawla, N. (2016) 'Hearthholds of mobile money in Western Kenya', *Economic Anthropology* 3 (2): 266–79 <https://doi.org/10.1002/sea2.12055>.

Ligon, E.A. and Sadoulet, E. (2007) 'Estimating the effects of aggregate agricultural growth on the distribution of expenditures', *SSRN* <https://doi.org/10.2139/ssrn.1769944>.

Morawczynski, O. (2009) 'Exploring the usage and impact of "transformational" mobile financial services: the case of M-PESA in Kenya', *Journal of Eastern African Studies* 3 (3): 509–25 <https://doi.org/10.1080/17531050903273768>.

Nation Correspondent (2014) 'Uhuru challenges youth to be entrepreneurs', *Daily Nation*, 21 November. Available from: <https://www.nation.co.ke/business/Uhuru-challenges-youth-to-be-entrepreneurs/996-2531070-k79wqtz/index.html> (accessed 7 June 2018).

Osei, R.D. and Jedwab, R. (2017) 'Structural change in a poor African country: new historical evidence from Ghana', in M. S. McMillan, D. Rodrik, and C. Sepúlveda (eds), *Structural Change, Fundamentals, and Growth: A Framework and Case Studies*, pp. 161–96, International Food Policy Research Institute, Washington DC <http://dx.doi.org/10.2499/9780896292147_ch4>.

Platteau, J.P. (1996) 'Traditional sharing norms as an obstacle to economic growth in tribal societies', Paper 173, Notre-Dame de la Paix, Sciences Economiques et Sociales, Namur. Available from: <https://ideas.repec.org/p/fth/nodapa/173.html> (accessed 1 July 2018).

Rodrik, D., McMillan, M., and Sepulveda, C. (2017) *Structural Change, Fundamentals, and Growth: A Framework and Case Studies*, International Food Policy Research Institute Washington, DC <http://dx.doi.org/10.2499/9780896292147>.

Scully, B. (2016) 'From the shop floor to the kitchen table: the shifting centre of precarious workers' politics in South Africa', *Review of African Political*

Economy 43 (148): 295–311 <https://doi.org/10.1080/03056244.2015.1085 378>.

Standing, G. (2016) 'The precariat, class and progressive politics: a response', *Global Labour Journal* 7 (2) <https://doi.org/10.15173/glj.v7i2.2940>.

Suri, T. (2011) 'Selection and comparative advantage in technology adoption', *Econometrica* 79 (1): 159–209 <https://doi.org/10.3982/ECTA7749>.

Suri, T. and Jack, W. (2016) 'The long-run poverty and gender impacts of mobile money', *Science* 354 (6317): 1288–92 <https://doi.org/10.1126/science.aah5309>.

Thurlow, J. and Wobst, P. (2014) 'The role of agriculture in pro-poor growth: lessons from Zambia', in M. Grimm, S. Klasen, and A. McKay (eds), *Determinants of Pro-poor Growth: Analytical Issues and Findings from Country Cases*, Palgrave Macmillan, London.

World Bank (n.d.) *Projects: Kenya Cash Transfer for Orphans and Vulnerable Children*, World Bank, Washington DC. Available from: <http://projects.worldbank.org/P111545/kenya-cash-transfer-orphans-vulnerable-children?lang=en&tab=results> (accessed 4 June 2018).

Zollmann, J. (2015) *Two Steps Back: How Low Income Kenyans Think About and Experience Risk in their Pursuit of Prosperity*, FSD Kenya, Nairobi. Available from: <http://s3-eu-central-1.amazonaws.com/fsd-circle/wp-content/uploads/2015/08/30095839/15-03-23_Kenya_Financial_Diaries_Report.pdf> (accessed 1 July 2018).

CHAPTER 3

Managing money: Meeting daily needs and investing for the future

Abstract

Managing money in a low-income household requires constant discipline both to meet daily needs and to invest in the future in an attempt to move slowly out of poverty. Those two financial jobs entail difficult trade-offs for families with limited savings capacities. This chapter reframes the challenge of managing money and draws on evidence from Kenya's vibrant, digital financial market to explore the real – if often marginal – role that financial devices play in solving the money problems of low-income people.

Keywords: saving, borrowing, financial management, financial health, financial capability

Patrick was the first respondent we visited for the Financial Diaries update study in 2015. Compared with most respondents, he was accessible. His dim, corrugated iron-walled workshop clung to the edge of a major road in an informal settlement in Nairobi. He was not just easy to get to, he was easy to talk to, patient with questionnaires that still required refinement. He was a patient man in many ways.

When we arrived, he greeted us with a massive, excited handshake and ducked inside his shop, emerging with a letter covered in smudged, red-soil fingerprints. One of his sons had been accepted into university. This was a first for the entire extended family. Patrick was exuberant. Here was the ultimate pay-off in pride for years of investing in his children's education.

Throughout the Diaries, we had seen him – like many respondents – put school fees above all other financial goals. A full 20 per cent of all his expenditures over the course of the study were for school fees. He was one of our higher-income respondents, earning about $200 per month, but still, fees were expensive.

Patrick and his wife had six children. Their agreement was that the children would stay with their mother upcountry for primary school and then they would come to Nairobi for secondary school, where he would take care of them and make sure that fees for this expensive stage of education were covered.

Of course, Patrick didn't have the luxury of worrying only about one money problem: school fees. There was also the reality of volatile income from his

http://dx.doi.org/10.3362/9781788531207.003

business selling charcoal cook stoves. His wife upcountry needed money to take care of the family members there. Once during the study his wife needed medical care after being spit on by a cobra, and he needed to come up with money quickly to help her see a doctor. There was rent to pay and food to buy, even when business was slow. And sometimes bad things happened, like the time he was accused of buying stolen metal to make his cook stoves and had to spend KES 50,000 (around $500) to defend himself in court.

Patrick used a wide range of financial services to navigate all these challenges. In fact, he used 17 different financial devices over the course of the study year, slightly more than our sample median of 14 financial devices per household.

Each of these tools did a different financial job for him. His rotating savings and credit association (ROSCA or 'merry-go-round') groups helped him build up money he could invest in school fees. His accumulating savings and credit association (ASCA) helped him accumulate and also borrow when he needed stock or to deal with unexpected expenses – this was borrowing function often more important than the saving function to our respondents. The importance he placed on each tool was not reflected in the frequency with which he used them or the balances he held in them. M-Pesa was hugely important to him, but it did only one job: transferring money to his wife at their rural home. He only rarely took goods on credit from an area shop, and, when he did, it was usually for goods worth less than $1. Still, the *possibility* of being able to do this was very important for him. Just knowing it was an option took away the stress of a bad day at his business. It also meant that his 'big' savings could be left alone to be put towards 'big' things.

For Patrick, that 'big thing' was school fees. Looking at Patrick's net worth graphed over time in Figure 3.1, we see that there is an annual build-up of wealth and a precipitous drop when the bulk of fees are paid. This was intentional. This was how Patrick was able to devote 20 per cent of his annual spending to his children's education even amidst major responsibilities, numerous risks, and constant income volatility.

What this graph does not show is a steady building of net worth over a lifetime of working years in the manner that is expected and encouraged in higher-income contexts. Patrick was not thinking about building a financial nest egg he could draw on in old age. Doing so in a serious way would almost certainly necessitate cutting back on his spending on the education of his kids, which did not even feel like an option. Instead, he invested in them. He secured a home upcountry before the children started secondary school and planned to keep his business running until the kids were all through school. Some might support him with remittances in his old age, but he will also invest in less labour-intensive income-earning strategies when he gets there and when the burden of school fees has been lifted.

Patrick did not live in a financial paradigm of 'earn and allocate', parsing set earnings out to a strict budget of spending and investing. That paradigm is more common in higher-income settings, where most people earn salaries and

Patrick's Daily Financial Flows (KES)

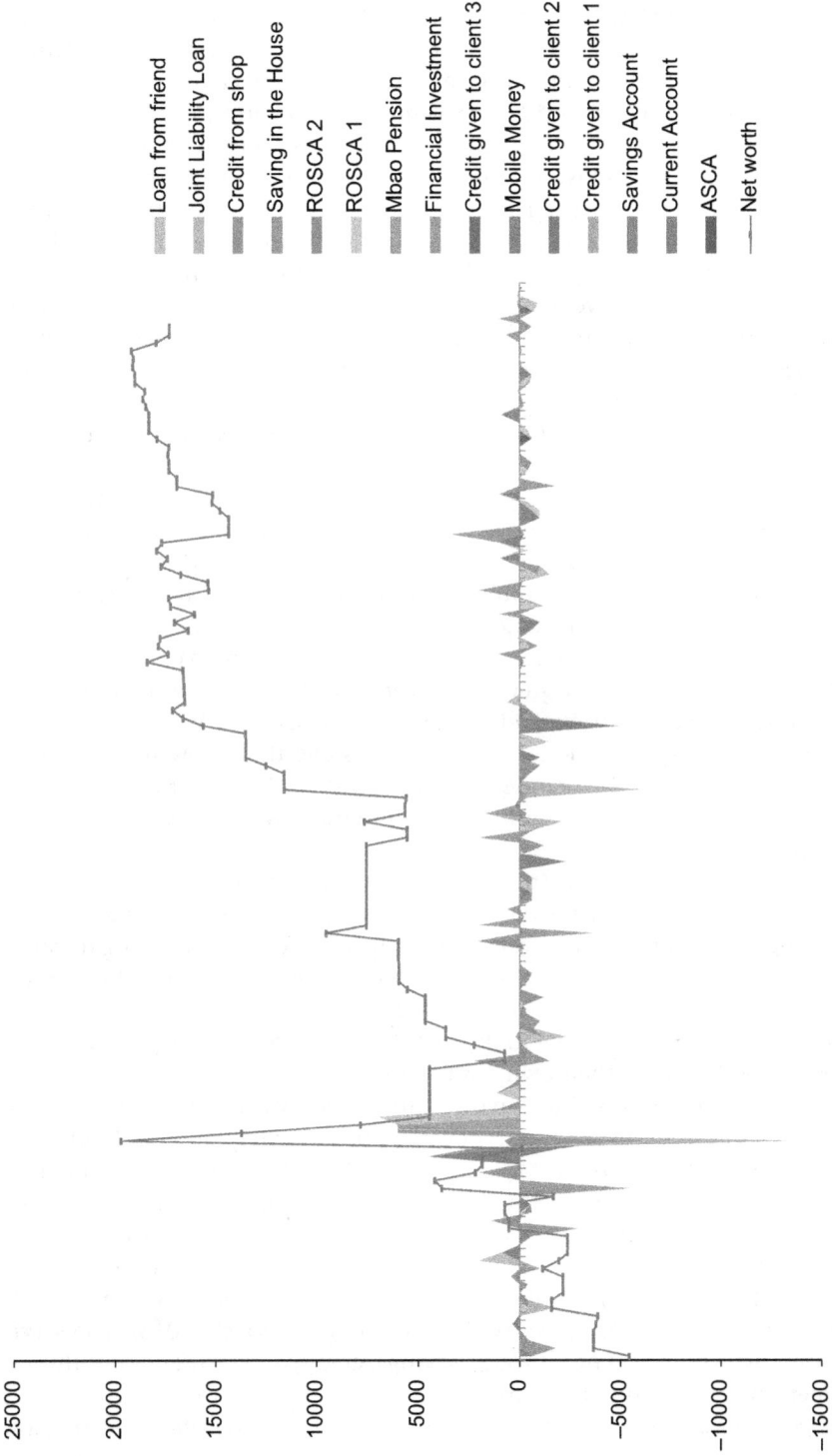

Figure 3.1 Patrick's financial tools work in concert to help him pay for school fees.

are able to think about 10- or 20-year – or longer – planning horizons, making analytical decisions about how to maximize long-term returns. Patrick's reality was starkly different. For him, earning and allocating were constants, a daily routine. Every time $2 or $5 came into his hands, he made a new set of decisions: what to spend on food, what to keep just for tomorrow, what to send to his wife, and what to lock up for school fees and other needs lurking just around the corner. These constant decisions meant that his biggest challenge was not around understanding compound interest, but rather in exercising constant discipline (Zollmann and Collins, 2010).

That discipline, we were often told, meant avoiding unnecessary spending and staying focused, with little frivolous spending on things like alcohol and *mpango wa kando*, literally 'side dishes', referring to extramarital affairs. In this world, being a good money manager was equated with being a good person (Zollmann and Collins, 2010). The good money manager was master over his or her own temptation.

Apart from navigating daily needs and challenges, our respondents were constantly thinking about how to earn more money. Financial investing alone wouldn't lift Patrick and his family into the middle class. They needed more money – and more earning potential – as quickly as possible. And that was unlikely to happen through wage employment within one generation. Instead, we found people like Patrick building up an income portfolio, not just a financial portfolio. They grew and diversified their income streams. Patrick was mostly focused on expanding his current business. When we saw him in 2015, he had a new design for his cook stove that allowed both normal cooking and grilling. He branded his stoves with a sticker. At their rural home, his wife farmed, complementing his remittances with extra food and cash income.

For Diaries respondents, the money management end game was not just to acquire a home and provision for old age. It was about avoiding severe hardship today and progressively increasing income, about working towards a more comfortable life in this generation and the next. It was about generating upward mobility on a very personal level, about earning more income. And, for that, traditional financial tools (such as bank accounts and business loans) were helpful, but, on their own, far from sufficient.

The good news was that – particularly in Kenya, where digital financial infrastructure is quite advanced – people no longer rely only on 'traditional' financial services. Consider M-Pesa. This mobile money solution, which was developed by the mobile network operator Safaricom, has changed real people's lives. Research from Billy Jack and Tavneet Suri has shown that using this system both protected low-income people from the impacts of health shocks (Jack and Suri, 2014) and, nationwide, lifted 2 per cent of Kenyan households above the $1.25 per day poverty threshold (Suri and Jack, 2016). The service accomplished this feat not through savings, credit, and insurance but through something else: remittances. In other words, it has increased the *incomes* of the poor. It moved money from those who had it to those who needed it, and, by doing so, helped solve the primary problem of poverty: not having enough money.

Similarly, Kenya's digital financial system has been enabling government and NGO cash transfers to some of the country's most vulnerable people. It has made it easier to recruit, manage, and pay remote workforces. It can smooth the functioning of supply chains. Good savings, credit, and insurance all matter, too. And to the extent that any of these tools open up new avenues for the poor to increase their incomes, they could be transformative.

Understanding how ordinary people manage money is important for developing the next generation of financial services – whether traditional or transformative. That is why we undertook this research in the first place. But this understanding also has broader implications. Money – and its absence – is integral to the business of living.

Box 3.1 A few notes on terminology

Kenyans mediate their finances through a blend of informal and formal financial services. Some of these terms may be new to readers not familiar with Kenya's financial context.

Informal finance groups, broadly called '*chamas*' in Kenya, were very common among our respondents. While the rules of these groups varied, they typically did one or more of the following functions:

- **Rotating savings and credit associations (ROSCAs)**, also known as 'merry-go-rounds', are groups in which members contribute regularly (daily, weekly, monthly), typically, but not always, a fixed amount. On each contribution date, one member takes the entire pot. Those early in the cycle are net borrowers, and the ones later in the cycle are net savers, although most in our study conceptualized these groups as a savings tool.
- **Accumulating savings and credit associations (ASCAs)**, also called 'table banking' in Kenya, tend to start a round with members either making one lump-sum contribution for the year or contributing slowly and regularly to build a fund from which the group makes loans to members. Members later divide the savings and earned interest through a share-out, typically once a year. Many groups had both a ROSCA and ASCA component.
- **Welfare groups**, or simply 'welfares', are groups that act like informal insurance pools for members. These can stand alone or be part of another group, and the rules vary from group to group. There may be fixed regular contributions to a group fund that is used in emergencies or members may be required to contribute to one another only in the event of an emergency. In some cases, unclaimed funds are redistributed to members.

Another informal tool that may not be familiar to all readers is the money guard:

- **Money guard** is a term we used to refer to individuals who held other individuals' savings on their behalf, returning the money on demand. This person was often a shopkeeper or relative. There is no specific term Kenyans use for this arrangement.

There are also several commonly used digital financial tools in Kenya:

- **M-Pesa** is a mobile money transfer system in which users deposit cash at thousands of small agents and their mobile wallets are credited with the sum. That money can then be sent from wallet to wallet, making it a major channel for remittances, but it is also used by some for personal savings or to make other kinds of payments over distances.

- **M-Shwari** is a bank account offered by Commercial Bank of Africa[1] that is linked to M-Pesa. You can save on M-Shwari in a very basic, interest-bearing account, or a 'locked' commitment account. Users can also borrow small sums for up to two months.
- **Okoa Jahazi** is an arrangement on Safaricom (there are similar arrangements on other mobile networks) to get an advance of airtime. The balance (with interest) is deducted the next time airtime is purchased, whether through mobile money or, more often, through a scratch card or voucher.

Financial management and financial inclusion

Decades of folk finance research that preceded our study gave our team a solid foundational understanding of some key money management challenges facing low-income people (Shipton, 1990; Collins et al., 2009; Rutherford and Arora, 2009). *Portfolios of the Poor* has been particularly influential in spreading that foundational understanding. Looking across multiple countries, the authors depicted the complex and intricate financial lives of ordinary people who were not living hand to mouth but rather dealing with complicated challenges with clever – but imperfect – solutions. The authors of *Portfolios* concluded that the poor faced a 'triple whammy' of low incomes, unpredictable incomes, and poor financial tools. They reasoned that the financial sector could have a real impact on poverty by providing a wider range of low-cost financial tools to low-income people, inspiring nearly a decade of work on these kinds of financial innovations (Collins et al., 2009).

Like the families in *Portfolios of the Poor*, our respondents struggled to come up with useful lump sums to do meaningful 'projects' and to solve problems. Their incomes were volatile from day to day and from year to year. They balanced their portfolios to deal with competing preferences for liquidity and illiquidity. Managing money when there is very little to go around is a complicated business.

But for us, the most pressing prescription was not for development actors to ensure that low-income people could be banked. Instead, we saw families struggling with more than three 'whammies'. Not only were their incomes too small and unpredictable, schools and healthcare were too expensive and often of low quality. Governance was extractive. Women were burdened with untenable responsibilities and deprived of a voice. In Kenya – where financial solutions were already quite diverse and more robust and accessible than in many other countries – the flaws in financial solutions (except when they place large amounts of money at risk) were often the least of people's worries. A much more worrisome problem for our respondents was that they simply did not have enough money.

What's more, they thought this was their fault. Social glorification of entrepreneurship and even finance reinforced the idea that those who had so little were failures and those failures were personal, not systemic.

Scarcity matters. And it matters not just in how much people eat or the quality of their homes. It matters to how they make financial decisions, how and where they save, and why they use or do not use insurance. It is easy to forget that the very definition of poverty is not having *enough* resources to meet basic needs. When we keep this at the front of our minds, the idea that people might move out of poverty by *consuming* more or different products – financial or otherwise – feels like putting the focus in the wrong place. Scarcity changes the very aim of a financial strategy, which for our respondents was not about surviving old age or avoiding catastrophe. It was about *improving* one's life as quickly as possible, mostly by *earning* more money.

It's not that finance was meaningless for our participants. But finance mattered only in so far as it successfully solved a real money problem. As obvious as this sounds, a lot of work has gone into trying to open bank accounts for every adult in Kenya (and in many other countries), measuring 'progress' without paying much attention to whether those accounts were solving – or even realistically could solve – deeply felt problems faced by the low-income majority. Slave to these metrics, the financial inclusion community has proliferated millions of dormant accounts that cost financial institutions real money and do little to help ordinary people (Venkatesan, 2015; Cheston et al., 2016). Over time, it has become clear that gains in 'access' (usually measured as the share of adults with a formal bank or mobile money account) are poor proxies for impact on the lives of low-income people. Financial inclusion practitioners have sought to remedy this by looking for more nuanced indicators, such as usage levels and quality of services, along with an increasing focus on developing measures of financial health to better capture the extent to which individuals are able to meet day-to-day expenses, manage risk, and plan for the future (Gallup, 2014; Gutman et al., 2015; Gubbins, 2017). The emergence of the financial health concept helps place the focus on real people trying to solve financial problems, but it also calls on development practitioners to think hard about the determinants of financial health. The latest FinAccess study in Kenya showed a deterioration in financial health metrics despite record-high access to formal financial tools (Central Bank of Kenya et al., 2019). Financial health may be more tied to income levels and broader economic factors than to personal behavioural choices, calling the development community to recognize that not all formal financial services contribute significantly to the outcomes in financial health that we care about (Porteous and Zollmann, 2016).

Financial service institutions interested in helping clients improve their financial health and in becoming more relevant in low-income clients' lives should orient themselves around helping those clients pursue their main money goal: improving their living standards. To develop better solutions, we need to keep pushing the boundaries of what we understand about what low-income people already do in managing their money and what they need from their financial tools.

Understanding the challenges

For the remainder of this chapter, let's focus on what the Kenya Financial Diaries tell us about that, focusing on five key lessons.

'You don't actually get two dollars a day'

Low-income people's incomes and expenses are unpredictable and complex. This is not a new finding. It was, in fact, one of the main insights in *Portfolios of the Poor*. Writing about the book, Tim Harford summarized: 'The trouble with living on two dollars a day is that you don't actually get two dollars a day. One day you might get five, then nothing for the next three days. Income is unpredictable. Outgoings, too, are irregular. Emergencies crop up' (Harford, 2009).

And it holds just as true for respondents in Kenya. As we have seen in Chapter 2, 'Looking for money', households piece together livelihoods, pooling resources from multiple activities simultaneously or in frequent shifts among different earning opportunities as they become available or when expenditure needs become pressing, forcing extra work or asset sales. The typical family in our study had five income sources apart from gifts and remittances.

This idea that incomes are unpredictable needs to be unpacked to fully appreciate the implications for managing money. One form of unpredictability is inter-month volatility. Why do we care about fluctuation from month to month? Many Kenyans think about their incomes and expenses based on a monthly time horizon, because that small share of Kenyans with salaries are paid at the end of the month and consequently pay their domestic staff, send remittances, and do the bulk of their spending at that time, providing a common sense of periods of punctuation. When we aggregate incomes and expenditures for our respondents, we typically see a quite jagged pattern, as in Figure 3.2. If we take the standard deviation of this monthly income, divided by the mean income for the household during the study period, we get a measure that tells us the percentage of average income that fluctuates – up and down – from month to month over the course of the project.

In our sample, this income volatility measure was 54 per cent for the median household. For a typical family in our study, income regularly fluctuated up or down from the average by 54 per cent from month to month. The average monthly income for the median household in our study was KES 7,120 ($84) at the time of the initial study. Regularly, they had to plan for a budget of $46 or $130, which made it incredibly difficult to afford fixed expenses such as rent, but also to consistently meet slightly more variable needs like healthcare.

Of course, spending needs were also quite volatile. Sometimes these went up and down with the availability of income. But at other times consumption had to jump simply because there was a new need. The roof could be leaking and require urgent repair. A medical emergency could crop up, either within the household or to a person – like an elderly parent – which required

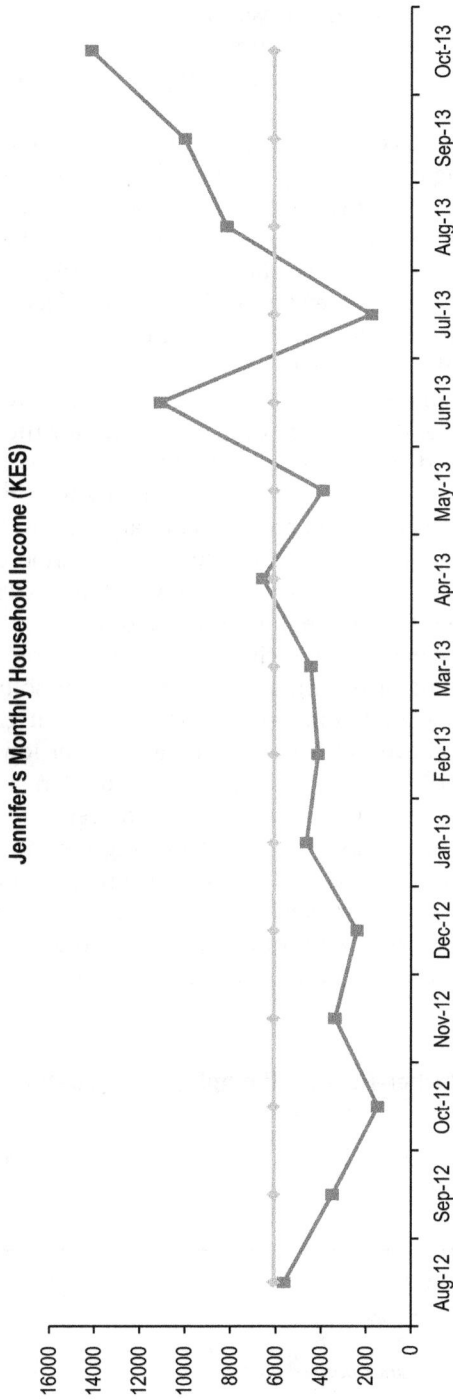

Figure 3.2 Jennifer's month-to-month income over the duration of the study.

household members to chip in. Consumption expenditure volatility at the median was 43 per cent across our sample. Households used financial services to help mediate against volatility in consumption even in the face of more dramatic income fluctuations.

Most respondents earned their incomes in high-frequency, low-value increments, like Rachel (Figure 3.3). Early in the study, Rachel was running a small business in a rural market, where she bought groundnut stock twice per week and sold the groundnuts daily in small increments – both fresh and fried – in her local market. On the days when she was able to work, her income was not exactly the same, but it was somewhat predictable. The challenge was that she had to force herself to allocate well every single day or she wouldn't be able to both feed her family *and* buy stock in larger amounts to keep the business going. She also had ambitions to grow her business and to buy some basic furniture for her house. It was really difficult to plan for the long term when money was so tight and arrived in such small sums.

Rachel had it pretty good. She had a small family with just two children, neither of whom had yet entered costly secondary school. Her business was fairly stable and her market quite busy. During the period of our study, the limits to the growth of her business were in how much stock she could afford, not whether she would have enough customers to buy it.

Just as Rachel's business was growing, in Nairobi, a woman whose neighbours called her a nickname meaning 'Auntie' was facing some serious trouble (Figure 3.4). She was a single mother with HIV and twin girls in secondary school. Things were already difficult when she lost her low-paying job at a small cybercafé. She didn't have enough savings to start a business. Nearly everything she had was going to school fees. It had been years since the family had taken a midday meal. So, she started looking for casual jobs – mostly washing clothes – in the slightly higher-income neighbourhoods not far from her own. The best place to go was Eastleigh, where women gathered on a curb they called 'the parking' and waited hopefully to be chosen to do washing and cleaning in people's homes for KES 150–300 ($1.75–$3.53) per day.

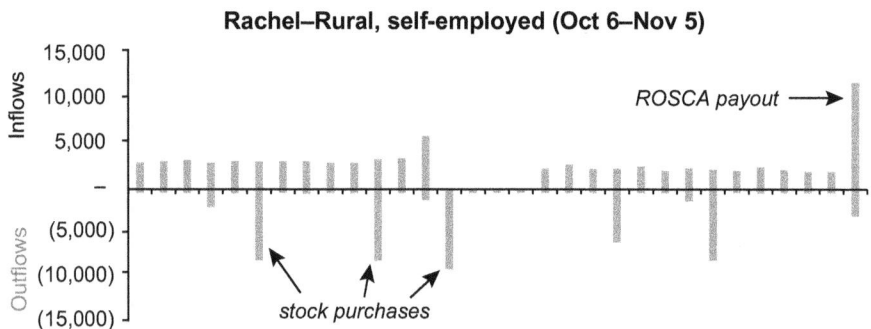

Figure 3.3 Rachel has fairly consistent, but daily cash flows.

"Auntie"–Urban, loses job and moves to casual work (Oct 6–Nov 5)

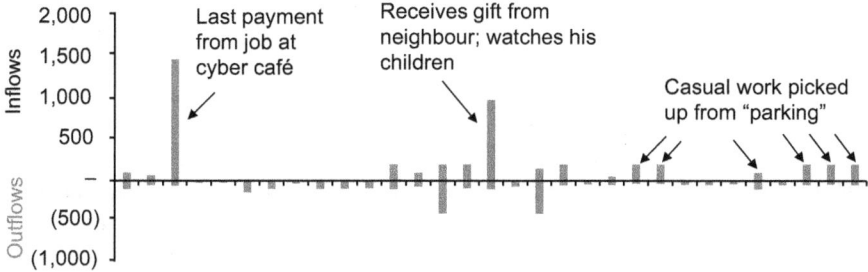

Figure 3.4 Auntie has very volatile income.

Middle and Upper Income: Already somewhat stable, inflows lumpier	Lower income: Very ustable, volatile, tiny and high frequency inflows.
Earn ➡ Allocate	Earning & allocating constant, inseparable cycle
Objective to maintain living standards over long periods, acquire and hold assets.	*Objective to simultaneously meet needs and dramatically increase income and security. Need to invest out of poverty.*

Figure 3.5 Lower-income families experience a unique financial management paradigm.
Source: Zollmann and Collins, 2010.

This was about a two-hour walk away, but she couldn't afford to pay for transport, not yet anyway. Some days she got work; some days she did not. She had to spend as if there would be no work tomorrow, just in case. That meant, like most of our respondents, buying foodstuffs and the other basics of survival in extremely small increments almost every day.

Things got bad. A neighbour gave her KES 1,000 ($11.76) to try to help out. One of her daughters was sent home for an outstanding fee balance. There was no money, so she stayed at home.

But even Auntie couldn't *just* think about meeting basic needs; she had to plan some way to get out of this vulnerable situation. If she were very lucky, she might get another job, like she had in the cybercafé. But, more likely, her route out would be through starting a business, and for that she would need to save or borrow to invest and get herself on more solid ground.

This nature of volatility, in the form of both large inter-month fluctuations and the reality of intra-month fluctuation with daily income cash flows, meant that, for most respondents, the foundations of money management were fundamentally different from those of middle-income people, especially those with a salary. Most low-income people in our sample simply didn't have a fixed income to budget around. Every single day, perhaps multiple times per day, they had to decide what could be spent, what could be saved, what could be used today for the most acute needs, and what resources had to go to the project of becoming less poor and vulnerable in the weeks and years ahead. The challenge was not primarily about analysing and maximizing portfolio returns; it was about discipline – the discipline to keep aside funds to earn tomorrow's income even when you are hungry today and your child has been sent home from school for unpaid fees.

Low-income people do not have enough money

Of course, income volatility was not the only reality – or even the most important one – that low-income families in our study contended with. Even when you sum up all the money they brought in, it was typically not enough to comfortably meet all of their needs.

When countries set a poverty line, typically it is based on the value of an essential basket of goods – or minimum caloric intake – considered necessary for survival. Poverty lines are used regularly to name and count the 'poor' and 'non-poor', even though in reality there is no such distinctive, low-level threshold above which the stress of scarcity evaporates (Pritchett, 2017). In terms of our Kenya Financial Diaries sample, 72 per cent of households were living below the $2/day consumption threshold and 95 per cent below $5/day. It's fair to say that nearly all of them were living in conditions of rather serious scarcity – and, for a significant share, serious deprivation.

It seems obvious to point out that 'the poor' are, well, poor. But it's surprisingly easy to lose sight of what this rather obvious statement of fact really means. There was a time when the dominant paradigm of thinking about these kinds of families was that they were in a very deprived state, and therefore they must live hand-to-mouth, make very few decisions, exercise little agency, and need public, top-down provision of all services to cater for their needs. *Portfolios of the Poor* recognized that all people, including 'the poor', have some money, have financial lives, and plan their own futures. Those insights fell on fertile ground, particularly among those already swayed by the work of C.K. Pralahad advocating for a more commercial or social enterprise approach to the problems of poverty. That paradigm saw the poor as full of agency and capable of improving their own lives by spending their own money and viewed private businesses and business principles as an engine for poverty reduction.

It was a seductive and empowering idea. It is very expensive to provide aid on a large scale. And, through the 1980s and 1990s era of Washington Consensus austerity, many countries were being forced to cut back on public funding of things like health and education. At the same time, a lot of aid simply did not work – or at least we had no strong evidence that it was having an impact. Governments and donors needed solutions that worked at scale, and perhaps that might be more possible by businesses motivated by commercial returns that would inherently be 'sustainable' because profits would make them continue to provide services in perpetuity. This movement asked: what if we could make it easier for the poor to invest in their own services, in improving their own lives? It seemed to be worth trying, and there have been some noticeable commercial successes through things including a famous Unilever-led hygiene campaign in India and even the rapid spread of mobile phone services fuelled by users buying airtime $0.05 or $0.10 at a time. The big insight was to sell things in units that ordinary people could make space for in their budgets.

However, there is a limit to this commercial approach. Low-income families simply cannot afford everything they need. They are constantly making trade-offs among *good* choices. Drinking alcohol and smoking cigarettes were – to most of our respondents – quite obviously wasteful. Such expenditures happened, of course, but at very minimal levels among our respondents.[2] But even without a shilling of waste, our respondents were making choices between things like sending a child to see a doctor and paying an exam fee, between paying rent or sending money to a relative in desperate need in the hospital.

The median household in our study had average monthly consumption expenditure of about KES 6,000 ($71). About 71 per cent of that went on food, housing, and education expenditures, leaving only about $20 for everything else: energy needs, transportation, stock for business growth, healthcare, and anything else that might come up. With that $20, a family had to make decisions – even among good options – about how to make the best use of those funds. And often, when that $20 is *not* left over every month, making sure that important things – such as school fees – are paid often means that spending must be reduced on other things, even essentials like food.

Let's look at one real-life example. Faith lived in rural Makueni County, and in a typical month during the study, she brought in KES 7,200 ($85), which was normal for the study, though higher than average among our respondents in this low-income, rural area. She lived with her father-in-law and four children. Faith taught nursery school by day, collecting erratic payments from parents who were also cash-strapped. In the evenings, she sold vegetables from a small *kibanda* or stand. Her husband also sent a little bit of money most months.

Over the course of the project, 46 per cent of her consumption budget went on food expenditures, even though she also grew her own maize at home. Another 24 per cent went on education expenditures. Housing consumed another 7 per cent; this was used to buy cement to plaster the inner walls of her home. Faith did have some wiggle room and saved a bit and made payments against loans. But we also saw that when she had a big school fees expense in February, she had to cut back on food spending. She, like most respondents, lived in a world of constant trade-offs even among *good* choices, even among things we would consider *necessary*.

In Figure 3.6, we see Faith's month-to-month net income, consumption, and financial flows over the core months of the project. One thing that stands out here is that, over the course of the year, she was able to do one big investment project. She bought a water tank for KES 14,000 ($164). Especially in this area where water is scarce and bore holes inconsistent and far away, this tank dramatically improved her quality of life and reduced her time spent fetching water. But it was a big commitment, which meant that she could only pull off these kinds of investments infrequently and typically one at a time.

Fundamentally, having too little money – especially in combination with income volatility – meant that there were constant trade-offs, especially when faced with unexpected needs. Consider just a few examples we first wrote about in our *Shilingi kwa Shilingi* report (Zollmann, 2014):

- When his baby came down with malaria in one of the slums of Nairobi, Gerard took him to the hospital immediately, using the money they had on hand, which had been earmarked for other needs. The hospital visit only cost about KES 200 ($2.35) or about 3 per cent of Gerard's consumption budget. Still, the family would have to cut back on food and other spending for a few days until Gerard was paid again.
- When heavy rains began in January, one household in Vihiga found their roof was leaking badly. They needed KES 600 to buy a new iron sheet to patch the leak. This would have required 10 per cent of their monthly consumption budget. They would have liked to sell a goat to buy a new roofing sheet, but their two goats were attacked by bees and died in December, just before the rains came. The family endured the leak and waited until May for a ROSCA pay-out to buy the roofing sheets they needed.
- A respondent in Nairobi lost a cousin in February and had to send KES 1,500 to help cover the burial expenses. This was about 25 per cent of his monthly spending budget, but because he lived in Nairobi, the family expected something substantial like this. He couldn't send less and lose face. He borrowed the money from colleagues at work, cut back on food for a time, and repaid his colleagues when he was paid again.

Not all families were capable of increasing their spending to accommodate these fresh needs, which is why so often we saw families forgoing expenditures on things like healthcare, education, and even food. A quarter of all households slept hungry at least once during the study and 9 per cent of them experienced hunger during at least three interview intervals.

Net income flows for Faith

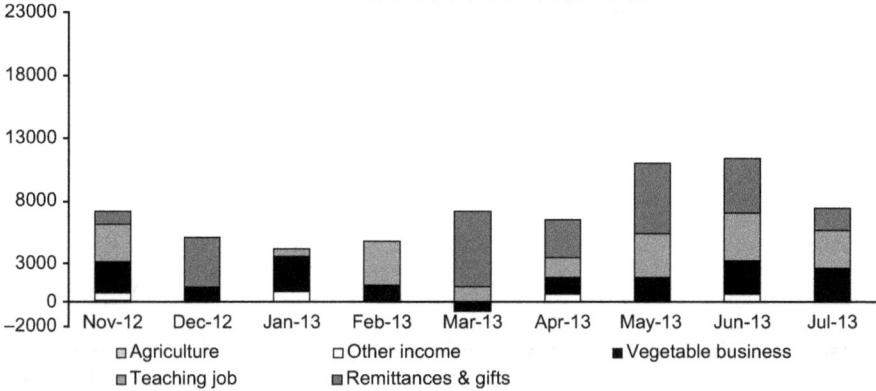

Legend: Agriculture · Other income · Vegetable business · Teaching job · Remittances & gifts

Net consumption flows for Faith

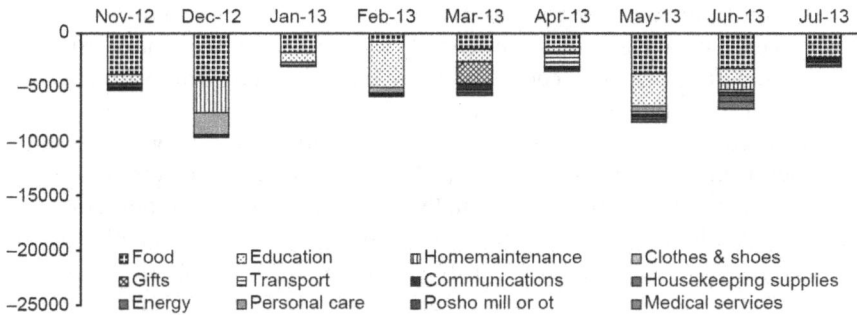

Legend: Food · Education · Home maintenance · Clothes & shoes · Gifts · Transport · Communications · Housekeeping supplies · Energy · Personal care · Posho mill or ot · Medical services

Net financial flows for Faith

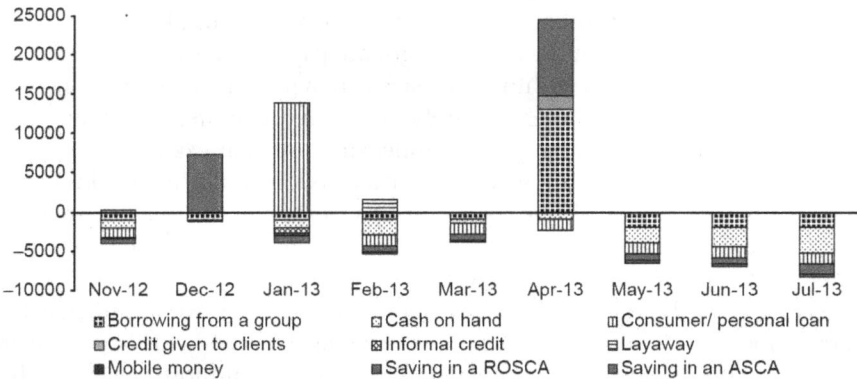

Legend: Borrowing from a group · Cash on hand · Consumer/ personal loan · Credit given to clients · Informal credit · Layaway · Mobile money · Saving in a ROSCA · Saving in an ASCA

Figure 3.6 *Continues*

Net physical asset flows for Faith

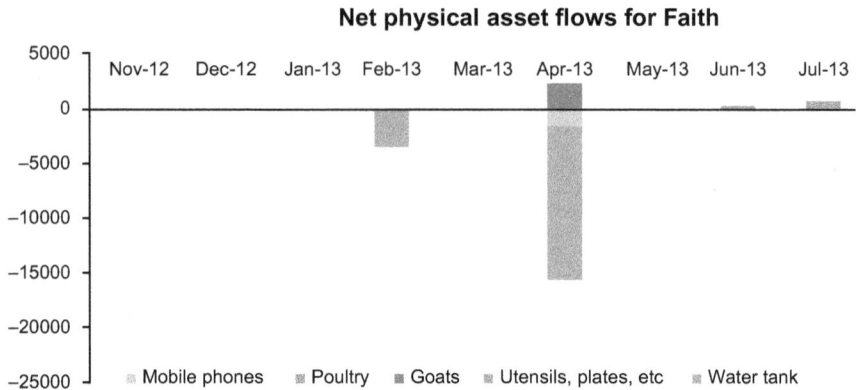

Figure 3.6 Faith's income, consumption, financial, and asset flows from month to month.

Thirty-eight per cent went without a doctor or medicine when needed, and 11 per cent of households experienced this across three or more interview intervals. Fifty-seven per cent had their children sent home from school because of unpaid fees at least once.

We might expect that low-income households would forgo these kinds of expenditures when the money needed to meet the need was substantial. However, many times, the need actually required very little money. For example, financial barriers to accessing healthcare were often very small, even relative to income. For example, Candy needed KES 70 ($0.82, or 1.7 per cent of her average monthly income) for medication to treat her malaria but she didn't have the money and postponed treatment for two weeks. In the meantime, her son developed malaria as well, bringing the total medication cost to KES 150 ($1.76) when the two were finally treated.

Similarly, many children have interruptions in schooling when they are sent home due to outstanding balances owed. However, unlike with medical care, parents seem to be more able to negotiate payment terms, allowing children to go back to school within a few days with a partial payment against the balance. But, sometimes, there's simply no money. Children can stay home for long stretches and miss important milestones, such as exams.

Our research participants would often tell us, 'I would like to do X, but there's just no money.' They were not exaggerating. The most important pressure relief valve was not saving or borrowing – although these were important – it was getting more money.

When we followed up with our respondents in 2015, we found that the most important driver of improvements in subjective well-being was – unsurprisingly – on the income side, earning more money. In most instances, this was from new or expanded small businesses. But having children complete their education (reducing a big expense), enter the workforce, and start remitting resources (increasing income) were also important for older respondents. Conversely, having an income drop – losing a job, closing a business, or a remitter losing their source of income – was the biggest driver of declines in subjective well-being.

In summary, income mattered. Having more money meant you could do more of the things that mattered to you. It meant having to make fewer stressful trade-offs among necessities.

Low-income people make trade-offs between financial tools that stretch their budgets and that grow their incomes

Our respondents understood this income imperative. So when it came to managing their finances, they devoted significant amounts of energy *both* to ensuring they could access the liquidity needed to meet immediate needs *and* to trying to invest – mostly in earning more money, but also in acquiring assets (like Faith's water tank) that made life more comfortable. But we found that, under such serious scarcity, these two goals – stretching and growing money – competed with one another.

What does this mean? It is most obvious when we look at savings. When starting this project, we were often told that Kenyans don't save. Regulators at the Central Bank would lament the low official savings rate as if it reflected irresponsible financial management and short-sightedness among the masses. But when we measured actual savings balances, we saw that families were consistently putting away substantial sums and later withdrawing those substantial sums for important projects. At the end of the project, the median household had the equivalent of 38 days (41 mean) of household income stashed away in savings. The median household had debts worth only about 16 days' of household income.

This may seem small. It was certainly not long-term, retirement savings. But, relative to low-income populations BFA has studied through Financial Diaries in other countries, this was quite substantial. Similar low-income samples in South Africa saved only the equivalent of one day's worth of income at the median (16 mean), 12 days in Colombia (41 mean), and zero days in Mexico (five mean) (Zollmann, 2014). Savings were important for dealing with income shortfalls and unexpected expenses, but they were most important for generating useful lump sums for investment. Our respondents were saving up for things like school fees, home improvements, expanding their businesses, and buying assets. They were saving to grow, not just to stretch.

This has some important implications. If your savings are intended to stretch, you want to keep them liquid and close at hand, maybe as cash in a secret hiding place or held in a mobile money wallet where they can be withdrawn quickly for any pressing need. If your savings are intended for growth, you likely want some distance. You want the money to be illiquid, protecting it from your own temptation to spend more. Remember, you already don't have 'enough', so the craving to spend never stops. Keeping money around means it will more likely be used for some of those needs or the claims of children whose shoes need to be replaced or who could use some pocket money for school. Spouses, siblings, and parents can all ask for money to meet their own shortfalls. And should you consistently give in, you would never get the lump sum you need to do things like buy a sewing machine, grow a business, buy a dairy cow, or build or repair a house.

We saw respondents simultaneously expressing liquidity *and* illiquidity preferences for these two different pools of savings. But the big money was illiquid, reserved for the growth function, for investments, typically called 'projects'. The median household held only 10 per cent of their savings in liquid form. The rest was tied up – intentionally – for those perceived higher-order needs.

We observed that when a household was forgoing basic needs because of a lack of even very small sums, it was often at a time when they had money in savings. It's just that these savings were inaccessible, locked up by design.

Perhaps that was why we saw so much effort going into non-savings means to stretch budgets where necessary. Stretching was all about creating elasticity in the budget to cope with short-term consumption needs and income shortfalls.

Since liquid savings balances were only about 12 per cent of the typical consumption budget, other tools need to be recruited for this work. One option was working more. As we know, income fluctuated about 54 per cent per month, sometimes upwards. Then there were the possible sources of credit: most often borrowing from friends and family, moneylenders, and groups. Often overlooked but very important were the opportunities to stretch by delaying payments to schools and landlords through personal relationships and negotiation (Figure 3.7).

And then there was the credit source deemed most important by an overwhelming majority of our respondents: taking goods – mostly food – on credit from the local shop. Even Patrick, with his higher-than-average income, who used this tool sparingly and only in very small sums, told us it was his most important borrowing tool. Being able to take goods on credit was a powerful pressure-relief valve. If Patrick had a bad day in his business or desperately needed to use his cash for some other pressing need, he could get the food he needed for himself and his boys and make it up to the shopkeeper within a few days.

Over time, our team noticed that respondents would go out of their way to keep the lines of some basic consumption credit open among small shops in the community. For example, Valerie deliberately bought food daily and from multiple shops and stalls around the community. She explained that this allowed her to maintain relationships with all those shopkeepers, so that she could access credit from multiple sources if the need arose. Each shopkeeper may let her borrow up to only around KES 200 ($2.35), but if she could get that from five places, she could cope with even a pretty serious problem. She never bought in bulk, even when she had the money. She wanted the

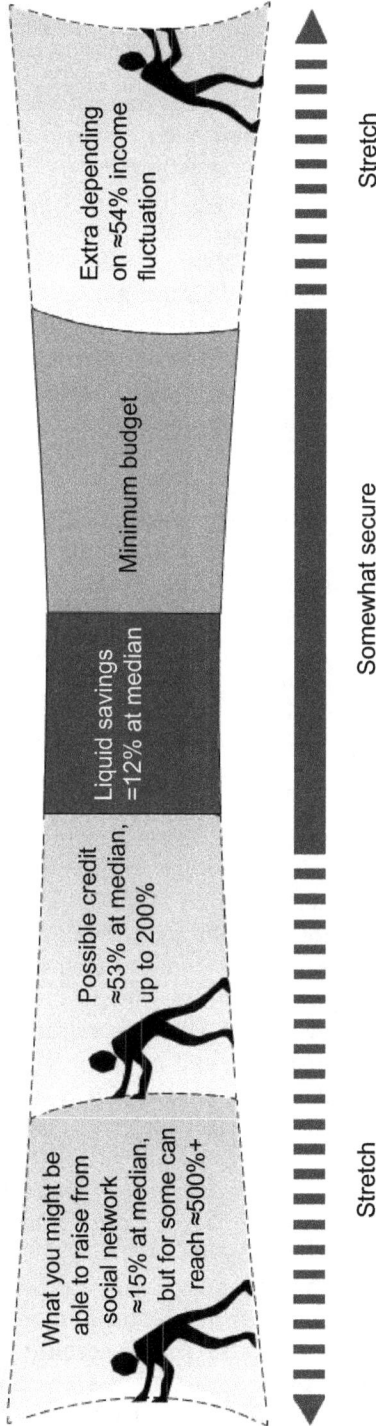

Figure 3.7 Respondents put a lot of effort into ensuring they can access liquidity – often on demand – to deal with budget shortfalls while saving is preserved for investment.

Text within figure:

Stretch

Somewhat secure

Stretch

Extra depending on ≈54% income fluctuation

Minimum budget

Liquid savings =12% at median

Possible credit ≈53% at median, up to 200%

What you might be able to raise from social network ≈15% at median, but for some can reach ≈500%+

shopkeepers to see her smiling face every single day. 'When they see you every day,' she told us, 'they believe you will repay.'

Bank or microfinance loans were not typically used for stretching. Instead, these tended to be rather large sums – an average of KES 15,000 ($176) – that were directed towards growth activities, such as purchasing productive assets, doing home improvements, and paying school fees.

But when the digital loan product, M-Shwari, entered the market in 2013, in the middle of the study, that started to change. On M-Shwari, respondents were able to borrow sums as small as about KES 200 ($2.35) instantly and privately, getting a month to repay at a flat interest rate of 7.5%.[3] Unsurprisingly, this was an enormously popular concept. The product grew to 7.1 million users in three years, including more than 3 million borrowers (Cook and McKay, 2015). Many had never used a formal bank account before. Practically overnight, millions were introduced to the formal credit market. M-Shwari had landed on a deeply felt, poorly met need for Kenya's low-income majority: on-demand liquidity.

The popularity of M-Shwari triggered an explosion of digital credit offerings in Kenya, including from both major banks and more specialized credit-only fintech companies. This huge growth has not been without its problems. MicroSave reported that 2.6 million people have received a negative listing on the credit bureau in the last three years, about 15 per cent of them because of outstanding debts of less than $2 (Mustafa et al., 2017). There have also been reports of many incorrect listings in the bureau, and some suggest that this may be intentional as a way of keeping competitors from 'stealing' their clients (Ngugi, 2017).

By the time we followed up with our respondents in late 2015, 92 had M-Shwari saving accounts and 52 were borrowing on M-Shwari. Of those 52, 17 had either been blocked on the service or received a negative listing in the credit bureau because of defaulting on M-Shwari loan payments. This was often not because they did not have the money to make payments on time, but because the consequences of non-payment were not understood. This digital lender felt so far away, unlike the shopkeeper who they knew, who trusted them, whose relationship they valued. Whether this massive negative listing of borrowers in the credit bureau will end up being problematic depends on how forgiving the system will be in practice. If it is sufficiently forgiving, it may turn out to be a massively successful exercise in experiential learning for first-time formal borrowers.

M-Shwari's compelling value proposition is one powerful example of the reality that different financial tools have different financial jobs, just as Patrick's case illustrated at the opening of this chapter.[4] The portfolio of instruments allows low-income people to manage competing priorities of stretching and growing. A single individual may have some long-term (six months plus) savings held with a money guard or in a fixed account. She may simultaneously belong to three ROSCAs that suck up extra liquidity on daily, weekly, or monthly intervals and provide lump sums back, also at different levels and intervals that she can thoughtfully plan around. Being able to borrow from the shop, M-Shwari, and close friends allows her to keep that savings group money building even as she rows her way through unexpected needs and income shortfalls.

Money needs to be working

A good number of banks and microfinance institutions have tried to mimic the characteristics of informal savings practices and then found that uptake and usage were relatively low. Because of low-income people's tight budgets and unpredictable lives, they need financial tools that have some characteristics that can be hard for formal providers to understand or deliver.

The people in our study wanted small, diverse pools of *liquid* savings. But they did not want to put large amounts of money there. They wanted very small fees to move money in and out. Historically, this has not been easy for traditional financial service providers to deliver. Financial institutions have tended to need either high balances or significant fee income to break even on providing savings services. This is another area where M-Shwari has broken new ground. By allowing savers to freely move money from their M-Pesa accounts, they provided Kenyans with a new liquid place to save, apart from mobile money wallets. While many of our respondents held very low sums there, the service reported in 2019 that they had KES 18.7 billion ($187 million) in savings, with the average saver keeping about KES 8,981 ($89) on the service for seven months at a time (Mutua, 2019). The explosion of digital savings wallets offered first by M-Shwari and then by others has made the growth in bank accounts overtake the growth in mobile money wallets in recent years (Central Bank of Kenya et al., 2019).

Our respondents needed *fungibility*. Given the unpredictability of their lives, to earmark savings – even insurance – for a specific purpose was problematic. Anything could happen and they needed the little that they had to be able to solve many kinds of problems. Asking people to lock savings specifically for school fees or health would most likely make them actually save less in that mechanism. People often saved in their ROSCAs with a broad idea of what they wanted to use the money for – maybe school fees, maybe some new furniture. But those plans changed over the course of a savings cycle, and often the funds were used for multiple purposes when the pay-out actually arrived.

Individuals in our study needed help being disciplined. Every time they saved, they were reducing their spending budget, which was already too low to meet basic needs. That was tough. They could not always live up to their promises to save every day, week, or month. What they seemed to value was *negotiable commitment*. Groups often afforded this to members. Yes, you were supposed to contribute KES 500 ($5.88) at each Wednesday meeting, for example, but if you could not, you could directly pay the member you owed on Saturday or Monday. You may have been scheduled to receive your pay-out turn on the 15th, but if something urgent arose, you could negotiate to receive your turn earlier. The penalties for bending the rules were small and typically were charged to your social account rather than your financial one. What we as outsiders might consider risks or losses in these groups, members themselves often viewed less negatively. This was also flexibility, a feature of the group that was allowed as part of the design. Sometimes you were the one who lost money or was forced to wait a few days for your lump sum. Sometimes you were the one who defaulted, out of necessity. And often these defaults were viewed more like very long delays (Johnson et al., 2010). They were debts that might still be repaid in money or in other ways 10 or more years in the future. Formal services work on a stricter set of rules that struggle to match this kind of flexibility.

Because people had so little money and because illiquidity was both necessary and difficult, we found that people wanted their illiquid savings to always be doing double duty. To allow money to sit and be idle was a sin! *Money should be working!* By this, our respondents meant that, even while money was being set aside for the future, it needed to also provide an immediate, tangible auxiliary benefit in order to compensate for the pain of pulling this money out of the operational budget. For example, when a person saved in their long-term savings with a savings and credit cooperative organization (SACCO) or deposit-taking microfinance institution, that money could be leveraged for a larger loan, allowing the individual to quickly accomplish some of their growth-oriented objectives. Even saving in M-Shwari built your credit score and loan limit with the bank, allowing you to borrow more, typically to accomplish stretching objectives. Even fixed accounts – though used relatively rarely and typically by extreme savers – become attractive when they offered very high returns.

The auxiliary benefits did not have to be personal or financial. ROSCA contributions are also viewed as 'active' money. When the group pooled its resources, it physically handed cash to a colleague or friend who took that money and tangibly and immediately invested it in doing something that propelled his or her life forward, whether it was buying a goat or water tank, sorting out a medical bill, or paying down the balance of school fees. The money was busy doing something good for someone you cared about. How selfish – and foolish – it would be to take your big savings and do something like bury it in the ground where no one could benefit from it until you decided on its use. Saving in a bank where the money was used by faceless borrowers who may or may not be in real need felt similarly wasteful to many of our respondents.

Money in the bank or on a mobile money wallet was idle, so you shouldn't keep very much there and it should not be there for very long. One respondent explained to us, 'Money cannot sleep on the phone,' meaning that she would not leave the money in her M-Pesa account overnight. 'We cannot sleep hungry while money is on the phone.' Money has a purpose – either spend it on the immediate needs you always face or preserve the value by putting it to work in active savings. Holding onto idle money 'just in case' was simply not compelling for most people.

Encouraging people to save more in a new formal account is often about finding a way to make that money *active* and meaningful even while it simply 'sits' on a balance sheet.

People face a large number of moderate-frequency, moderate-severity risks

We have already talked about the day-to-day volatility that respondents faced in their incomes and expenditures. Alongside that, families also faced a wide range of risks that sparked more substantial fluctuations and where small bits of saving and borrowing were often insufficient to contend with the shock.

Over the course of the Diaries, we tracked when our respondents experienced a shock, what we called a 'major event'. Such events triggered us to tag coping strategies for managing the direct costs and lost income related to these events. We also conducted a module survey around risks using recall data over five years to understand a larger universe of shocks and responses. In both cases, we ended up with a distribution similar to what we see in Figure 3.8. There are two outlier risks: the death of the main income earner, which is low frequency but very high cost; and outpatient medical care, which is very high frequency but low cost. And then there is a cluster of risks with moderate frequency and moderate cost. Any number of misfortunes may befall a family in any given year: someone might be hospitalized, the home or business could catch fire, livestock can get sick and die.

Traditionally, we associate risk management with insurance. In theory this makes sense. By expanding the risk pool, everyone can manage risk at lower cost. Actuarial analyses, like that of Nigel Bowman, have shown that individual micro-insurance policies can deliver tangible client value beyond alternative mechanisms such as microcredit loans (Bowman, 2014).

But if we look at the big picture, we see that the diversity of the risks people face means that they need risk management strategies that are fungible. Even if every insurance option available was very high value, a poor person could not possibly pay a premium for health, fire, livestock, legal, disability, and crop insurance simultaneously. Nor could an insurer actuarily design and provide cost-effectively a kind of cover that covers 'anything that comes up'. So, quite understandably, savings, credit, and asset sales will continue to be important risk management tools.

There was also another important resource for poor families coping with big shocks, and that was other people's money. The great thing about other people's money was that it was new income infused into severely resource-constrained households. It did not require trade-offs in the same way that other coping mechanisms did. There were no fixed premiums; beneficiaries cultivated their social network within their own means. Why would a resource-constrained

All Households Incidence & Severity

Probability of Population at Risk Experiencing Event in One Year (%) by Median Cost of One Event (KES)

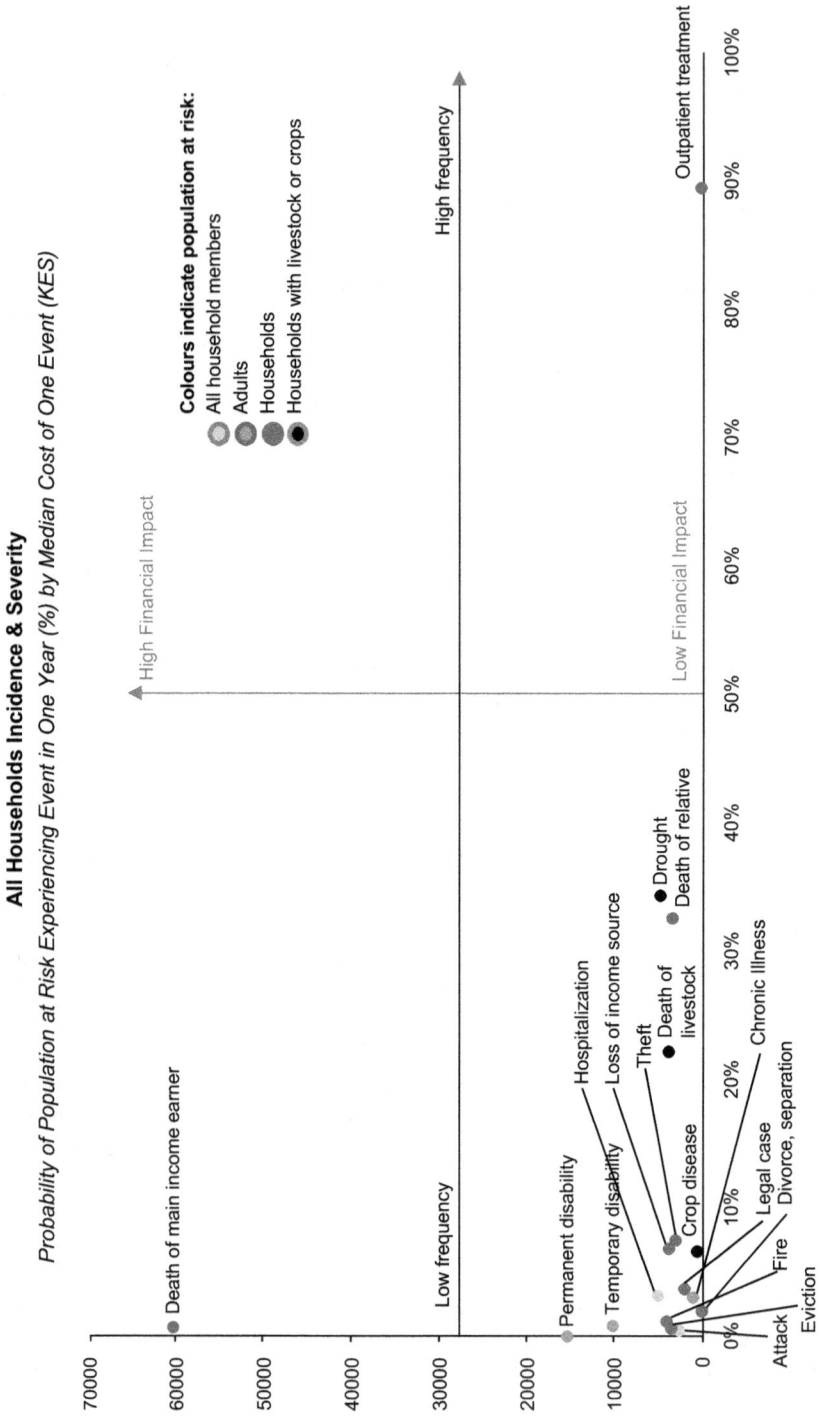

Figure 3.8 Frequency and costs of risks as observed in the five-year recall module.

person pay his or her own money to insure against risks that could be covered by other people's money?

When we look at a heat map (Figure 3.9) of the tools respondent households drew on to get through different kinds of shocks, two tools stand out. Saving in the house – that small pool of liquid savings – was hugely important. It was immediately available for urgent things. But it was also small, so usually only covered part of the cost for the urgent need. The other was 'resources received', our fancy term for remittances and gifts, also known as 'other people's money'. The importance of other people's money increased with the financial size of the shock. It had a very high upper limit that could reach many multiples of household monthly income.

Social networks made it possible for many to cope with shocks that would otherwise be unbearable. But they were not perfect, a theme explored throughout this book. To manage the many simultaneous risks they faced, our respondents drew on a wide range of tools simultaneously. No single device was sufficient or perfect for covering all of these needs, but social

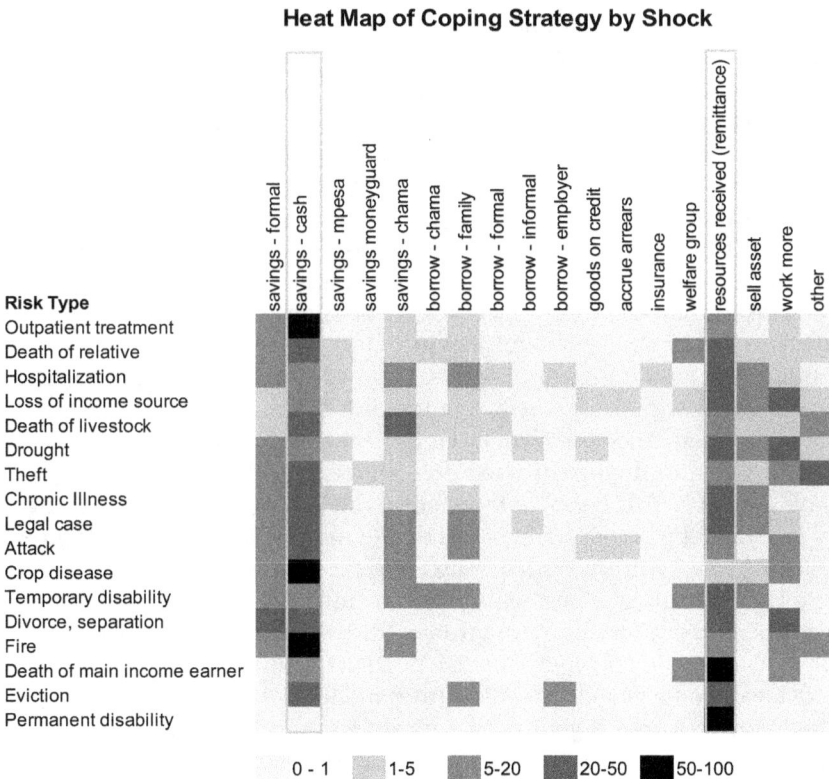

Figure 3.9 Saving in the house is the most used financial tool for small shocks and remittances the most used for larger ones.

networks – infusing new money into the budget – played a disproportionate role in managing big risks.

The future of financial inclusion

We often assume implicitly that low-income people are doing something wrong with their money and that there must be a better way to optimize their saving and borrowing behaviour. And that may be true, although I do not know what that prescription would entail. Some have argued for 'financial education' as a prescription for behaviour change. Apart from financial education's limited efficacy in low-income settings (Kaiser and Menkhoff, 2017), is it possible for experts to even know the optimal strategies to prescribe in the face of these complex realities? How should a family balance all of their competing needs? How can they know with confidence whether it is better, for example, to first invest in a water pump or to build a stronger house? How can they know beforehand whether investing in installing electricity might make it difficult to keep their child in school during exams months later?

Designing better tools that help people manage the real challenges they face, that make up for some of the shortcomings in the existing financial offerings available today, requires both an appreciation of the complexity of the challenges people face and humility about knowing all the answers. We have ideas about what might be helpful, but ideas need to be tested in the messy contexts in which they are meant to work.

The future of finance in Kenya looks bright. Advanced digital infrastructure means that incredible new things are possible. It is now conceivable to think beyond simple banking products and towards systems that solve money problems for schools, health facilities, and businesses. On the back of digital payments, we can build systems that introduce a new era of digital efficiencies in things like tracking medical stocks, improving healthcare quality by tracking diagnoses and records, reducing fraud in businesses, and better tracking moveable assets, allowing a wider range of collateral and also helping secure some of the most important assets of low-income people.

We are particularly excited by opportunities that get closer to solving the key problem of poverty: not having enough money. Digital channels promise greater efficiency in things like delivering cash transfers and targeted subsidies. They already enable remittances but might do so at even lower cost. They open up opportunities for greater redistributive person-to-person giving and crowdfunding for important causes. Digital value chains could mean that more low-income people can efficiently participate in markets and potentially earn higher returns. Digital payments alongside other kinds of technology can open up new opportunities for earning through distributed workforces, like that of Uber and other emerging platform companies. What is perhaps striking about some of these new digital financial opportunities is just how little they even look like the 'finance' we are used to in terms of basic savings, credit, and insurance. Where they will have an impact is where they can be efficient and reliable, and where they can solve the real, rather than imagined, problems of the poor.

Endnotes

1. CBA has since merged with NIC Bank to form NCBA.
2. Less than 1% of expenditure in the sample went on alcohol, and those expenditures were concentrated in 8% of households with more than five alcohol expenditures during the course of the study year. Readers should note that our sample is a bit biased in that those with severe addiction problems would most likely opt out of the study or drop out before completion.
3. Loans could be rolled over for one additional month at an additional flat rate of 7.5%. After the second month, the loan needed to be paid in full to remain in good standing.
4. As a flexible tool, M-Shwari could be used for many different financial jobs. In reality, the short-term liquidity fix has proved most exciting for the largest number of users.

References

Bowman, N. (2014) 'How low can we go? A discussion note on whether life microinsurance schemes offer value at low claims ratios', Cenfri, Cape Town. Available from: <http://cenfri.org/microinsurance/how-low-can-we-go-a-discussion-note-on-whether-life-microinsurance-schemes-offer-value-at-low-claims-ratios> (accessed 16 September 2017).

Central Bank of Kenya, KNBS, and FSD Kenya (2019) *2019 FinAccess Household Survey*, Central Bank of Kenya, Kenya National Bureau of Statistics (KNBS) and FSD Kenya, Nairobi. Available from: <https://www.centralbank.go.ke/wp-content/uploads/2019/04/2019-FinAcces-Report.pdf> (accessed 7 February 2020).

Cheston, S. et al. (2016) *The Business of Financial Inclusion: Insights from Banks in Emerging Markets*, Institute of International Finance and Center for Financial Inclusion, Washington DC. Available from: <https://www.centerforfinancialinclusion.org/the-business-of-financial-inclusion-insights-from-banks-in-emerging-markets> (accessed 10 March 2020).

Collins, D. et al. (2009) *Portfolios of the Poor: How the World's Poor Live on $2 a Day*, Princeton University Press, Princeton NJ.

Cook, T. and McKay, C. (2015) *How M-Shwari Works: The Story So Far*, Consultative Group to Assist the Poor (CGAP) and Financial Sector Deepening (FSD) Kenya, Washington DC. Available from: <http://www.cgap.org/publications/how-m-shwari-works-story-so-far> (accessed 7 February 2020).

Gallup (2014) *Corruption Tops the List as the World's Most Important Problem According to WIN/Gallup International's Annual Poll*, Gallup International, Sofia. Available from: <http://www.gallup-international.bg/en/Publications/71-Publications/181-Corruption-Tops-the-List-as-the-World%E2%80%99s-Most-Important-Problem-According-

to-WIN-Gallup-International%E2%80%99s-Annual-Poll> (accessed 25 August 2017).

Gubbins, P. (2017) 'Building a better compass: creating financial inclusion measures that are allied with people and their well-being, Part 2', Financial Sector Deepening (FSD) Kenya, 9 November. Available from: <https://fsdkenya.org/blog/financial-health-measurement-part-2/> (accessed 12 December 2019).

Gutman, A. et al. (2015) *Understanding and Improving Consumer Financial Health in America*, Center for Financial Services Innovation (CFSI), Chicago. Available from: <https://s3.amazonaws.com/cfsi-innovation-files/wp-content/uploads/2017/01/24183123/Understanding-and-Improving-Consumer-Financial-Health-in-America.pdf> (accessed 12 December 2019).

Harford, T. (2009) 'Does nobody want to take money from the poor?', *Financial Times*, 14 February, p. 13.

Jack, W. and Suri, T. (2014) 'Risk sharing and transactions costs: evidence from Kenya's mobile money revolution', *American Economic Review* 104 (1): 183–223 <https://doi.org/10.1257/aer.104.1.183>.

Johnson, S., Malkamaki, M., and Nino-Zarazua, M. (2010) 'The role of informal groups in financial markets: evidence from Kenya', Bath Papers in International Development and Wellbeing 7, Centre for Development Studies, University of Bath, Bath. Available from: <http://opus.bath.ac.uk/34557/> (accessed 16 September 2017).

Kaiser, T. and Menkhoff, L. (2017) 'Does financial education impact financial literacy and financial behavior, and if so, when?', *World Bank Economic Review* 31 (3): 611–30 <https://doi.org/10.1093/wber/lhx018>.

Mustafa, Z., Wachira, M., Bersudskaya, V., Nanjeroand, W. and Wright, G.A.N. (2017) *Where Credit Is Due: Customer Experience of Digital Credit in Kenya*. MicroSave, Nairobi. Available from: <http://www.microsave.net/files/pdf/Where_Credit_Is_Due_Customer_Experience_of_Digital_Credit_In_Kenya.pdf> (accessed 7 February 2020).

Mutua, J. (2019) 'Mobile-based M-Shwari lends Sh430 billion in seven years', *Business Daily*, 11 December. Available from: <https://www.businessdailyafrica.com/corporate/companies/M-Shwari-lends-Sh430-billion-in-seven-years/4003102-5382230-bjmgke/index.html> (accessed 12 December 2019).

Ngugi, B. (2017) 'Banks warned on inaccurate borrowers data', *Business Daily*, 1 May. Available from: <http://www.businessdailyafrica.com/markets/news/Banks-warned-inaccurate-borrowers-data/3815534-3910130-qr5t7g/index.html> (accessed 16 September 2017).

Porteous, D. and Zollmann, J. (2016) 'Making financial markets work healthily for the poor', *Enterprise Development and Microfinance* 27 (1): 5–20 <https://doi.org/10.3362/1755-1986.2016.001>.

Pritchett, L. (2017) 'Getting kinky with chickens', *Center for Global Development*, 28 March. Available from: <https://www.cgdev.org/blog/getting-kinky-chickens> (accessed 30 July 2018).

Rutherford, S. and Arora, S.S. (2009) *The Poor and their Money*, Practical Action Publishing, Rugby. Available from: <https://sites.google.com/site/thepoorandtheirmoney/the-book> (accessed 26 August 2017).

Shipton, P. (1990) 'How Gambians save and what their strategies imply for international aid', Policy Research Working Paper WPS395, World Bank, Washington DC. Available from: <http://documents.worldbank.org/curated/en/120041468771037897/How-Gambians-save-and-what-their-strategies-imply-for-international-aid> (accessed 27 August 2017).

Suri, T. and Jack, W. (2016) 'The long-run poverty and gender impacts of mobile money', *Science* 354 (6317): 1288–92 <https://doi.org/10.1126/science.aah5309>.

Venkatesan, J. (2015) 'In the case of India's PMJDY, considerations for avoiding account dormancy', *Center for Financial Inclusion*, 3 September. Available from: <https://cfi-blog.org/tag/account-dormancy/> (accessed 27 August 2017).

Zollmann, J. (2014) *Shilingi kwa Shilingi: The Financial Lives of the Poor*, FSD Kenya, Nairobi. Available from: <http://fsdkenya.org/publication/kenya-financial-diaries-shilingi-kwa-shilingi-the-financial-lives-of-the-poor/> (accessed 7 February 2020).

Zollmann, J. and Collins, D. (2010) *Financial Capability: Are We Missing the Mark?*, FSD Kenya, Nairobi. Available from: <http://fsdkenya.org/publication/financial-capability-and-the-poor-are-we-missing-the-mark-fsd-insights-issue-02/> (accessed 7 February 2020).

CHAPTER 4

Growing up: The challenges of low income for children and young people

Abstract

Childhood experiences set the stage for adult outcomes. Scarcity often means that children are raised by adults who are not their parents and are deprived of educational opportunities. Families struggle to pay steep fees for their children's educations, limiting upward mobility for all but the luckiest of low-income children. Young people living in poor families – especially once they are forced to end their education – face the same temptations and challenges as young people anywhere, but a childhood of deprivation can make it more difficult to avoid them. Low-income young people simply do not have the resources to buy second chances. Overlooking the important social role of education, programmes aiming to 'economically empower' youth can be misguided.

Keywords: youth, education, early childhood, youth transitions, youth development

Christine's daughter Wambui was 19 years old when we started the study. One of Christine's proudest achievements was getting Wambui a scholarship for secondary school, which she had recently completed. Christine hoped Wambui would have a different path from her own.

Christine was born in Mathare, a slum area of Nairobi. She spent her early childhood there, until she was sent to live with relatives on the coast to finish primary school. Even they could not provide much support; she was forced by financial circumstances to leave school after class seven (at about 13 years old). Soon after, she got a job filling jerrycans with kerosene for KES 130 ($1.50) per day. Looking for a way to advance, she moved to a larger town on the coast. However, desperation soon led her to prostitution, a period of constant abuse and no income. When a 'kind' client paid her directly, she used the money to flee back to Nairobi, the home she knew best.

Although Christine moved in and out of different types of work, prostitution – which she discreetly referred to as her 'supermarket business' – remained an important source of income for her throughout our study. She found it both necessary and shameful. She hid the business and her HIV-positive status from her daughter. When Wambui got a job as a waitress in an upmarket Nairobi neighbourhood, Christine was so excited; it seemed that Wambui would have a very different life.

http://dx.doi.org/10.3362/9781788531207.004

But when we came back for the update interview two years later, things had changed. We found Christine distraught and on her way to visit Wambui in the hospital. Wambui had lost her job; heartbroken, Christine disclosed that her daughter, too, had turned to prostitution. She had moved in with a man Christine considered lazy and abusive. Wambui was then eight months pregnant, and he had beaten her so badly that she had been hospitalized with a broken pelvis. Christine was terrified about Wambui's future. This was not what she had hoped for her only daughter. What would come next?

Young people and the success of a family

Throughout the Financial Diaries, but especially in our two-year update, we found many of our respondents agonizing – and sometimes delighting – in key milestones of their children's transitions into adulthood. Would their children be hurt as they began to exercise new independence? Would they make the wrong choices? Marry the wrong partners? Get mixed up in the wrong company? Parental anxiety relating to such transitions is universal.

But the pressures are intensified for those living on little. Parents in our study understood that their own conditions of poverty made it even harder for their children to stay in school. They understood the trade-off between working in the present for a little cash versus staying in school to earn more in the future. They understood that, for their children, mistakes were harder to recover from.

They worried about their children's financial futures. Our respondents viewed the exit out of poverty as a multigenerational process. They placed their bets on their children, investing huge shares of their personal income and wealth in education. That investment, parents believed, would not only launch their children, but also enable these young adults to help pay the school fees of their siblings, nieces, and nephews; ensure growing levels of family wealth; and help care for them in old age. This expectation was explicit, often with nuclear and extended families discussing the family's 'development' together in concrete terms, making the obligations of each actor clear, and plotting shared investment and allocation decisions.

'*Maendeleo*' (development) was the goal of every family in our study. *Maendeleo* reflected a family's continuous improvement of economic status, the accumulation of new assets, improvements in housing, and the achievements of children. Development was not done alone; it was a product of the shared effort of relatives, which explained the webs of giving and obligation described elsewhere in this book. Its central importance within every family made it the yardstick for happiness and dignity, while its absence was the cause of jealousy and conflict. 'Things are good, we are developing.' 'Things are bad, we have not been developing,' respondents told us. Our researchers conveyed the same: 'They must be so happy. They have a cow! They are developing.' 'The second wife has accused the first of witchcraft, because her children are developing and the second wife's children are not.'

Young people in our study were the hope of their families. In our two-year update, we asked whether respondents expected life to be better, worse, or the same in five years. Eighty-two per cent believed things would improve, and the leading reason was that their children would finish their education and begin working, both reducing the number of mouths to feed at home and increasing returns through remittances.

Like many countries in Africa, Kenya's population is young. Today, about 80 per cent of Kenya's population is under 35 years old and 42 per cent under 15 years old (Awiti and Scott, 2016; World Bank, 2018). As young people reach working age, this poses real risks and opportunities. On one hand, in many countries, like Kenya, these young people have higher levels of education than previous generations, which can be a rich source of human capital driving economic growth and increases in long-term productivity. On the other, many argue that if the economy cannot adequately provide jobs and entrepreneurial activities with sufficient returns, disgruntled youth can become a destabilizing force, leading to increased crime or political disruption. The instability of this generation may stagnate investments in education and healthcare for the next generation. Policymakers are constantly debating the policies that will determine whether a youth bulge generates a 'demographic dividend' or becomes a 'demographic curse'. The question is: are investments in creating the demographic dividend focused on the right kinds of interventions? The lives of Diaries respondents offer up some clues.

Childhood matters

Often, policies aimed at addressing Kenya's youth bulge focus on adolescents and young adults, when the reality is that life trajectories are influenced by factors much earlier in life. There is broad consensus that nutrition, health, security, and relationships in childhood – especially early childhood – are critical to a child's ultimate physical and social development (WHO, n.d.). More broadly, we know that home-life conditions shape the opportunities young people have later in life, their expectations for the future, and the push factors that may see them scrambling for a life of independence before they have the human capital and other resources needed to live successfully on their own.

In recounting their own life stories, many of our adult respondents went back to their childhoods to explain why they have been unable to live up to their fullest potential. Many felt that the seeds of their poverty were planted before they had any control over their own futures.

Jennifer, who we met in Chapter 2, 'Looking for money', told us that things were never easy in her large family in Western Kenya. Even from the time she was six years old, she had to pick up casual work and sell groundnuts to help the family. She was forced to leave school after class three (at nine years old) because the family could no longer afford school fees. Her parents sent their nine-year-old daughter to stay with her older sister. Her sister was better able to take care of Jennifer, but she lived in a notorious Nairobi slum. After a time,

Jennifer's sister struggled financially and sent Jennifer to work as a 'house help' for another aunt, also in Nairobi. Jennifer mixed with the wrong crowd. At 18 years old, she married a man she told us was 'one of Mathare's most wanted criminals'. When their second child had complications after birth, her husband disappeared, abandoning her at the hospital. By 2015, she was raising her children alone and got by by selling hot coffee in the morning and washing clothes for some long-standing clients.

Many features of Jennifer's childhood experience were not unique. It was very common for children to be raised by relatives who were not their parents and even for children to be passed from home to home depending on the relative capacity of related households to care for the child in any given year. The responsibility for caring for children often fell to grandparents, with or without much financial support from the children's birth parents. According to Kenya's most recent Demographic and Health Survey, about 9 per cent of Kenyan children were living with grandparents as their primary caregivers. Thirty-three per cent of household heads aged 55 and over were raising grandchildren. In our own sample of Diaries households, 73 per cent of children aged 18 and below were the biological children of household heads. Another 19 per centwere grandchildren and 8 per cent were other relatives, including nieces, nephews, and younger siblings.

This trend in non-parental caregiving was due in part to the HIV epidemic. The death rate from the disease has slowed and prevalence among those aged 15–49 has declined from a peak of around 10 per cent in 1995–96 to 5.4 per cent in 2016. Still, the epidemic has left 840,000 children orphaned (UNAIDS, 2016).

However, respondents' life histories indicate that children have been raised by relatives long before the rise in HIV. The extended family was often asked, or offered, to take in a child when his or her parents were struggling, when one parent died, forcing the surviving parent to seek work in a higher-cost, less stable, urban environment, when marriages dissolved, or when a mother remarried and could not bring her children into the new husband's household.

Such situations may not necessarily be 'bad' for children if they find acceptance, love, and resources in their alternative homes. However, we observed a number of children in our study who lived with grandparents who could not always provide them with adequate food, housing, and education. Others lived with relatives who treated them as an unwanted burden or merely as a source of free labour. The effects of these situations were certain to be long-lasting.

Maggie, for example, has never had enough money to live comfortably, and things got even more challenging in 2011 when two of her children and one of her daughters-in-law passed away. At that time, Maggie took in two grandchildren, even though she struggled to buy food and pay rent on her small one-room house in an informal settlement in Nairobi. She often found herself drawing on the working capital from her small grocery business just to meet basic needs, causing the business to shrink over time.

When we visited Maggie in 2015, she had recently moved back to her rural home and was now living with a third grandchild. No longer paying rent provided some financial relief, and the large farm enabled her to produce more of her own food, further cutting costs. But Maggie had few options for earning cash income. The market to support a small business in this rural area was very small. Although only 58 years old, Maggie was too worn out to endure the frequent travel to the nearest town that a business would require. Plus, she had no access to capital to get started.

Two of the three grandchildren in Maggie's care had a surviving parent who helped with school fees. One, Franklin, did not. The headmaster at the rural, public primary school insisted that, as a new parent in the school, Maggie pay all of Franklin's fees for the year at once. Public primary school is supposed to be free in Kenya, but many schools still charge some fees to bridge the gap between government funding allocations and what school leaders determine is the actual cost of running a school. Maggie could not pull together the required KES 2,200 ($22) at once to secure his admission. Instead, Franklin repeated nursery school (the equivalent of kindergarten) three times. Although nursery school was not free, the school allowed her to pay those fees in small instalments.

Maggie's inability to cover the most basic of education expenses for her grandson is extremely troubling. A key feature of nearly all of our adult respondents' life histories was regret over their premature exit from school. Many came from large families where education had to be rationed. Others came from homes where investing in education was limited by alcoholism, divorce, and abandonment. In some cases, parents died while their children were still young. Relatives provided support – especially for education – for a time, but not all the way through secondary school and beyond, the way a parent might.

And that matters. Numerous studies have demonstrated that returns on education in developing countries such as Kenya are high. One recent paper estimated that economic returns from education are about 13.5 per cent per year for Kenyan women and 14.9 per cent for Kenyan men. In our own study, although our sample was small and non-representative, we found that respondents with higher levels of education had higher earnings than those with lower education, even in the informal economy.

Education – especially for girls – produces substantial social returns, even when learning outcomes are poor. For example, girls with more years of education have fewer and healthier children (Oye et al., 2016; Sandefur, 2017). Education is key not just for building human capital for productive purposes, but also in delaying risky behaviours and avoiding circumstances that change the course of young people's lives. For our respondents, navigating the complicated, crocodile-infested stream of 'youth' was seen mostly as what must be done *after* a young person leaves school.

Nearly all of our adult respondents viewed leaving school as a turning point in their lives, and an early exit was never a good thing. For young men, leaving school early often meant getting trapped in low-skilled work. Young men who travelled outside their familiar homes at least gained skills and exposure, although often by engaging in high-risk activities. Young women who were forced to leave school early most often worked as domestic workers for a short time and began families before they had a chance to advance their education, build livelihoods of their own, or gain the empowerment that comes from knowing and navigating the world.

The partner a girl chooses at age 17 may be far different from the one she chooses at 27; the nature of the relationship is also likely to be very different. Among our respondents, many of the relationships forged at this young age dissolved, and those women were stuck with the lifelong reality of low earning potential that is associated with low educational attainment and early motherhood. To go back to school, paying school fees would be only the beginning; these women would also need money to sustain their children and someone to care for them. After two or three children, the future life choices and trajectories of individuals who were forced out of their education early – especially girls – became significantly more constrained.

Education

Parents and grandparents in our study understood that education was an important determinant of lifelong achievement. Often having been deprived of a full education themselves, the overwhelming majority prioritized the education of their own children, seeing this as an important endowment for their children and a necessity for the *maendeleo* (development) of the family.

One woman in rural Vihiga explained:

> When I got married to my husband, he was working in a certain company. I told him that I wanted him to buy a piece of land for me. I started farming it, which has helped me to educate my children. This is important to me because at least I want my children to know how to read and write so that when they are walking, they should not ask people [for help] because they are not able to read and write ...
>
> The most significant thing that I have ever done is educate my children. All of them have reached up to form four [the end of secondary school], and one has been able to go to college.

Education was a priority for our respondents in spite of its high cost. Formal education in Kenya starts with preschool. While not compulsory by law, many primary schools (both public and private) require preschool prior to enrolment. This is followed by eight years of primary school, exams, then four years of secondary school, followed by another set of exams. Students may continue to colleges or university thereafter. In 2003, the government of Kenya instituted free primary education, which led to a big bump in enrolment. In 2008, they eliminated 'tuition' fees at secondary schools. However, in reality, while the government pays a per-pupil amount to secondary schools, fees continue to be charged to parents up to a government-allowed maximum (which some report is exceeded).

The public primary schools our respondents' children attended often charged supplementary fees imposed by the school to cover extra teachers (often called 'PTA' teachers, since they are paid by the Parent–Teacher Association instead of the Ministry of Education), school meals, school investment fund contributions, and other fees as decided by the headteacher and his or her school's board of governors. Parents also paid for pens, notebooks, and school uniforms, which was a burden for poor families. For respondents in our study, the annual costs of public primary school were in the ballpark of the KES 2,200 ($22) charged by the headmaster in Maggie's community.

Secondary school was a much heavier burden. Even the lowest-cost public schools charged around KES 10,000–20,000 ($117–$235) per year per student. In comparison, households in our study earned a median income of about KES 7,120 ($84) per month. Paying fees for the first of four years of secondary school was particularly stressful. Many headteachers requested that first-year students pay in full for the entire academic year at the start of the first term, with instalment payments allowed for more senior students. Many secondary schools – both public and private – were boarding schools, which had a reputation for being higher quality than day schools. For students going to boarding school for the first time, parents incurred the additional lumpy expense of purchasing a trunk for their belongings and a number of other living necessities required by the school.

The median household in our study – irrespective of the schooling level of children – dedicated 11 per cent of their expenditure budget to education-related expenses. A quarter of households with children in school dedicated more than 24 per cent of all their spending to education. These families were typically struggling just to meet their most basic of needs.

The enormous expense of secondary school helps us understand the dramatic drop in enrolment rates in Kenya between primary and secondary school. As of 2012,[1] the gross enrolment ratio[2] in primary school in Kenya was 116 per cent, indicating enrolment levels higher than would be age appropriate (World Bank, 2012a). Gross enrolment in secondary school was only 67.6 per cent (World Bank, 2012b). In the 2017 elections, both major national parties pledged to work towards free secondary schools, but such a policy was not yet in place at the time of writing.

Despite its expense, low-income families know that education can be transformative, so they stretch as much as they possibly can to enrol their children in schools at the very edge of the affordability frontier. Parents often associate more expensive schools with better schools, and there is reason to worry quite a bit about quality. An Uwezo educational assessment of more than 130,000 students country-wide in 2015 found that only 30 per cent of class three students could do the work of a class two student in English, maths, and Kiswahili (Uwezo, 2016).

Often, families in our study enrolled their children in schools they knew they could not independently and sustainably afford with the explicit intention of periodically fundraising, hustling, and otherwise 'looking for money' each term. Sometimes, they started early, allocating a one-time income source towards enrolling their children in relatively expensive nursery schools, investing in private schools in the years when that was possible, or splurging on higher-quality schools for one or two children at a time.

The high cost of secondary school held back some of the most promising students. Daniel was one. Daniel was the youngest child of Violet, a single mother in our study. Violet supported her three children – two in secondary school during the study – with a small grocery stall and occasional stipends for her part-time work as a community health worker. Daniel had scored highly on the national exam and was offered a place in a prestigious school. Violet managed to put together the minimum requirements to get him enrolled for Form 1, but then struggled to come up with the rest of the fees. Basic fees alone – apart from his living expenses, shopping needs, and pocket money – were KES 37,000 ($435) per year. Daniel thrived at this school; he had his eye on university, where he hoped to study law.

But, as his second year came around, Violet still carried over a debt from the first year. Her total bill had grown to KES 72,000 ($847). She had no idea where to get that kind of money. Daniel stayed home from school for several weeks while she searched for money, even joining some new savings groups in the hope that they would give her a loan of about KES 20,000 ($235) to at least get him back through the door. She failed. Unable to clear her debt or pay the new fees, Violet moved Daniel to a local day school where fees were only around KES 9,000 ($105) per year.

Violet was ashamed of this failure. When we visited in 2015, she told us that even these lower fees were a strain. One year, she was able to convince some local politicians to help her get a partial bursary to help with the costs. At this lower-quality school, Daniel lost motivation. He was not learning and no longer felt stimulated. University no longer seemed like a real option. With less motivation to study after school, he started picking up casual work and raising guinea pigs to help bring some extra cash into the household. His grades dropped dramatically. He was about to sit his final secondary school exams the last time we saw him. He had no particular plans but was very eager to leave home and figure something out.

Violet wished things could be different, but she ran out of options. It was not as though education was not important to her. Twenty per cent of all her spending throughout the Diaries went on school fees. She has had a painful, orange-sized growth just under her left breast since 1997. She has been advised that it will cost KES 10,000 ($100) to remove it. When we saw her in late 2015, she told us that maybe she would finally have the money once Daniel finished school. School came first. But for her most academically promising child, a *good* school was out of reach.

Parents didn't give up easily on their children, especially these very promising students. It was not uncommon for low-income families to hold *harambees* (large fundraising events where large numbers of contributors make small, public donations) to collect funds for school fees, especially to cover the large sums needed to enter secondary school or to finish paying for exams and clearing debts. They turned to their better-off relatives for help. They pleaded with politicians for special favours, like securing local Constituency Development Fund (CDF) scholarships. They looked to churches and NGOs for 'sponsorship' for specific students. And they drew as much as they could on their own resources, from income, savings, borrowing, and planned and unplanned sales of assets including livestock – and even trees and land when push came to shove. The general approach appeared to be to secure the student's place in school and then to tackle one payment at a time – step by step – until the child finished.

But finishing also has begun to stretch beyond secondary school to college and university. Students with the very highest marks on their secondary school exams secure places in public universities where fees are not substantially more than secondary school and where there is often a government loan (from the Higher Education Loans Board or HELB) available to support the costs. However, many other students do not receive this support and still aspire to continue their education at either universities or training colleges (for professions such as nursing, teaching, secretarial work, and even information technology). While likely very good for the long-term finances of these individuals and the human capital of the country, the extended financial burden for the family is often unbearable.

Sarah was the widow of a police officer. Since her husband's death, she had managed to put her kids through secondary school with a combination of pension money and income from a posho mill where she ground maize for neighbours. When we visited her during the update, four of her daughters had finished secondary school with good grades, and she really wanted to send them to college, knowing this would be helpful for their long-term earnings.

Because none of Sarah's daughters received scholarships or government loan assistance, paying for college was up to her. She was able to raise the money for only one of the girls by convincing her son-in-law, a soldier in the Kenya Defence Forces, to pay the fees for one daughter to go to a teacher training college. Sarah viewed this as a partial payment against the dowry her son-in-law would eventually pay for marrying her daughter. The other three daughters were all working as housekeepers in Nairobi, which broke Sarah's heart. When she was forced to drop out of school at class seven, she also worked as a housekeeper and found herself married within two years. She had hoped that all of her sacrifices to educate her daughters would mean that they would have different, better options.

Pressures to earn

The cost of secondary school is perhaps the most important barrier to low-income children getting a secondary school education, but it is not the only one. In the last year of primary school, Kenyan students take a national examination that determines their eligibility for secondary school. Schools of varying quality then offer them places based on those scores. Unsurprisingly, the best public schools – a set of 'national schools' – are stocked with the highest performers, who are often overwhelmingly from better-off families.

However, in our study, a fair number of young people – 24 per cent of those who took the exam in 2015 – did not achieve the minimum scores required to advance into secondary school (Aduda, 2016). For low-income students with low scores, it was very difficult for parents and extended families to be motivated to raise and sacrifice significant sums of money to send them to secondary school anyway. Some found their way – typically after a couple of years out of school – to technical training programmes in skills such as tailoring and catering for girls and driving, carpentry, and auto mechanics for boys. But many did not, often entering a period of idle drifting. 'I'm just at home,' was a common phrase. They picked up bits of low-skilled work that didn't seem to lead anywhere.

Another subset of young people left secondary school by choice. Often, they were not good students. They were uncomfortable with the structure and confines of a school environment. They did not expect to continue their education, and as a result sometimes felt guilty about consuming family resources with school fees. These young people preferred to go out in the world, earn an income, help the family, and start their own, independent life.

During our 2015 update, a number of our adult respondents worried about children who were losing interest in education and choosing to engage in livelihoods their parents thought to be either risky or inadequate in the long term.

One example was Brian, Alice's second of three sons. Alice always struggled to make ends meet. She had been disabled by an illness and could no longer walk normally, making it difficult to find and keep regular work or even pick up casual jobs. During the Diaries, Brian helped out, earning some money fetching water for other families and doing many of the household tasks Alice couldn't manage herself.

Brian's father had not been very involved in his life, but his paternal grandmother stayed in touch. The year prior to the update, his grandmother called Alice and offered to take Brian in and pay for his school fees. The two women also hoped the change of scene – from urban Mombasa to rural Rift Valley – might help him focus on his studies. But when Brian reached his grandmother's home, he begged to be enrolled in a driving course instead of finishing his final year of primary school. (Brian was still below the legal driving age of 18.) Neither Alice nor Brian's grandmother thought this was a good idea. They had already paid school fees and the fees for the national examination.

But then one day, well before the close of the school year, Brian just showed up back at Alice's home in Mombasa. She said he smelled terrible and that his clothes were tattered and stained. She wondered how he had possibly made it back home from Rift Valley with no money at all, but she didn't ask any questions.

Brian refused to go back to school and started washing motorbikes for *boda* (motorbike taxi) drivers around the neighbourhood. When the owners left their bikes to be washed, Brian would play around with them, teaching himself to drive. Eventually, he was able to convince a few *boda* drivers to lend him their bikes at night, so that he could start picking up some shifts. This worried Alice. He could be harassed by the police for being too young to drive or for not having a licence. He could be injured driving late at night. He could be attacked by thugs. But she felt she couldn't change his mind and begged her brother to try to talk to him – 'as a man'. Brian continued riding the bikes.

One night, at around two in the morning, Alice was woken by a neighbour. There had been an accident. Both Brian and his passenger were in the hospital, badly injured. It seemed Brian had also been drinking. The two had been hit by a lorry and the bike was destroyed. The lorry driver agreed to pay the hospital bills. Luckily, the owner of the motorbike never came looking for compensation. Alice hoped this close call would make Brian change his ways. But, as soon as he was able to move around, he was back driving motorbikes at night.

Alice was extremely worried but didn't know what else to do. She would much prefer that Brian finish school first. But she couldn't convince him to forgo the small bits of money he could earn and freely spend today in hopes of something more substantial in the long term. Having so little for so long made it extremely difficult to forgo the opportunity to make money. Alice gave up trying to convince Brian to finish school. She prayed he would do something safer, rather than run the risk of a permanent disability – or worse.

Patrick could relate to this. One of his sons was not an enthusiastic student and failed his secondary school exams. He was eager to be out in the world, working and earning his own money. Patrick explained: 'These days, he gets KES 500 [$5] in a day, and he thinks it's a lot of money. There's nothing else he wants.' But Patrick knew that the same KES 500 wouldn't feel like enough once his son had a family. If his son insisted on doing construction, Patrick hoped he would try to learn a special skill on the site, so that he could at least earn more money and be able to work even as he ages. He worried that his son was short-sighted, holding himself back from what could be a much better life.

The lure of crime

In urban environments, where gangs are prevalent, the temptation for quick money lured a number of respondents into crime, most commonly theft.

John grew up in Siaya, in Western Kenya, and was a bright student, so bright in fact that he was invited to a highly selective national school for his secondary education. But his father had recently passed away and his mother had no way to pull together the money for his fees while trying to raise eight children on her own. After leaving school, he tried to earn a living fishing, but the money was not very good, and his mother disapproved. He ventured to Nairobi, hoping to find work. After a few years in construction, he met a metalsmith who agreed to take him on as an apprentice, and he soon found a lucrative market in making guns. But when another gunmaker in the area was caught by the police, he stepped away from that trade. Then things became really hard. He ran up a debt with his landlord and had to go back to construction. That was when, he told us, he became a 'thug'. In 2009 he was arrested for violent robbery and spent a year in jail where he was 'saved', becoming a born-again Christian. When he got out of jail, he returned to his wife and their three children and focused squarely on using his skill in metalwork to construct the boxes so many Kenyan children use to pack their things when they go off to boarding school.

Like John, several male respondents in Nairobi also walked away from lives as self-described thugs. Some wake-up call – an arrest or close call with death – was often the impetus. Salvation, the ritual of being 'born again', provided a pathway for dramatic change acceptable to their gang colleagues. It provided a new identity and simultaneously demanded avoidance of a certain set of behaviours (especially alcohol, drugs, and – at least nominally – infidelity) and the social reinforcement of those norms within the community of church members.

Not all young men escape their close call, commit to change, and proceed to live full, productive, even inspiring lives. Many court significant risks every day. A civil society group in Mathare (one of Nairobi's largest slums, and one of our study sites) documented the extrajudicial killing of 800 young people from 2013 to 2015 (Mathare Social Justice Centre, 2017). Across the country, violence accounted for 6.4 per cent of deaths of men aged 15–49 in 2015. That is more than deaths from road accidents and more than double the average rate for the same age group in other low- to middle-income countries (2.95%).[3]

Addiction and mental health

The lure of crime was not the only thing that threw young people off course. As in many countries, Kenyan young people also struggled with addiction and mental health challenges. Although we did not quantify these experiences in our study, a number of our adult respondents shared their challenges and fears relating to their children struggling with these issues.

Alcoholism was a particular concern. A number of respondents had sons aged between 20 and 35 with such severe drinking problems that they began to terrorize the home, stealing anything from the house that could be used to buy alcohol, including cash, household utensils, and even food from the *shamba* (farm) before their families could harvest it.

Anna's 33-year-old son had been in and out of rehabilitation centres multiple times, at Anna's expense, but he was never able to shake his drinking habit. During the Diaries, he left another programme before finishing. He complained: 'I felt like I was lining up for medication like an HIV-infected person.' Last time we saw Anna, she lamented that her son had gained a partner in her grandson. The two stole whatever they could get their hands on in order to drink. When they were drunk, they harassed her for more money and even threatened to kill her. Her son's repeated theft of the family's farm produce led Anna's other children to stop buying inputs for cultivation, replacing farm produce with bulk purchases of food that could be locked in Anna's bedroom. Anna decided not to open a shop as she had planned, afraid that more cash would give her son more reason to steal from her. Despite her fear and frustration, she was resigned. She could not force her son to leave. She lamented:

> This is a burden I must live with until I die...My blood pressure keeps rising. I keep taking diabetic medication and there is no change. When we are in the kitchen, they come in the main house and steal maize. They sell anything they find so that they can buy liquor.

Bendetta had a similar problem with her stepson, Clemence. After his father died, Bendetta stayed in the home (and on the land) she had shared with her late husband. Clemence had been living elsewhere, but when he returned, he became difficult to live with. He stole whatever he could find in order to buy alcohol. Some of his uncles had intervened in the past and had taken him to their homes, where they tried to give him a new environment away from his drinking buddies and usual drinking spots. But they, too, eventually gave up. Bendetta was afraid of Clemence. She tried to appease him by giving him a little money every day to go and drink. But, still, she was afraid. When we came to visit Bendetta in 2015, she claimed that one of the friends Clemence drinks with had raped Bendetta's 15-year-old niece. Bendetta was afraid to confront Clemence or the friend, or even to seek help from the police. Instead, she turned to her late husband's relatives. Their options were also limited; in their culture, a son cannot be forced off his father's land.

In addition to alcohol, young people worldwide are vulnerable to mental health problems. Adolescence is often the time when existing issues become more apparent and the strains of transition into adulthood can cause additional problems (WHO, 2019). Undiagnosed and untreated, such problems can derail low-income young people's life journeys. This was particularly apparent with one young man, Tim, in rural Vihiga. Tim was in secondary school during the study. He was a bright student, and his parents had high hopes for what he might do after school. But things took a turn when he was badly beaten by a teacher at school. (Corporal punishment in schools is illegal, but it continues in practice and often has the support of parents (Mwai et al., 2014).) The beating sent Tim to the hospital and into depression. Following a quarrel with a classmate, he attempted to kill himself by drinking acid. His mother rushed him to the hospital in time for successful treatment, though at a significant cost of KES 16,500 ($194). Although extremely worried about him, his mother was afraid to talk to him about his future, worried he might try to kill himself again.

When we followed up two years later, we learned that Tim had passed his secondary school exams with flying colours and had been offered a position at Egerton University (a prestigious public university). His parents were thrilled and began raising money to make sure he could attend. But Tim refused to register and went to stay with his elder brother in Nairobi. He started learning the basics of driving and vehicle repair, but then ran away from his brother's home. Eventually he called his mother. He told her that he had got a connection to work in one of Nairobi's hotels. Tim's mother still worries about him constantly: 'I don't know what to do. It's like he is possessed.'

Partnership

Parents the world over worry about the risks of sexual activity for their adolescent children. For our respondents, there were good reasons to worry. Young mothers are at a greater risk of dying during childbirth, and their children are less likely to survive past their fifth birthday (Levine et al., 2008; Lloyd and Young, 2009; Temin and Levine, 2009; Hardgrove et al., 2014). As of 2014, 40% of young Kenyan women had been pregnant at least once by age 19. That proportion has not changed since 2009 (KNBS et al., 2014). Six per cent of Kenyans were living with HIV, with prevalence rising upwards of 20 per cent in some counties in the western part of the country (KODI, 2015).

In Chapter 5, 'Being a woman', we explore the profound, lifelong implications of marital relationships on the shape and course of the lives of women and their children, many of which start when the women are still girls. Children born during those early relationships typically constrain the future opportunities of the mother far more than the father. If a girl gets pregnant while in school, often she will keep the child but not continue a serious relationship with his or her father. Among our young respondents, the girls seemed to partner intentionally shortly after dropping out of school. When a girl reached the end of her educational journey, both she and her community viewed partnering as the logical next life step. Parents started expecting their daughters to get married and start their own lives. For their part, girls dropping out of school sometimes felt that they also need to leave home to stop being a burden to their parents.

Sometimes these were formal marriages in which spouses were introduced to each other's parents and a dowry paid. Quite often, though, they were so-called 'come-we-stay' relationships in which couples began living together without any formalities and were still considered 'married' from a social perspective. Those relationships were typically sealed when the couple had their first child, although dowry payments formalizing the relationship could be delayed for years.

Partnerships formed in youth have implications beyond the challenges of raising children. The needs, expectations, and wisdom that a 17-year-old brings to bear rarely set the stage for building a healthy long-term relationship. Older individuals (and this is particularly important for girls) have the advantage of being clearer about their expectations from marriage and can enter a relationship with more equal negotiating power. An older woman might enter a relationship with more skills and financial wherewithal, which affords her the ability to walk away if things do not work out. Girls who leave school early and partner very young often start at a disadvantage that is difficult to correct; they can find that their bargaining power in the relationship, weak to start with, erodes over time. And we saw from our respondents who were just a few years older that this compromised position matters.

A number of our respondents who married men close to their own age seemed to have fairly stable and respectful relationships when both of them were staying together in the village, where they had relatively similar levels of opportunity and exposure. We saw divergence increase when men – unhindered by childcare responsibilities – spent more time away from home and were able to continue pursuing new opportunities, even if this was through low-wage jobs outside the village. In such cases, it appeared more likely for expectations between partners to shift.

For example, Matthew, a young man in our study, was really struggling to get by in the Diaries, but he was also investing, trying to put himself through college. He rented a one-room house in Mathare with his brother, his wife Marie, and their small child. When he met Marie, they were largely in the same place socially and economically. Together, they shared the financial burdens of running a household in Nairobi, and Marie's family even helped Matthew with his college fees, which were around KES 70,000 ($823) per year. To complete his tuition payments, he maintained an online business doing homework and writing papers for other students worldwide. He explained:

> I also befriended a lady [Marie] whose family was a bit rich. I tried to figure it out to pursue my education; I had to rely on her so that the family could sponsor me partially, because I knew the brother had some reliable income … It's true that the lady was in love with me, I can't deny that. Even me I was a bit in love, but not so much.

Although they had a child together, by the end of the study Matthew had sent Marie to live with his mother upcountry. He had become ashamed of his decision to start a life with her:

> It's a shame for a learned man like me to have a wife below my education level … I have learned that it is not good to marry at a tender age. You will have a burden because, you know, now where I am, there are some more beautiful girls. So, you know, it's as if I made a mistake by marrying a long time ago, and now I am crying, 'I wish I knew.'

Matthew finished college and landed a high-paying job in a Nairobi café. During the update, he told us Marie was still at his rural home. He sent her only KES 500 ($5) per month and told us he was actively shopping around for a new wife. We were not sure if Marie knew that Matthew was seeking a new partner or what she thought about it. The fact that she continued to stay with Matthew's mother suggested that she considered herself his wife and would most likely not be happy with the prospect of him seeking a new one. It could be years before she even found out. While it was easy for Matthew to change his mind, it would be much harder for Marie. She had a child and had pulled back from the workforce to help Matthew's mother at the rural home.

Like many young men, Matthew had flexibility that young women like Marie did not. It's hard to imagine Wambui, introduced at the opening of this chapter, choosing to have a child with the same abusive boyfriend if she had not lost her job, if she had first had a few years of independence and some savings in the bank. Instead, this one very important choice of partner has closed off options she might have had in her life.

Charting a course towards independence

Which is not to say that Wambui is doomed. Young people did start over and move on. But now, still unable to walk normally and with a child, things will be harder for her.

One young woman from the study was particularly determined not to let the birth of her first child prevent her from living a full and happy life. Lilyan had her first child before she completed form four (the end of secondary school) but was committed to finishing school. Her mother agreed to watch the baby so that she could attend classes. But, after passing her exams, things got harder. Her mother had not agreed to become the baby's full-time caretaker. Lilyan had to turn down a job in Mombasa, since she was unable to bring her child. After a year or so, she moved to Nairobi with the child to work as a teller at an M-Pesa agency. The baby's father had recently finished university. Lilyan thought that would be her path too, but there was not enough money. She was only admitted into a university programme in early childhood development, a course she was not excited about pursuing. The father of the baby wanted to marry Lilyan. Her mother agreed, asking, 'What's the point in looking for another?'

Lilyan was afraid that if she agreed to marry at that time, she would be sent to live at her husband's rural home with his parents. How would she earn an income there? How independent could she be there? She was willing to marry her baby's father, but she insisted on finding a good stable job in Nairobi first, to avoid having to move upcountry with her in-laws, which would involve losing much of her independence and her sense of personal and professional possibilities.

Very often, we saw that charting a course towards independence and happiness was about overcoming the barriers of everyday life, the severe constraints imposed by having few resources and limited access to jobs. With few obvious breakout opportunities, many young people felt like they walked away from school into an economic abyss. However, in our study, a few of them turned that uncertainty into lucky opportunities, benefiting their entire families. One young woman, Leah, finished form four but did not do particularly well in her exams. Leah's first bit of luck was landing an internship that paid KES 6,000 ($60) per month. She was also able to pick up occasional jobs doing some modelling work. At the end of her internship, she was offered a full-time job at the modelling agency, and her earnings increased to about KES 75,000 ($750) per month. Her life and that of her mother were transformed. Leah helped her mother to slowly pay off her many debts, both to Leah's school and to Kenya Power for long overdue electricity arrears. Once the power was reconnected, Leah's mother was able to get a tenant for her extra room, increasing her personal income. The young woman herself moved from the slums of Dandora into the middle-class neighbourhood of Kileleshwa, in Nairobi's suburbs.

While Leah's story was very happy for her personally, it was also a demonstration of the ways in which merit was overshadowed by luck in shaping young people's futures. More than a few bright students were moved from good/expensive schools to poor/cheap ones due to family finances. Not all of those students offered competitive admission to universities were able to take advantage of the opportunity. One of the most transformative stories we heard in the 2015 update was that of a young man securing a job as a soldier in the Kenya Defence Forces. That job was bought with a substantial bribe, rather than the young person's qualifications.

Luck was fickle and unfair in the way in which it shaped life pathways for youth. Yet there was another path towards livelihood security, even if it did not lead all the way to Kileleshwa. That was the incremental building of one enterprise on top of another. Looking for clues among our most successful respondents in their thirties and forties with less than a college education, it seemed that investing in multiple layered businesses was key to living a better life (see Chapter 2, 'Looking for money', for a more detailed treatment of this topic). Some young people's parents and extended family prepared them for that life, and it seemed to have made a difference.

Geoffrey, for example, grew up in Korogocho, one of Nairobi's roughest neighbourhoods. His father was an alcoholic and his mother struggled to keep him in school. Perhaps knowing she couldn't afford secondary school, she tried to teach Geoffrey business from a young age. During school breaks, starting when he was only 12 years old, she had him set up a kiosk. She would buy Geoffrey a small supply of fruits to sell and ask him to calculate the profits to keep for himself after returning her capital. When he was in his final year of primary school, his mother sent him on a two-week training course to learn to be a barber. There was no money for secondary school, so he kept up with his fruit kiosk, adding cigarettes and candy to his inventory. But he felt like this business left him with too much free time and too many of the wrong kinds of friends. 'The kind of friends that I kept were not good. Some used to smoke *bhang* [marijuana] and do many filthy things that were not good.' He claims that their influence turned him into a 'gangster', but he wanted to walk away from all of that after nearly dying in a shootout with police.

His mother encouraged him to try selling potatoes. This kept him busy and helped him save enough to buy someone's fully equipped barber shop. That barber shop helped him save and open an M-Pesa agency, then a church (which was meant to be a source of income), some rental homes, and a restaurant. He attributed all of this success to his mother's guiding hand:

> Generally, life in slums is highly influenced by peer pressure and many other bad things. Since my mother didn't want me to be influenced with such things and because she couldn't afford to take me to school further, she saw that it was better to introduce me to business while still young and train me on how to manage, save, and also how to be independent. This helped me a lot, because I remained sober and focused to date. So I am very happy for that. Even though I didn't have the opportunity to continue with my education, at least I have something to be proud of.

Building better bridges

Navigating the transition from childhood to adulthood is challenging in every country and culture, but the stakes – and expectations – are raised for Kenya's large, low-income youth population. Securing durable investments in their personal development is not easy. Temptations to abandon education early to have money today – through both legal and illicit means – are powerful. It is easy to make decisions that one will later regret, that reduce their long-term odds of leading long, full, and happy lives. And even if they do everything 'right', the jobs and other opportunities that await them are often limited. All of that is problematic and stressful for young people, their parents, and government alike, because the stakes are so high. So much is riding on their success.

And yet the proposals to address the challenges of youth transitions in so many countries have been narrowly focused on vocational training and access to credit. Kenya is no exception. The three recent flagship government programmes in Kenya aimed at addressing the burgeoning youth population have been: 1) a Youth Enterprise Fund providing business loans to young people at subsidized interest rates; 2) the National Youth Service, a corruption-plagued initiative to provide young people with paramilitary training and then rotate them between vocational training and deployment on development projects such as building pit latrines in urban slums; and 3) a pledge by the president to allocate 30 per cent of government tenders to youth-owned businesses.

The data we have about young people's lives beg the question: are these the right investments, the right places for attention? Opening credit access and vocational training (for what are often a limited set of careers) can be part of the problem, sending the message that work, rather than school, is how a young person should be spending his or her time. Such programmes can lure youth away from what might be a long-term future with higher returns.

Given the returns on schooling – even with limited learning outcomes – it is important to carefully compare the costs and benefits of subsidized youth lending funds versus policies and funding that keep young people in school longer. The high cost of secondary school education creates burdens on families that amplify the temptations of young people to leave school in search of an income of their own. Policies that cut the cost of education – and even give direct cash transfers to students or their families – would be incredibly powerful in building human capital and helping build safer bridges from adolescence to adulthood. Reliable, merit-based scholarships can also encourage young people to invest in their educations and ensure that bright students stay in good schools and fulfil their potential.

What about targeting youth-owned businesses for government contracts? This sets up an incentive for young people to start their own businesses and inevitably privileges those with access to capital (both financial and social) to start and grow those businesses. It encourages young people to start endeavours without the requisite skills and experience needed to be successful. NGOs are often complicit, offering up their own youth solutions in the form of entrepreneurial training of questionable quality for young people, ignoring the bigger contextual challenges that make it difficult for young people's businesses to thrive.

One thing we learn from many of our respondents with successful businesses, is that they learn to operate them often as employees in the same kinds of enterprises (see Chapter 2, 'Looking for money'). Apprenticeships and 'attachments' (internships, often mandatory for university graduation) can be powerful tools, not because they translate into long-term employment, but because they help young people learn skills and make contacts. They help young people learn from the inside how to operate a certain kind of business. They can also be a helpful tool for keeping young people on an educational track just a bit longer. Perhaps instead of sending business to youth-owned enterprises, government should incentivize the *hiring* and retaining of young people who will learn new skills on the job.[4]

Governments and development practitioners cannot take all of the risk out of young people's transitions into adulthood, but they can certainly work to build better bridges.

Endnotes

1. The most recent year for which both gross primary and secondary enrolment ratios are available is 2012.
2. The United Nations defines the gross enrolment ratio as: 'The number of children enrolled in a level (primary or secondary), regardless of age, divided by the population of the age group that officially corresponds to the same level' (UNICEF, n.d.).
3. See IHME (2017). More detailed data focused on young men are not available.
4. Of course, for those incentives to work, they need to be operationally functional, which is no easy task given the governance challenges in Kenya.

References

Aduda, D. (2016) '200,000 KCPE candidates unsuitable for secondary admission', *Daily Nation*, 1 January. Available from: <http://www.nation.co.ke/news/200000-KCPE-candidates-got-less-than-200-marks/1056-3017328-ydk9eh/index.html> (accessed 6 October 2017).

Awiti, A. and Scott, B. (2016) *The Kenya Youth Survey Report*, Aga Khan University, Nairobi. Available from: <https://www.aku.edu/eai/Documents/kenya-youth-survey-report-executive-summary-2016.pdf> (accessed 6 February 2020).

Hardgrove, A., Pells, K., Boyden, J., and Dornan, P. (2014) *Youth Vulnerabilities in Life Course Transitions*, UNDP, New York. Available from: <http://hdr.undp.org/sites/default/files/hardgrove_boyden_hdr_2014.pdf> (accessed 6 February 2020).

IHME (2017) *Global Burden of Disease Comparisons*, Institute for Health Metrics and Evaluation (IHME), Seattle. Available from: <http://vizhub.healthdata.org/gbd-compare> (accessed 6 October 2017).

KNBS et al. (2014) *Kenya: Demographic and Health Survey 2014*. Kenya National Bureau of Statistics (KNBS), Nairobi and Rockville MD. Available from: <http://dhsprogram.com/publications/publication-FR308-DHS-Final-Reports.cfm> (accessed 6 February 2020).

KODI (2015) 'HIV situation in Kenya – open data blog', Kenya Open Data Initiative (KODI). Available from: <http://blog.opendata.go.ke/hiv-situation-in-kenya/> (accessed 6 October 2017).

Levine, R., Lloyd, C.B., Greene, M., and Grown, C. (2008) *Girls Count: A Global Investment and Action Agenda*, Center for Global Development, Washington DC. Available from: <https://www.cgdev.org/publication/girls-count-global-investment-action-agenda> (accessed 6 October 2017).

Lloyd, C.B. and Young, J. (2009) *New Lessons: The Power of Educating Adolescent Girls. A Girls Count Report on Adolescent Girls*. Population Council, New York. Available from: <http://www.popcouncil.org/uploads/pdfs/2009PGY_NewLessons.pdf> (accessed 6 October 2017).

Mathare Social Justice Centre (2017) *Who Is Next? A Participatory Action Research Report against the Normalization of Extrajudicial Executions in Mathare*, Mathare Social Justice Centre, Nairobi. Available from: <https://drive.google.com/file/d/0B2NZry_SioNhWEFyQWNuVVBJV2M/view?usp=sharing&usp=embed_facebook> (accessed 6 October 2017).

Mwai, B.K., Kimengi, I.N., and Kipsoi, E.J. (2014) 'Perceptions of teachers on the ban of corporal punishment in pre-primary institutions in Kenya', *World Journal of Education* 4 (6): 90 <https://doi.org/10.5430/wje.v4n6p90>.

Oye, M., Pritchett, L., and Sandefur, J. (2016) 'Girls' schooling is good, girls' schooling with learning is better', Background Paper, The Education Commission, New York.

Sandefur, J. (2017) 'The world needs more bad schools', Center for Global Development, 25 April. Available from: <https://www.cgdev.org/blog/world-needs-more-bad-schools> (accessed 6 October 2017).

Temin, M. and Levine, R. (2009) *Start with a Girl: A New Agenda for Global Health*, Center for Global Development, Washington DC. Available from: <https://

www.cgdev.org/sites/default/files/1422899_file_Start_with_a_Girl_FINAL_0. pdf> (accessed 6 October 2017).

UNAIDS (2016) 'Kenya 2016 HIV and AIDS estimates'. Available from: <http:// www.unaids.org/en/regionscountries/countries/keny>a (accessed 6 October 2017).

UNICEF (n.d.) 'Definitions'. Available from: <https://www.unicef.org/infoby-country/stats_popup5.html> (accessed 19 January 2018).

Uwezo (2016) *Are Our Children Learning? Uwezo Kenya Sixth Learning Assessment Report*, Twaweza East Africa, Nairobi. Available from: <http://www.uwezo. net/wp-content/uploads/2016/12/UwezoKenya2015ALAReport-FINAL-EN-web.pdf> (accessed 16 December 2019).

WHO (2019) 'Adolescent mental health', World Health Organization (WHO), 23 October. Available from: <https://www.who.int/news-room/fact-sheets/ detail/adolescent-mental-health> (accessed 31 December 2019).

WHO (n.d.) '10 facts about early child development as a social determinant of health', World Health Organization (WHO). Available from: <http://www. who.int/maternal_child_adolescent/topics/child/development/10facts/ en/> (accessed 6 October 2017).

World Bank (2012a) 'Gross enrollment ratio, primary, both sexes (%)'. Data available from: <https://data.worldbank.org/indicator/SE.PRM.ENRR> (accessed 6 October 2017).

World Bank (2012b) 'Gross enrollment ratio, secondary, both sexes (%)'. Data available from: <https://data.worldbank.org/indicator/SE.SEC.ENRR> (accessed 6 October 2017).

World Bank (2018) 'Population ages 0–14 (% of total)'. Data available from: <https://data.worldbank.org/indicator/SP.POP.0014.TO.ZS> (accessed 6 October 2017).

CHAPTER 5

Being a woman[1]: How social norms affect women's lives and livelihoods

Abstract

Low-income women's lives and livelihoods are shaped profoundly by their social roles, including expectations for raising children, caring for the sick, and managing day-to-day household expenditures. Their own agency and behaviours are tightly circumscribed by thick webs of social enforcement that make it particularly difficult for women to drive their own financial and economic lives. Getting more financial resources into the hands of women and helping couples learn to cooperate on finances appear to be important mechanisms to improve welfare outcomes for women, men, and families.

Keywords: gender, women, intra-household bargaining, marriage, gender roles

Ruth lived in Western Kenya, where she – somewhat exceptionally – headed her household of seven, which included herself, her husband Jackton, and five of their six children. The sixth, a son, married and moved out on his own. Ruth served as both the main income earner and chief household strategist. She had two children in secondary school and also needed to be prepared to cover unexpected shocks, such as when her son fell from a tree and broke his jaw or the time her brewing operation was raided by the police.

That day, the police caught her in the house with a batch of alcohol brewing. There was no way to deny the charges or run away. But Ruth knew that if the police hauled her off, Jackton would be unable to negotiate with the police or raise the money needed for her release. So as the police demanded answers and confiscated her equipment, she pointed the finger at her confused husband. He had always been the Robin to her Batman. Once her husband had been taken away to the police post, Ruth got on the phone, hysterical, dramatically telling her siblings that she had been taken to jail, that it was awful inside, and that they should send money quickly to bail her out.

They did as she asked. Ruth was the eldest daughter of seven siblings; their mother died when the siblings were young, and Ruth dropped out of school to help raise them. Having finished school, her younger siblings were doing relatively well economically and seemed to understand that they owed Ruth for her sacrifice. They helped to pay school fees for Ruth's children and sent money when things went wrong. 'If they are late paying for school fees,' she said, 'I tell them I will send my children to their houses in Nairobi to be maids.'

http://dx.doi.org/10.3362/9781788531207.005

So when she called for help after the arrest, they also sent money, about KES 5,000 ($59) in total. However, Ruth negotiated with the police until they agreed to release her husband for a bribe of just KES 2,000 ($24).

Ruth both bucked and leveraged gender norms. She was the main income earner for the household and made most financial decisions for the family, usually with the support – but not the close involvement – of her husband. She also knew how to deploy her gendered identity to solve problems and how to exercise agency in the limited spheres of influence she has been afforded by society.

The Diaries study showed us many ways in which gender played a powerful role in allocating both responsibilities and resources, whether related to inheritance or to claims to remittances and other social benefits. Gender shaped how individuals earned a living, managed resources, and negotiated with their spouses. It shaped what they did to earn money and how much they got from that work. It coloured life aspirations, Susan Johnson argued, and even individuals' very 'capacities to aspire' (Johnson, 2015).

Ruth's story – her sharp thinking, her tenacity, her savvy in negotiating with police and tapping the resources and sympathy of her siblings – often elicited laughter when we recounted it at public events. It brought some levity to what was typically a more sombre discussion of the role of women in Kenya's low-income households. Being a Kenyan woman was difficult, which is not to say that being a man was easy. As we argue throughout this book, poverty itself caused enormous strain for everyone. Being a man meant managing some difficult – often impossible – financial responsibilities and expectations. Men, like women, were trying to build lives that made them feel successful, happy, and proud. As in relationships everywhere, men were also sometimes betrayed by and let down by women they loved. Many men in our study went to extraordinary lengths to earn, save, and invest in their family's future prosperity.

But, as this chapter will show, they did that with significantly more resources and freedom than were available to women. Men's incomes were higher and more secure over their lifetimes. Men's obligations were loose; women's were tight. Women struggled to manage their obligations in a context of constrained social and economic freedoms.

The women in our study were not powerless victims. Our unique view into household cash flows helped us see women's remarkable resilience and capability to leverage resources – such as social networks, community groups, and personal financial devices – to pursue their own ambitions within society's gender constraints.

Gender inequality and development

Gender inequality is a challenge worldwide, and Kenya is no different, although some of the ways in which those inequalities manifest themselves are unique. While the education gap between boys and girls at the primary school level has nearly closed, important differences remain at secondary and tertiary levels. Agency within the household – although it has been improving quickly in recent surveys – remains limited. Only 56 per cent of women in 2014 participated in key decisions about their own healthcare, major purchases, and visiting family (KNBS et al., 2014). The same study found that 42 per cent of women believed that husbands were justified in beating their wives.[2] Thirty-eight per cent of women who had ever been married experienced domestic violence, and it appeared that neither being part of urban society nor being wealthy provided much protection: 35 per cent of urban women had been victims as well as 29 per cent of women in the highest wealth quintile (KNBS et al., 2014).

Our research participants placed a very high value on motherhood, but Kenya has made very slow progress on women's reproductive health. Five women in Kenya die for every 1,000 live births, only a modest improvement over the 1990 estimate of about 6.8 deaths per 1,000 live births (World Bank, 2017). A nurses' strike in the first half of 2017 doubled the rate of reported maternal mortality over the previous year, showing just how vulnerable such gains can be (Murumba, 2017). As of 2014, only half of rural mothers had a skilled attendant or facility-based birth (KNBS et al., 2014). Although it appears to be declining among younger women, 21 per cent of Kenyan women have been circumcised, and this is not isolated among remote, disconnected, and pastoralist communities.

Global leaders have signalled the importance of gender equality by including it as a sustainable development goal.[3] Still, the pathways to achieving equality are not necessarily clear. Some research suggests that equality will flow naturally from growth. Increasing household income reduces pressures to ration resources – food, education, and healthcare spending – by gender (Duflo, 2012). While evidence supports this in certain forms and contexts, we also know that inequality can take new forms as economies grow and shift. For example, women's entry to the workforce has introduced the 'double burden' of women's work inside and outside the home. Women in advanced economies still receive unequal pay for equal work and face workplace discrimination.

Others argue that giving priority to empowering women delivers faster development gains. There is evidence that increasing women's education, labour force participation, and control over resources improves economic, educational, and health outcomes of families. In other words, closing gender gaps can in fact lead to some desirable development outcomes (Bery et al., 2011; Cuberes and Teignier, 2011; World Bank, 2012). Evidence suggests that men and women have different priorities, and that when women have a voice in the use of resources, they make different, often pro-human development choices: girls in homes of grandmothers with pensions in South Africa experience improvements in nutrition; Zambian women who could conceal a contraception choice from their husbands were more likely to seek family planning; women leaders in India were more likely to focus on development initiatives – like improved access to drinking water – that were prioritized by female constituents (Duflo, 2012).

Table 5.1 Changes in key gender indicators over time.

Indicator	1990s		2000s		Most recent	
	Women	Men	Women	Men	Women	Men
School enrolment, primary (% gross)	99%	102%	95%	96%	112%	111%
School enrolment, secondary (% gross)	36%	45%	38%	40%	65%	70%
School enrolment, tertiary (% gross)	1%	2%	2%	4%	3%	5%
Literacy rate, adult (% of adults aged 15 and above)			78%	87%	75%	81%
Women participating in the three decisions (own healthcare, major household purchases, visiting family) (% of women aged 15–49)			26%		56%	
Women who were first married by age 18 (% of women aged 20–24)	31%		25%		23%	
Female genital mutilation prevalence (%)			38%		21%	
Women who believe a husband is justified in beating his wife (any of five reasons) (%)			68%		42%	
Maternal mortality ratio (national estimate, per 100,000 live births)	687				510	
Labour force participation rate (% of population aged 15–64) (modelled ILO estimate)	70%	80%	63%	73%	63%	73%

Source: World Bank, 2017.

Still others argue that gender equality is important in and of itself. It should not matter whether your country or your family is rich or poor. Equality is about human dignity. It should not be forced to wait for economic growth to reach some threshold value. Nor is equality important because it helps your economy grow faster or for your society to more quickly improve other human development goals.

It is hard to argue against this idea. However, divorcing equality from economics glosses over the complicated and very real power that money exercises within interpersonal relationships. This chapter attempts to tell more of that story – mostly through the lens of money – trying to illuminate in a small way what women's and, to a lesser extent, men's lives are really like, showing how ordinary people navigate gender realities and dynamics day in and day out in a context of scarcity.

Gender shapes life experience

A peek at the life histories of any one of our respondents shows that gender plays a key role in shaping many facets of ordinary people's lives. Carol was a great example.

Carol was raised by her grandmother. Her father left her mother before she was born, and her mother decided to remarry.[4] When a Kenyan woman remarries, she is often forced to leave children from outside her new marriage behind. Another respondent explained, 'No man wants the responsibility of caring for another man's children.' Children are viewed as 'belonging' to their father's family, especially if the father has paid dowry,[5] even if the father's family doesn't claim them. So, Carol was left behind with her maternal grandmother, unclaimed by her father and unwelcome by her mother's new husband. She was a child no one claimed, a rejection that affected her deeply.

Carol was never sent to school. When she was nine years old, her grandmother sent her off to become a maid, or 'house help' as Kenyans say. Carol was eager to get married, hoping that marriage would give her love, family, and a home, things she felt she never had. When she met Amos in 2002, at age 18, she thought he seemed like a reasonable enough choice. The early years of marriage were difficult. She lived with her husband's mother and had her first baby upcountry, relying on irregular remittances from Amos to get by. But a year later, her husband invited her to move to Mombasa where he had been living and working. In this urban setting, her growing family all together, Carol began to feel a new sense of freedom and hope. She could earn some of her own money by plaiting hair and picking up casual work. Her husband provided her with some cash every day to manage the day-to-day household needs. Living together, it was easier to talk about plans for the future – although the two did not always agree.

Carol thought that they should buy the house that they were renting. Like most homes in their informal settlement, it was a simple, cramped place constructed with simple wooden poles and mud bricks and roofed with a patchwork of second-hand corrugated iron sheets. The house – like all the others in the community – was informally owned, but Carol asked why they should pay KES 500 ($5.88) per month to a landlord when they could buy the house outright for a total of KES 10,000 ($118). Amos didn't believe that they could come up with that kind of lump sum. For now, he thought, they needed to focus on meeting their daily needs. Plus, the government was threatening to demolish the houses in their row, claiming that they blocked emergency vehicle access to the wider informal settlement.

Between housework and childcare, Carol braided hair, picked up casual jobs, and took adult education classes, trying to keep up with what her own kids were learning in primary school. She also joined three different *chamas*[6] or savings clubs. She hated the groups, feeling that the meetings too often descended into shallow gossip. But she stayed because they worked. They helped her get her meagre earnings out of the house, away from her husband (who had stolen her savings before and often took whatever loose money he could find to buy cigarettes), and away from her own temptation. When it was her turn to collect the group fund, she took the money, KES 1,500–2,000 ($18–$24) at a time, straight to a bank agent nearby who would deposit the funds into her bank account.

When she had saved KES 10,000 ($118), she went back to the owner of the house and tried to make a deal. He was reluctant to sell to her without her husband's permission, so she sent a friend to pose as the buyer. She ended up paying a premium – KES 15,000 ($176) plus some extra bribes to local officials to transfer the paperwork[7] twice (once to her friend and once to her) – but she got her house. For months, she was too scared to tell her husband that she had bought the house. While Amos knew that there was a new landlord, he never suspected it was his wife.

When we saw the couple two years later, Amos had come around and was proud of Carol for buying the house. The investment had more than paid off. They had expanded the house and installed electricity. Carol had earned more of her husband's respect, but something else had changed that again shifted the power dynamics in the family: Amos got a formal job as a cleaner in a government office, earning KES 10,000 ($118) per month. This was a bit less than he used to earn as a casual worker in construction, but it was more stable and less physically demanding. Now that Amos's pay came in as a lump sum and only once per month, suddenly all the money available for future-oriented decisions in the family was Amos's. Responsibility for daily expenses shifted to Carol, making it difficult for her to save. She had to stop her own education, unable to pay the monthly fees of KES 350 ($4.11) from her own earnings. Amos was thrilled about landing a new job; Carol was frustrated. 'At least he's quit smoking,' she told us.

Carol wanted more leverage in the family decisions, but, to get it, she needed more income. Her dream was to open a 'modern' salon and cosmetic shop, but she would need KES 100,000 ($1,176) to do it, almost 10 times more than she had been able to save to buy her house. Meanwhile, Amos had his own plans. He opened a bank account and was saving much of his salary there, hoping they would soon top it up with a loan so he could buy a piece of farmland upcountry, also for KES 100,000.

Carol and Amos were both trying to do the best they could. But, as in many marriages, they wanted different things, faced different constraints, and viewed the world in very different ways. Both through her mother's experience and her own, Carol has seen that a woman finds meaning and belonging in marriage. She has learned that if a woman wants influence in any decisions beyond day-to-day spending, she has to earn her negotiating power by bringing her own money to the table. Culturally, a husband had the right to control his earnings; investing was his responsibility and discussions or negotiations with a spouse about such decisions were not common. And that was complicated: Carol had to find ways to earn that accommodated her skills and education as well as the many hours per day that had to be spent on cooking, cleaning, and childcare. It was well within a husband's rights to make his own decisions about how to invest the money he earned. Culturally defined gender roles meant that it never even occurred to many men to discuss those decisions with their wives. Investing was typically viewed as the man's responsibility, even if men and women rarely saw eye to eye on what 'good' investing meant.

Money, power, identity, and responsibility were tangled up and made especially complicated by scarcity. There were not enough resources to cover all the bases, the things both men and women valued. So, in lots of households, there was more competition than collaboration. Usually, in household financial decisions, someone won and someone lost.

Life journeys

Women's life journeys are a helpful place to start in understanding many of the economic gaps we see between men and women in Kenya. Women's journeys differ from men's. A typical life story for men in our study involved them leaving school and beginning to work. Men's first jobs were often as low-level employees in the informal sector until they learned some skills and saved some money, often with the aim of transitioning to self-employment. We saw, especially in men's younger years, searching behaviour, including moving around geographically and from job to job, although these transitions were nearly all *within* the labour force. Throughout this journey, men progressively built their assets – some financial, but most physical (land, homes, business equipment and stock, motorbikes and vehicles).

Women's paths were different. Most notably, women's lives, in comparison to men's, were marked by a large number of transitions, by many instances of starting over, especially economically. Our adult female respondents typically left school earlier than men (though this is changing today) and found themselves pregnant and de facto married within a year (this is *not* changing today).[8] In that short interim, a woman was likely to have lived with her parents or other relatives and also to have dabbled in some informal work, but motherhood forced a pause in income earning. For many women – and men – this pause was incredibly stressful. Suddenly the husband – typically a young man without a sufficient, stable income source – must independently provide not just for himself but for three people: himself, his wife, and his new child. Scarcity often caused tensions in the relationship and sharp disagreements over the use of resources. Once they were able, new mothers typically started looking for ways to supplement their husbands' income and earn some resources of their own. Constrained by childcare and household duties, low-income women typically looked for casual work near home (such as helping on others' farms, fetching water and firewood, and washing others' clothes) or tried to start small businesses that allowed them to simultaneously mind their children. Growing these activities was constrained by capital, time, and inevitable interruptions: additional childbirths, caring for the sick, and organizing cultural and social events (weddings, funerals, and other ceremonies). Some of these interruptions required months or years of geographic displacement, with wives moving upcountry to care for elderly in-laws or to raise the children in a lower-cost environment.

In two-parent families, women's incomes were supplemental. When finances were particularly tight, or when there was an urgent, pressing need for school fees or medical care, women pulled the capital out of their businesses to plug the gap. The business stopped or declined until there was enough breathing room to invest again. Starting over from scratch multiple times made it difficult to grow a business, build an asset base, or earn a good income. Consequently, a woman's typical life journey thwarted her desire to build agency in household decisions, something that was dependent on her ability to bring her own resources to her marriage.

When we began dissecting women's life stories in Kenya, we were surprised at the similarities across narratives (Figure 5.1). Even seemingly idiosyncratic life events were surprisingly common. For example, being rejected by in-laws after a husband's death was not unusual; rather, it was the norm, a trend reinforced by incentives created by inheritance practices. Typically, inheritance of assets – especially land – passed from a man to his sons. If the husband had not already added his wife's name to the land title (assuming there was one; often there wasn't), a struggle over who actually owned the land often ensued. If the man's sons were still young, in-laws were likely to reclaim the property and any of the deceased person's financial assets, promising to distribute them later among the sons. Things got especially complicated when the deceased had multiple wives or mistresses, especially if they had children together.[9] Wives battled to inherit property and resources from their husbands, even when there was a written will that included them. Without inheritance, starting over was very stressful for widowed women.

One particularly heart-wrenching case was Gloria's. When Gloria was in the hospital delivering her fourth and last child, she was tested for HIV as part of routine hospital procedure. She tested positive. She later learned that her

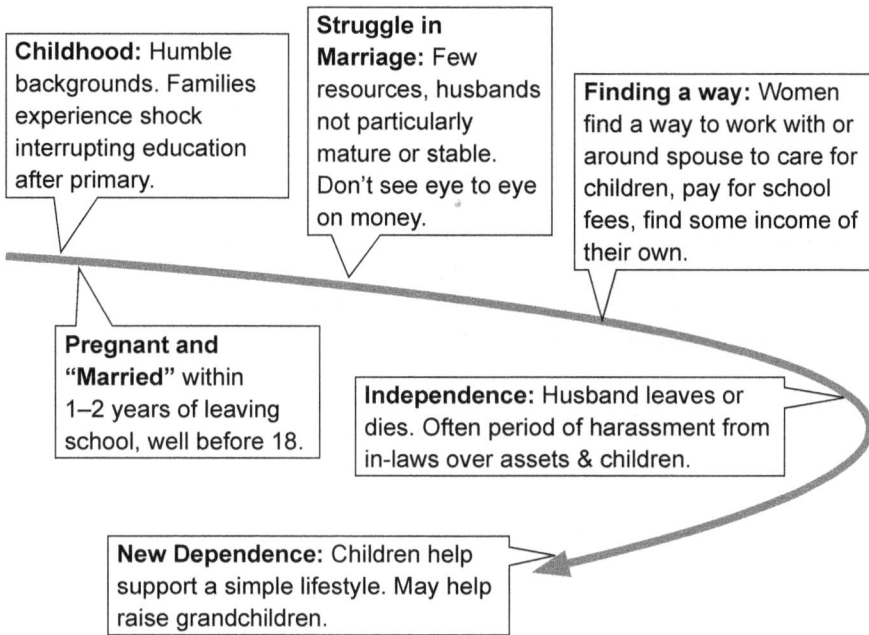

Figure 5.1 Stylized depiction of a typical life journey for a woman in the Diaries.

husband had known that he was positive for some time but hadn't disclosed his status. Not long after the birth, her husband became quite sick. He told her he was battling TB and 'typhoid' (in this case most likely meaning chronic diarrhoea that was probably not diagnosed as actual typhoid). Gloria also became ill and was admitted to the hospital. Her husband's relatives helped care for him but he died. Her husband's relatives accused Gloria of keeping him from taking his antiretroviral (ARV) medications. While she was still in the hospital, they sold all of her belongings and kicked her out of her house and off the family land. They took custody of her three boys, while Gloria's sister took in her daughter.

When she finally recovered, she was able to get back her older two boys first. It took some fighting, but eventually the in-laws agreed to give back the youngest as well. Her sister bought her a small piece of land for KES 40,000 ($471). In this new area, neighbours would not know her HIV status, so she could get some casual work beyond the shadow of stigma. The ARVs worked, she recovered, built a small house on the plot, and told her sister she wanted to take her daughter back. The sister beat around the bush, finally revealing that she had placed the girl in another family. However, it was not clear whether the daughter had been adopted, was working as a maid, or something worse. Finally, the sister agreed to meet Gloria in Nairobi to help her at least visit her daughter.

Gloria saved money and made her way to the city. But her sister didn't show up at the meeting point. She turned off her phone – going *'mteja'*, as Kenyans say. Gloria waited for two days – as long as her money lasted – before she had to return home. Her sister continued to send Gloria a monthly remittance of KES 2,000 ($23.52) but only on the condition that she stop asking about her daughter. When we saw Gloria two years later, she had lost hope that she would ever find her daughter. Once in a while, the sister put a young girl on the phone, but Gloria knew it was not the right one.

Gloria has rebuilt her life, struggling without help from her in-laws and without any inheritance from her late husband. The support she received from her sister came at an unthinkably high cost.

Others, like Rebecca, have been able to put up more of a fight. When her husband committed suicide, her in-laws blamed her for their son's death. They burned all of her belongings and tried to chase her off the plot. But she refused to leave. When the family denied her a plot to grow food, she earned an income from brewing. According to her, she defiantly made the market into her *shamba* (farm). She was determined to keep the 'permanent house' made of bricks and metal roofing sheets that she and her husband had built. She wanted to ensure that her sons would one day build homes of their own on their father's land. After many years, the in-laws seem to have accepted their stubborn daughter-in-law.

Like other women, Rebecca, Carol, and Gloria have found a way to make their lives work, to keep their children fed, to build their lives with – or around – obstacles thrown up by their husbands and in-laws. They developed new strategies to adjust to new realities. Those strategies and that resilience served them well when they entered another phase of life: the period of independence created by their husband's death or his abandonment for another woman, another family, or another life.

Independent livelihoods

Usually, the life phase of 'finding a way' (Figure 5.1) involved earning an independent income. Knowing that having only one income earner can be a serious constraint on family welfare, most men in our study, but not all, were supportive of their wives' income-generating activities. A few husbands forced their wives to leave jobs or step away from businesses to keep them closer to home. Leah remembers waiting a long time to start her business, afraid to negotiate with her husband after he initially rejected the idea.

> **Leah:** I was expecting that even if I was getting married, I could at least be able to provide for myself, not just rely on my husband to provide everything...I wanted to have my business but my husband didn't like the idea. I wanted to have my own money so that I could even be able to send some to my parents.
>
> **Interviewer**: Why didn't you start the business way back then?

Leah: Because I was still a fool at that time! I was afraid. I realized I have stopped fearing him, and I can now tell him any opinion that I see can work. He is a good person. I don't have that fear I used to have in the past so I can just tell him anything.

Leah knew she needed to supplement the family income somehow. Often there was not enough money to cover basic household needs. Many respondents told us that women's earnings were meant to fill gaps in the household budget. And the ways they got money were shaped by a number of gendered economic realities and family responsibilities that resulted in lots of starts and stops in livelihood activities. Women took jobs that offered easy entry and exit. They started businesses with very little capital. They were rarely able to stick with them for long periods before life obligations interrupted and working capital was repurposed.

It was common for women to live at families' rural homes with their children while their husbands worked elsewhere. This was the case for 30 per cent of the rural households in the Diaries. Women tended the farm, earned supplemental income, and cared for children while husbands worked in cities. Viable livelihoods in less densely populated rural areas were substantially different from those in urban areas. Wage labour in rural areas was restricted almost entirely to farm work and very low-paying jobs like fetching water, hauling firewood, and washing others' clothes. Market opportunities for businesses such as tailoring, selling vegetables, or hawking second-hand clothes in rural areas were limited.

One might think that women in rural areas must be farming. That was true. But while women did much of the work on farms, they did not always control the resulting income. In our research sites, much of the cultivation was done for consumption rather than for sale. Yet eating from their own production did not offset food expenditure as much as we expected. Even when we considered farm consumption as income, only 24 per cent of rural households counted on farming as their main source of income.[10] Agriculture was the main income source for 13 per cent of men in our sample and only 6 per cent of women, even though many more of our female respondents were living in rural areas.

Figure 5.2 shows the main sources of income for women and men. Self-reported main livelihoods from the 2016 FinAccess survey appear on the left. On the right is the main source of livelihood as calculated by actual cash flow earnings of individual Diaries respondents. As discussed in Chapter 2, 'Looking for money', we found that respondents viewed farming as an identity even when it played only a minor economic role in the household. Consequently, we hypothesize that FinAccess respondents may overestimate their reliance on agriculture and underestimate their remittance income. Still, some interesting patterns hold across both samples.

In both studies, women were much less likely than men to have regular jobs. Even in cities, where market access was larger, the time women could invest in earning income was limited by household responsibilities. They

Main income sources of men and women in Kenya

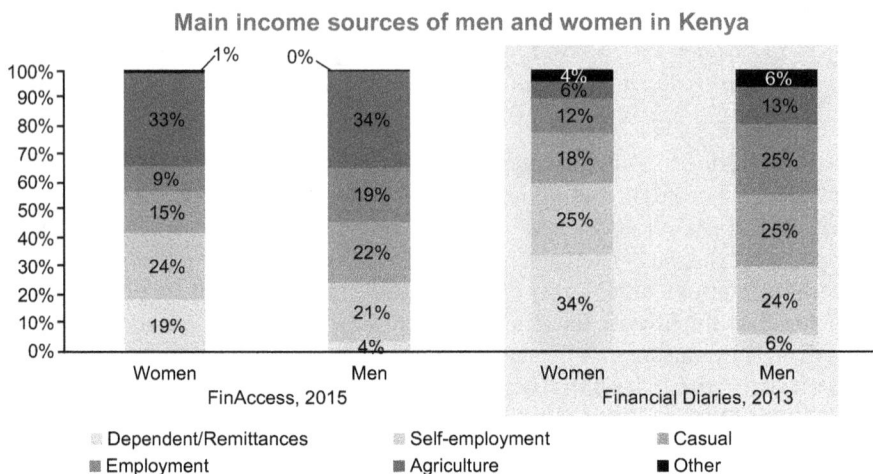

	Women	Men	Women	Men
FinAccess, 2015			Financial Diaries, 2013	

- Dependent/Remittances
- Self-employment
- Casual
- Employment
- Agriculture
- Other

Figure 5.2 Women and men get their money from different sources.
Source: for FinAccess 2015 Central Bank of Kenya et al., 2016.

looked for earning opportunities that could be shaped around those responsibilities. As we see in Figure 5.2 and Chapter 2, that was often through small, informal businesses.

Women were much more likely than men to both receive remittances and count them as the largest share of their income. There were many reasons for this. Many remittances were sent by children to their parents, and children may have felt greater obligation to take care of their mothers in their old age. They may have intended the remittance money for 'upkeep' (e.g. food and other basics), which tended to be the types of expenses that women managed.

Box 5.1 M-Pesa, remittances, and financial inclusion.

The now ubiquitous mobile money service offered by Safaricom in Kenya plays an important role in facilitating remittances. When the mobile money service entered the market (starting in 2007), it increased the total amount and frequency of remittances in Kenya by reducing transaction costs. This had the effect of decreasing household vulnerability and decreasing poverty (Jack and Suri, 2014; Suri and Jack 2016).

The usefulness of M-Pesa – for men and women, for high-income and low-income people – has meant that the gap in formal financial device access and usage in Kenya is quite small (16.8% of men are financially excluded, compared with 18.6% of women). This gap is smaller for mobile money than it is for banking (Central Bank of Kenya et al., 2016). M-Pesa has given women a low-cost way to receive remittances more efficiently. It is often the first private, formal means women have to receive, store, and spend their own money. Because M-Pesa facilitated the movement of money into the household and often from men to their wives, women were often encouraged to open accounts and taught how to use them by their husbands and sons.

Sources: Jack and Suri, 2014; Heyer and King, 2015; Central Bank of Kenya et al., 2016; Suri and Jack, 2016.

Individual monthly income levels by gender in Kenya (US$)

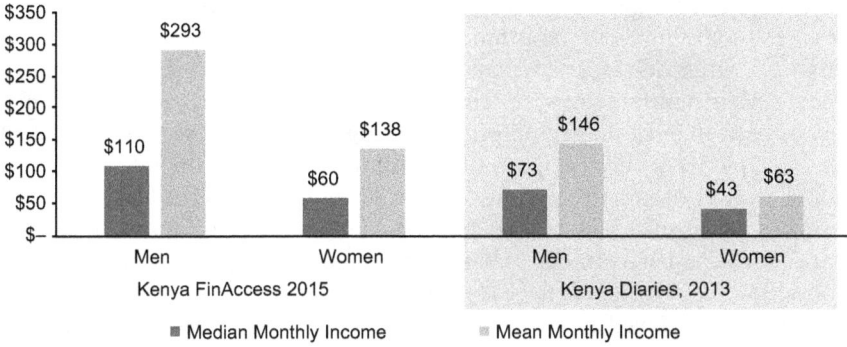

Kenya FinAccess 2015 / Kenya Diaries, 2013

- Median Monthly Income
- Mean Monthly Income

Men (FinAccess): $110, $293
Women (FinAccess): $60, $138
Men (Diaries): $73, $146
Women (Diaries): $43, $63

Differences in Diaries respondent monthly earnings by education & gender ($)

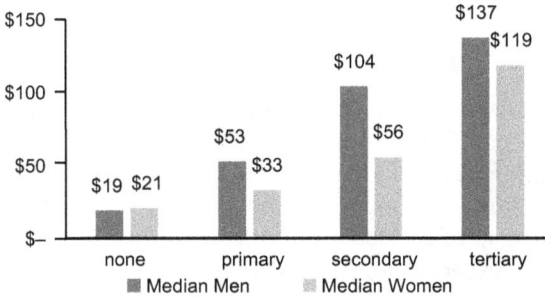

none: $19 / $21
primary: $53 / $33
secondary: $104 / $56
tertiary: $137 / $119

- Median Men
- Median Women

Differences in Diaries respondent monthly earnings by main income & gender ($)

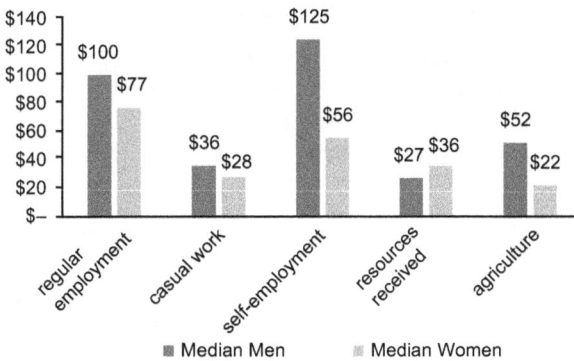

regular employment: $100 / $77
casual work: $36 / $28
self-employment: $125 / $56
resources received: $27 / $36
agriculture: $52 / $22

- Median Men
- Median Women

Figure 5.3 Female respondents earned substantially less than male respondents, and that holds at similar levels of education and by main income source.

They may have felt that women were more likely to spend the money 'wisely' on real needs for the family. And, in many cases, the father may have been deceased or absent. Some remittances were meant to care for those who could not care for themselves, and women were more likely to fall into that caregiver group. Other remittances were sent on an as-needed basis, and here women may have been both more comfortable asking for help and seen as more legitimate recipients of such support, like Ruth, whose story opened this chapter.

Still, overall, men had higher incomes than women. This held for every form of income apart from remittances and for every level of education (Figure 5.3). This is not a challenge unique to Kenya, of course; wage gaps persist across most economies. As in other parts of the world, women's movement in and out of the labour force played a role in that gap, though in Kenya, that was more about the small scale of enterprises than wages. When women took formal jobs, their social obligations often pressured them into low-paying jobs with easy entry and exit. Also, in our study, working-age women were more concentrated in rural areas, where they had access to smaller markets for their businesses.

Expectations and realities in marriage

Women's lower incomes in Kenya are not particularly surprising given women's and men's circumscribed roles in the family. Women's primary responsibilities are to have and care for children, to manage household chores, to take care of day-to-day finances, especially in terms of daily food needs, to care for the sick, and to organize cultural events like weddings, funerals, and other ceremonies. Men are expected to be breadwinners. They are supposed to ensure that the family has enough resources for basic needs, housing, school fees, and investments for the future such as land, home improvements, livestock, motorbikes, and vehicles.

Women and men in our study mostly agreed on these culturally dictated responsibilities. Dennis, a young father in a rural community, explained:

> A woman should welcome me well when I come back from work. When I send her, she should be able to go very fast. She should take water to the bathroom for me to shower. That's supposed to be the woman's job. Men should just look after their family because they are usually the head of the family.

Dennis was a good husband by these standards. Dennis was initially attracted to his wife because she was young, and, as he says, 'She didn't know many things.' She was not very sexually experienced, and he felt that she was likely to be subservient. After she had their first baby, they moved in together. He did not want to pay dowry, yet; he wanted to give her a trial run first. 'When a woman takes care of you well, and you get satisfied, that is when you decide to take the dowry to her home ... you should first stay with the wife and know how she is before paying dowry.' While Dennis would have been free to leave during that period, his wife, with a baby to care for, was stuck.

While men expected complete fidelity from their wives, the reverse was not true. As long as the man continued providing sufficient resources for his wife and children, a woman was expected to accept her husband's infidelity, although it often caused emotional distress. Dennis explained when infidelity was acceptable: 'It depends on your capability and the wealth that you have. Like for me, I cannot.' Men are allowed to cheat, he said, 'Because a woman came from a man's rib. And men are usually very jealous; they don't like seeing their wives having another husband. It is hard for a man to forgive unlike women who forgive easily.' He didn't offer any reflection on why women might be more inclined to forgiveness, but women's stories showed us that 'forgiveness' often grew from the feeling that leaving would be impossible economically.

When Beauty married her husband, Keith, she understood that he had an ex-wife. She felt secure, though, because he paid dowry for her. He seemed to have his economic house in order. Her minimum expectation was, she told us, 'One has land, a house, and can buy assets like cows.' But things didn't go as planned. Telling Beauty that he was working (as a lorry driver), her husband continued his relationship with his first wife, even having additional children with her:

> **Beauty:** He even lied to me that the land adjacent to this one belongs to him. We only have this small space here [where the house is situated]. I am the one who bought iron sheets for this house. It was grass thatched. The timber that he has been saying will be used to construct a house was taken from his father's farm. He has not bought any of it.
>
> **Interviewer:** Why did you stay?
>
> **Beauty:** I tried to leave, but I heard that my children were having problems because he would leave them alone in the house and go for a whole week. I had even applied for a job in Saudi Arabia, but I came back for the sake of the children. I have tried to do a lot of things, but he is not supportive. I have bought cows with my *chama* payout, but I had to take them to my mother's place because he started accusing me of stealing his money to buy them...I have also leased land for cultivation, but he does not help with purchasing the farm inputs. He does not help with the child that I had before getting married, but I have managed to take him through school.

Beauty didn't intend to become a second wife, but after the dowry was paid and she had a child, leaving was harder than staying; she simply had to try to make the best of it.

Collins had only one wife but has had many girlfriends throughout his marriage. This was very painful for his wife in the early years. She caught him cheating a number of times and grew desperate when he stopped sending money home, diverting it to his mistress. His wife came to the town where he was working, pleading with him to help. He yelled at her and told her to go home but didn't give her any money. When he woke up the next morning, he found that she had cleared out the box where he kept his savings along with funds he had been asked to hold for others. His wife was making her way home when he caught up with her and pleaded for her to return the funds. She refused and threatened to throw their new-born baby into the river if he wasn't going to be sending money to help her raise the child. He watched her walk away along the railroad tracks and disappear into the woods towards the river. When she emerged from the woods without the child, he panicked, rushing to the river only to find the baby lying safely in the grass. For him this was a wake-up call to take his responsibilities at home more seriously, even if he would never become sexually faithful.

'A good husband should provide for the family every day, should always leave money behind every day when he leaves the house for the expenses and food for the family,' Collins conceded. 'But wives,' he told us, 'shouldn't expect fidelity. [Men will] take any decision they want.' And, no matter what, a wife should just accept it. 'A good wife should respect her husband.'

When Sally found out she had gonorrhoea, she was both angry and sad. How could her husband do this to her? He had told her he was going to work, travelling as a lorry driver, and left her a bit of money for food during his absence. She used all of it to seek treatment at the district hospital. When her husband came home, the two had a huge fight. Sally yelled at him for cheating and infecting her with a sexually transmitted infection. She accused him of lying about the job and leaving to stay with another woman in town. In response, her husband kicked her out of the house. 'She is so hard-headed,' he said. He wanted to teach her a lesson. 'Let her pay rent and food all on her own. She needs to appreciate all I do in the house.' A few months later, the two were back together.

Even if women expected infidelity, it took an emotional toll. Ella's struggling marriage made her sad and ashamed:

> I have not met my expectations [in marriage]. I expected an understanding partner and an enjoyable time with my family, but mine did not go that way ... I served as a women's leader in church, and I got to know that women suffered lots of challenges at home. But I felt I had even more challenges ... I felt it was not good that I be leading people and yet I have my own serious challenges.

She was disappointed that her husband didn't provide for the family, but, in her case, she says, she was looking for love, since her father was not around growing up and her mother remarried, making Ella feel quite alone. The infidelity stung:

> The Bible says forgive and forget. I don't know whether it's possible to forgive and forget. As for me, since 2005 when I was wedded in a church officially, I tell you there is nothing I have forgotten when he was unfaithful. I can count all the women he has been with.

Infidelity has real economic consequences. For one, family resources can be unilaterally diverted to mistresses and new children, without the wife's consent. But just as importantly, our younger respondents emphasized, the broken trust makes it harder for husbands and wives to collaborate on 'projects' for developing the family. Millicent explained that she thought the main problem facing couples today was trust.

> If we don't trust each other, we won't do any development together. The woman will decide to do her own projects because of lack of trust. She might leave one day and does not want to leave behind what she has worked hard for. The same applies to a man who does not trust his wife.

A few men agreed. Patrick told us that he feared infidelity would change a man's relationship with his children, something that really mattered to him:

> Children learn from observation. They are likely to do what they have seen their parents do. That is why it is good to be a role model. I hope my children will learn from my marriage and treat their spouses with respect ...
>
> There are different stages in a marriage: at first there is a lot of love, then you start taking care of the children. When they have grown up, they leave, and you remain the two of you. That is when marriage gets better ...
>
> The children are more attached to their mother and the way a man treats his wife will determine the relationship a man will have with his children. When the children are all grown-up, your wife can decide to go and stay with one of them and help with the grandchild while the man is left behind. A man should humble himself before his wife so that he can also benefit in later years.

Others seemed to concede that infidelity was unkind but normal. Wives and children would accept it and forgive, because they must. First and foremost, our respondents told us, a man's job in the family is to provide. A woman's job, they said, is to 'persevere'. Even when the man is not contributing enough. Even when he is not faithful. Even when he is abusive. We asked Leah if she had ever heard of a woman leaving her husband because she is being beaten: 'No,' she said, 'in case they leave, there has to be another issue.'

Women rarely left, we were told by men and women alike. They did not have the independent resources to care for the family alone. If they returned to their families, their brothers and parents would be angry, since they were likely to arrive with more mouths to feed and might make claims on family resources. One respondent, for example, left her husband and returned home. Her father decided to do something unusual and put her in his will to inherit a piece of land alongside her brothers'. Ever since then, her brothers have conspired to find ways to remove her. In their eyes, that land was their birthright.

A husband could also insist that his wife leave the children behind. Collins reminded us: '[Many women] don't have enough money to go and start life afresh. In the past, it was a rule that when a woman leaves the marriage, her children pull her back.' Women's parents and brothers could be asked to return the dowry if a wife left her husband. And women who left their husbands were socially ostracized.

A good woman perseveres, our respondents told us. Esther explained:

> What makes me feel proud is that I persevered in my marriage. I am proud of my achievement, because when I got married my husband was not working. I found him when he did not have any bedding or blankets. When I gave birth to my children, I was taking banana leaves and squeezed water out of them to lay the leaves down on the floor. That is where we used to sleep. So I feel proud of myself because of the patience and the perseverance that I had, because many people then that got married at the same time did not tolerate that kind of lifestyle. It was too much for them, so they left their marriages, but for me I stuck by it. So that makes me feel very proud. When I got married I gave birth very fast so it's because of my children that made me persevere because I could look at my children and ask myself should my children suffer just because of what I am going through? So I had to hold on to my marriage to see if things would improve.

Many respondents drew on cultural and religious teachings to reinforce this expectation of profound female perseverance. Ella, while struggling in her marriage, explained to us:

> I would think of going away, but you see, God created a woman to stay in her family ... I realized that God created a woman for a man. How else would my mother get married after 20 years [following Ella's birth]? As much as I would like to run away, I would end up getting married to another man. So I just pray that [my husband] will change.

Talking of a friend, she continued:

> She gave her husband everything – children and care – and then the man was not faithful. She is so faithful, but the husband is not. She does not understand why. Like, she called me, and she talked negatively about her husband. Myself, I never hurl abuses at my husband, I don't talk to him rudely ... I just wanted to be with him. I personally respect my husband as the Bible says – respect your husband like God, for the man is closer to God. He was created first. That's how it is with me.

Later, she expressed some resentment over the way in which the cultural cards were stacked against women:

> You know, men believe in themselves so much. They even read the Bible and tell you, you know, Solomon had many wives, so it's not bad. In Kikuyu, we even have a proverb that there is never only one hen for any cock.

Bernadine persevered, too, for 10 years. The first six years of their marriage were good, she recalled, but things changed when her husband lost his job and the two moved to Nairobi. He started drinking and beating her and stopped paying rent. She was eager to find a job, and his employer offered her one. Her husband was humiliated by the prospect of his wife working in the same company. He beat her and forbade her to work outside the home. At one point, her husband hadn't paid rent for an entire year. 'The landlord knew the situation I was in. I was struggling to get food for my children and he never asked me for rent. He would only ask about my husband's whereabouts.'

The beating wasn't the main thing pushing her out of the door. But she felt like she was being beaten for no reason, and that, combined with his failure to provide – after 10 years – drove her to breaking point. She called her brothers, and they approved of her decision. She rented a small room for herself and her three kids and got casual work helping with the horses at wealthy foreigners' farms. A month after leaving her husband, she realized she was pregnant. 'I was very devastated. I was even thinking of aborting the pregnancy ... but my brother told me that I should just keep the pregnancy and that he would help me with the baby.' Luckily, three months after giving birth, she found a job as a housekeeper and then moved to a better-paying, foreign family for two years. When that family decided to return to their home country, they gave Bernadine a sizeable sum that allowed her to go upcountry, buy a plot of land, and once again start over. 'I was not happy to leave my husband. I still have his contacts, and I sometimes call him since I have his children. Sometimes he picks my call and sometimes he doesn't.' Sometimes she thinks about getting back together with him – 'But, only if he has changed.'

While beatings were not necessarily a reason for leaving a marriage, several women did confide in us their fears of husbands sexually abusing their daughters, especially daughters from previous relationships who may have been allowed to come along into the new marital home. Here, every woman seemed to draw a line. Ella explained her fears of remarrying with daughters from another man:

> I knew whoever would marry me would hate my children. They were girls. He would harass them, and I did not like that ... What makes every woman stay and persevere is their children ... Like now I have six children. Where will I take them? I will not be peaceful if I go away. I love them. So that is why we have to persevere. Even if he tells me to go, I will not leave.

Gendered family roles and their enforcement

The very clear and circumscribed social roles and responsibilities ascribed to men and women were enforced in starkly different ways. Men's behaviour was meant to be self-governing, enforced only by their shame or pride.

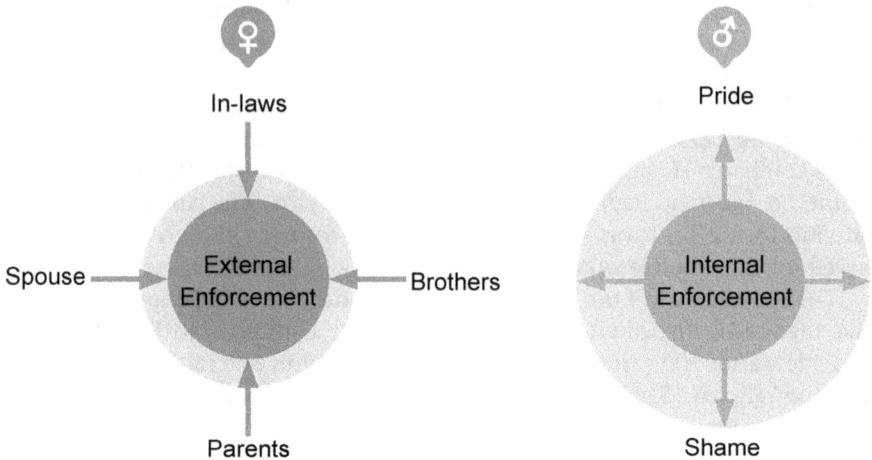

Figure 5.4 Women and men face very different levels and types of enforcement of their social roles.
Source: Zollmann and Sanford, 2016.

Occasionally, extended family members stepped in as negotiators when men were not adequately providing for their families or were otherwise breaking norms about their behaviour. Yet often the behaviour was simply ignored. It was not uncommon for a woman to be living with her children next to her in-laws on shared land, where parents saw first-hand that their sons were not providing adequate support, but the parents did not intervene.

Women, on the other hand, were policed in quite a different way. Many participants felt that beating women was justified when they disobeyed, made independent decisions without informing their husbands, or qualified somehow as 'bad' wives. Our study included several cases in which husbands punished their wives' disobedience by kicking them out of the house or threatening to take another wife.

Women were also 'disciplined' by brothers and parents, especially when they left their marriages. In one case, a respondent bragged about beating his sister because she was not being a good mother. (She had disappeared with a new boyfriend in the city, leaving a sick child behind with his grandmother.)

If family responsibilities were enforced equally in communities, men's disproportionate decision-making power might not induce such significant risk for the lives of women and children. A key area where this plays out is in family size. The number of children in a low-income household has a profound effect on the resources available for each one. Large families must spend more on food, a major preoccupation for women, and not all children get to go to secondary school. Ordinary people recognize this, which is why fertility rates in Kenya are declining.

Of course, negotiations over family size are gendered. Our female respondents were often pressured to have more children than they wanted or to have them closer together than they would choose. In many countries, when researchers ask men and women separately about their fertility preferences, there is often[11] disagreement between spouses, and women report wanting smaller families than men (Mason and Smith, 2000; Wambui et al., 2009; Tilahun et al., 2014; McCarthy, 2015). In a small study of urban couples in Kenya, 31 per cent disagreed about whether they wanted another child, with husbands more likely than wives to want additional children.[12] Men and women may also disagree on when to have children. Although it was not necessarily the case that husbands applied direct pressure, we saw that if a Kenyan couple did not yet have a son, birth intervals shortened. Shorter birth intervals are associated with increased risk of infant and child mortality (Fotso et al., 2013).

Although spouses in our study typically did talk about the number of children they wanted and how to space them, our respondents – men and women alike – told us that men often changed their minds and wanted more children later. It was women, however, who bore the welfare consequences when men were unable (or unwilling) to increase household contributions to accommodate the additional children or who later abandoned the family physically and/or emotionally.

One of the more extreme examples in our study was Diana, from a rural area near the coast.[13] During the Diaries, she took care of her two youngest children, aged 11 and 14, as well as four small grandchildren left behind when an adult son went to work in Mombasa and a daughter remarried and was unable to take her children with her. Diana's husband, Kenneth, sometimes picked up casual work or earned some money trading cows. None of this income was allocated to Diana or the family. Instead, Diana would leave well before dawn every morning to buy fish from the boats as they came in and hawk them in the area surrounding Kilifi town, returning late in the evening to cook and take care of household duties, all on her own. Meanwhile, Kenneth had become notorious for sleeping around. During the study, he impregnated a standard seven pupil (about 12–13 years old). Later in the study, Diana found out about two mistresses he was keeping as well. Neighbours had found him bringing the mistresses sacks of *unga* (maize meal) from their home, even when his own children were hungry and had been sent home for unpaid school fees. Diana was frequently frustrated but felt trapped. Where would she go? How could she feed her children and grandchildren while also paying rent somewhere? Where would her sons settle if they left and her husband gave the land to the new children of his mistresses? By the end of the study, she finally sought help from the local government's Child Rights Office, asking for them to demand some support from Kenneth. This action pushed him to help for a time, but two years later that help remained limited. He had stopped selling cows because his trading partner had returned to Somalia. Diana's business also collapsed. She believed that Kenneth's family had bewitched her in retribution for her reporting Kenneth to the Child Rights Office.

Another respondent, Cassandra, had six children with her husband, Victor, who lived and worked in Nairobi. His parents did not approve of her, so they had not given her land to cultivate to feed the kids. Victor sent home just KES 600 ($7) per month from his job as a watchman. Secretly, he married another woman and had a child with her. Cassandra met this new wife by accident when she was visiting the in-laws, who lived only a few hundred metres from Cassandra's home. Cassandra's husband had told the new wife that he had only two children and that his previous wife had run away. Yet, there she was. Where do you go with six children? We visited Cassandra just a week or so after her last birth. She had gone into labour at night in the middle of a rainstorm. She had no money for transport to a health facility and no way to get out along the muddy path anyway. She sent one of her oldest children to call a neighbour to come and help her and gave birth on the floor of their two-room mud house. Her husband sent nothing extra to help with the costs of delivery or to get the baby to the hospital for a check-up afterwards. She explained, 'He told me, "I didn't tell you to give birth."'

Sometimes negotiations are subtler, though still unequal. Milly, one of our respondents from Eldoret, had one child when we met her. Her uncle had brought her to Eldoret to work in his bank agency shop while he pulled some money together to send her to college. When she got pregnant, she had to run away for a week until her uncle could cool down. He was so disappointed in her and worried for her future. But for her, being a mother was also a good option, and she loved her new husband, Calvin. 'I thought we would be happy forever,' she told us. After the Diaries, her husband was spending a lot of time outside the house. Calvin would call and tell her that the lorry he drove ferrying goods between Eldoret and Nairobi had again broken down. She believed him, although his co-workers hinted that there was another woman. Then one day she called and a woman answered his phone. Milly was so upset that she went to Calvin's aunt and asked her to intervene. Under the guise of a family ceremony, the aunts and uncles lured the couple upcountry and confronted her husband. He agreed to stop seeing the mistress but had a condition: he wanted another child immediately.

He had been talking to some friends and they told him how to inspect a woman's arm to see if she had a birth control implant. He came home, searched Milly's arm and found the small device. All night, he tried to claw it out from under her skin, insisting that they have a child right away. The next day, she had it removed. For a time, she secretly took birth control pills, but she was not completely consistent and was soon pregnant again.

'Were you ready?' I asked.

'No. I wanted to wait until [my other child] was in class one. But when I realized I am pregnant, I had to accept. Now I am happy.'

Men had an awful lot of authority over decisions that had an outsized impact on women's health and well-being. A similar problem affected the financing of maternal healthcare. While culturally men were responsible for the costs of labour and delivery, they did not always budget appropriately or express a willingness to pay for the care their wives felt was essential. At the lowest end of the income spectrum, free labour and delivery services at government facilities (a policy that came on stream late in the Diaries) were easing part of this burden, ensuring that women who could get to facilities would receive free care.[14] However, there was no guarantee that women could manage to travel to a facility (as was the case with Cassandra), that they would find medical staff available on arrival, or that the costs of complications would be covered (see the case of Sandra in Chapter 6, 'Staying alive').

We visited Ellen once just before she was scheduled to deliver her third son. He was due just days after Kenya's 2013 national elections, and she feared election-related violence. She had gone into labour during the post-election violence in late 2007/early 2008. The couple had to close their businesses amid the chaos, and her husband quickly ran through his cash reserves just making ends meet. When she went into labour, there was no money left. She had to give birth in a notoriously bad government facility, where she says women were lying on the floor, no one was helping, and she thought she would die. Desperate to avoid such a situation again, she secretly saved up for her next birth, including enough money to take a taxi to the hospital (even at increased rates, assuming violence broke out again) and for delivery at a 'decent' facility. Although culture assigned this responsibility to her husband, if he didn't come up with the money, she was determined not to be stuck again.

The problem of financing women's health was made particularly difficult by women's relative isolation. When women married, they moved in with either their husbands or their in-laws, often very far away from their own relatives. We saw how difficult this was for Zainabu after she experienced a late-term miscarriage. Her husband didn't live with her regularly. She wasn't sure where he went and suspected he had another family. 'I don't mind as long as he provides,' she told us. But when she needed help, she was on her own in a rural coastal village. Eventually, it was her own relatives who came to the hospital to care for her, rather than her husband or his family. She was hospitalized for two months and then stayed with her parents for another two months to recover before she returned to her marital home.

The last doctor she saw warned her that her uterus was too weak to carry another baby to term. If she wanted to try again, they would do a C-section at eight months. The last time we saw her, she had only one child, and she felt like the other people in her community were now gossiping about her infertility. She hoped her husband would keep her even if they did not have another child.

That was not necessarily a safe expectation. If a woman couldn't have children, our participants felt that it was acceptable for her husband to either leave her or simply take a second wife. Leah explained:

> **Leah:** If the [fertility] problem is with the wife and the husband still loves her he will marry another wife for them to get children.
> **Interviewer:** What if the problem is with the husband?
> **Leah:** They will just stay.

Even progressive Patrick told us:

> [Children] are the most important thing in marriage. When you get old
> you need someone to take care of you. One of my uncles died without
> having any children and no one cried at his funeral.

The high stakes placed on bearing children help us understand some of
the extraordinary lengths women suffering from infertility would go to
to have a child, even when their husbands were not particularly invested.
Pamela was the second wife of a man from Western Kenya. It took her
about 11 years to get pregnant. She was so excited, but she lost the baby.
The doctors recommended surgery (likely a dilation and curettage or
'D&C', although Pamela wasn't exactly sure). The procedure at that time
(in 2010) was set to cost KES 28,000 ($329). She did not have the money,
and her husband did not offer it either. She went without, though it seems
to have triggered some lasting health problems. Pamela still longed for a
child of her own.

When we interviewed her for the update, she had moved to Kisumu where
women from her husband's church claimed that a local healer cured them
of infertility. To make the move, she left her business and her stepchildren
behind. Their mother went back to stay with them. Pamela had not found
a new source of income for herself in the city. She used all of her savings for
an X-ray that the healer told her she needed to start her treatments. When
we last spoke, she had been receiving treatments for a year with no success.
She told us, 'Since it has been a long illness, it will require a long treatment.'
She had no idea what this treatment would cost. She told us she would just
have to figure it out when the time came. At least, the cost of healers could be
negotiated, unlike at the hospital.

The good news for women – and for men – is that norms can change. We
saw a few glimpses of what that change might look like coming from a perhaps unlikely source: churches.[15] Both women and men explained their marital roles with church teaching and through Bible verses, as did Dennis when
he explained that men's marital infidelity was acceptable because biblical
Adam provided a rib for the creation of Eve. But a handful of couples – mostly
younger and mostly urban – had found a more reflective form of spirituality,
when the church – and especially men's participation in the church – created
some openings to think about and discuss with their partners how to build
relationships that worked for the good of the entire family.

Millicent and her husband actually met in church. The two were in a youth
group together. They dated for two years before they agreed to get married:

> Being in church helped a lot. When we attended the youth seminars,
> they would guide us per our age groups. For those of us who were about
> to get married we were told what to expect. Like for my case, I am a first
> born and he is the last born. I'm used to being in charge, and he proba-
> bly used to be treated as the young one in the family. So there were a lot

of differences, but we were told how to handle such issues and to deal with each other's weaknesses.

At one point, her husband went a long time without a job. Millicent was paying for all of the family expenses, and after a few years she grew frustrated. She felt he wasn't trying hard enough to help financially. When she vented, her husband turned to the church to mediate:

> I told him to pull up his socks and be the man of the house or I move out and live on my own ... He talked to the church pastors and some elders in the church to come and talk to me. I did not like this as I felt it was a private matter, especially since all the blame should have been on him. When they came, I never told them anything because it would have been embarrassing for my husband.

Patrick also credits the church for his own successful marriage:

> The Bible says that marriage should be respected by everybody. That includes the men. On my side, salvation really helps. The devil does not want to see people living happily and that is why a lot of people are tempted to go outside their marriage. I have boundaries that I cannot go beyond. The people who are not saved do not have boundaries.

Salvation could be quite a powerful force, offering, to men especially, quite literal 'come-to-Jesus' moments, most of which led them to stop drinking, leave gangs, or end extramarital affairs – most of which ended up being pretty good for the women in their lives.

Building a future together

Women's lower average incomes and bargaining power within the household made it difficult for them to be full partners in making future-oriented decisions for the family. When men and women described their visions of a good life, we heard many things in common. Both wanted land, through allocation from the husband's family and purchase of additional farm ('*shamba*') and housing ('plot') land. Land was an asset with many purposes including cultivation, construction of rental housing, accumulation of wealth, and inheritance for children. Both wanted their children to be educated as far as and as well as possible.[16] Both men and women wanted to run their own successful businesses, to gain secure cash flow well into old age with the freedom and independence of self-employment. And both shared a dream for a permanent house, with brick walls and a metal roof, even if it took several iterations of semi-permanence to get there. For those living in the city, a home upcountry was important both to have stable housing in their old age and as a symbol, especially for men, of their adulthood and success.

But with very low incomes, few families could invest in all of these things at once. As a result, most deployed some common phasing strategies. First, they told us, as a couple you should have children, cementing your relationship. Then, you should begin investing. Make as many investments as you can before children enter secondary school and school fees crowd out other projects.

Beyond that rough schedule, men and women differed on how they prioritized the various parts of their shared visions. Typically, men in our study prioritized business and land investments and women housing and education. Women waited to see what their husbands made plans to do, tried to nudge them towards their own priorities, and when that didn't work, tried to supplement men's investing with their own in the areas that mattered most to them.

We often saw women saving in secret, borrowing, and planning, hoping to gain some leverage or opportunity to undertake their priority projects. How Carol saved to buy her house is a great example. Ellen, who was secretly saving for a dignified childbirth experience, is another. Beyond healthcare, she and her husband disagreed on family investments. Her husband wanted to buy a car. She was subtly and persistently nudging him instead towards building a house first with their shared savings.

With lower incomes, women often set their sights on investing in small things: a new piece of furniture for the house, a goat or cow (sometimes kept secretly at a relative's house where their husband wouldn't know about it), a few new roofing sheets. Savings groups of various forms have proved particularly helpful in building up sums for these types of purchases, as well as making women, like Leah, feel encouraged and supported to take on more active economic lives.

Upfront, transparent cooperation was the exception rather than the rule in our sample. For example, Mark and Fiona (Zollmann and Sanford, 2016), though married for many years, were managing their own savings separately and in secret. When the two married, Mark was unprepared for the pressures of caring for a wife and child. His brother gifted him a business that he ran into the ground. Often without enough food in the house, Fiona made her way over to a Somali neighbourhood in Nairobi where she picked up casual work washing clothes. Her family found this shameful; they were deeply disappointed that she had chosen to marry Mark, who didn't seem serious about life. Fiona stood by him, and Mark began to change after the couple had their third child. He got work as a newspaper vendor, then built up connections to become a distributor. He began saving one shilling from every paper sold through an automated deduction scheme at the paper, and he started making plans.

Meanwhile, Fiona had been entrusting everything she could save to a money guard,[17] Mark's brother. Once Mark announced that he had saved enough to start building a home upcountry, Fiona joyfully offered up her own savings to help move the construction along. This was a major milestone, proving to her own family that they had 'made it' as a couple and solidifying Mark's status as a 'man' in his community. Two years later, they also pooled funds to at last pay Fiona's parents for her dowry. Mark said he finally felt like Fiona's parents accepted him, and Fiona was thrilled to have won her family's respect and approval. While both the dowry and the home were Mark's responsibilities, Fiona sought secretly to fill the financial gaps to accomplish goals that were deeply important to her but out of reach on her own.

Although Mark and Fiona ended up cooperating around these investment priorities, they saved separately and secretly. Mark didn't want to inflate his wife's expectations. Fiona wanted Mark to first fulfil his responsibilities and see where he was headed before committing her own savings, which, after all, might be needed to fill other gaps – like buying food if business was down or paying school fees. For both, privacy was imperative. A joint financing mechanism would not have served either very well.

There were a few households in our study where the spouses had more open communication about their projects and plans for the future. The men in these families tended to have a deep respect for their wives, including their capacities to manage money, work, and make financial decisions. These households were somewhat idiosyncratic. They weren't necessarily younger or more urban than others. They weren't necessarily higher earning. And, statistically at least in our small sample, we did not find that levels of intra-household cooperation correlated with increases in per capita income two years after the initial study. What they achieved together was something more intangible in the health of their relationships as partners.

Conclusions

Equality in terms of human value and self-determination should not be based on how much individuals earn. The indicators around the sustainable development goals for gender equality recognize that, measuring things such as violence, discrimination, and access to leadership opportunities. Getting to equality requires shifting long-standing cultural norms. That is important work, but it takes time.

In the short term and in the relationships negotiated in the homes of our respondents, money mattered. Women with their own earnings and savings were better able to negotiate financial decisions. Money gave women more power to choose the right partner (or no partner) and to delay marital decisions. It gave women more of a voice within the family and enabled them to wield a realistic threat of leaving abusive or otherwise intolerable relationships. Shifts in these realities can help change long-standing cultural norms as well.

Even as we work towards greater fundamental equality for women, today we can make an immediate impact by finding better ways to help more women earn and control more money, even in the face of serious cultural and lifecycle constraints.

Endnotes

1. The analysis in this chapter originated first in a presentation I prepared to discuss with colleagues at the Gates Foundation in 2014. That work was also the foundation of a subsequent report my colleague, Caitlin Sanford, and I wrote for the Omidyar Network, reporting insights from

three countries (including Kenya) that explain the financial inclusion gender gap (Zollmann and Sanford, 2016). We are able to explore this topic in such depth both because of the careful notes of the field team and thanks to a set of in-depth life history interviews collected from our respondents by Dr Susan Johnson. Susan's work was so enlightening that we were inspired to extend life history interviews across our entire sample. In November 2016, my colleague Catherine Wanjala and I conducted a small set of follow-up qualitative interviews to ask respondents more directly about the institution of marriage. In those conversations, we particularly targeted male respondents, making sure we were accurately reflecting their perspectives in what can seem at times to be an antagonistic portrayal. My intention is not to cast blame on Kenyan men. Culture is something women and men create, sustain, and alter together.

2. While this comes from Kenya's Demographic and Health Survey – which is not necessarily easily comparable across countries – the World Values Survey found similarly high proportions of men and women approving of domestic violence. Kenya was not part of that study (Aizenman, 2015).

3. Kenyan lawmakers' commitments are more ambiguous.

4. Having more children, being part of a 'complete' family, is important to many women for a host of reasons: it means some financial security, it means being respected as a mother and wife in society, it means belonging in a way that single mothers often don't.

5. In Kenya, men pay dowry to the father or other relatives of their wives. In theory, this is supposed to be done before the couple begins to live together or have children, but it often comes later. The wife's family traditionally keeps some responsibility for or ownership over children born to the couple until the dowry is paid. For example, the infant child of one of our respondents died during the study. The father had not yet paid a dowry, so the baby could not be buried at the father's home and was instead interred at the mother's family farm.

6. A 'chama' is a general term for a group or political party. This is the most common word that our respondents used to refer to all kinds of informal financial clubs, including ROSCAs (rotating savings and credit associations) and ASCAs (accumulating savings and credit associations).

7. There is no formal title for the property, but many communities try to create some protection over this kind of informally held land via letters from area chiefs acknowledging possession of such property. While this does not prevent the entire community from being pushed off the property and cannot serve as formal collateral, such documents are typically respected within the community.

8. Socially, they are considered married once they are living together, but they may not have a legal marriage certificate or have undergone any kind of marriage ceremony, and their partners may not have paid a dowry yet. Legal marriage rights – like inheritance claims – are weak at this stage.

9. The controversial Marriage Act signed into law in 2014 further entrenched this practice. It enshrined men's right to marry multiple wives without the consent of their first wives, although this has enormous economic implications for the first wife and her children. Many female MPs boycotted

the vote and walked out of parliament in disgust as the legislation was debated.

10. It was the main *monetary* source of income for only 11 per cent of our rural households. When we add in the value of the food grown and consumed at home, that rises to 24 per cent.
11. Some researchers consider 20–30 per cent of couples disagreeing about family size to be a low incidence of discordance in fertility preferences. We consider that quite substantial.
12. See Irani et al. (2014). Of course, couples can also disagree about the intervals between births; in Kenya, women without sons have shorter birth intervals, for example (Mace and Sear, 1997). However, we don't know as much as we should about how divergent women's and men's fertility and birth interval preferences really are since surveys often only ask women, even though husbands clearly have an important say in such decisions in many countries.
13. Diana's story is also found in the original Diaries report (Zollmann, 2014).
14. At least, this is the case when doctors and nurses are not on strike and facilities are able to accept women.
15. 'Unlikely' because of their more typical reinforcement of patriarchal gender roles.
16. Tertiary education is increasingly recognized as important for long-term earning potential.
17. A 'money guard' is a person who is asked to hold money for safekeeping on behalf of another person.

References

Aizenman, N. (2015) 'Alarming number of women think spousal abuse is sometimes OK', NPR.org, 18 March. Available from: <http://www.npr.org/sections/goatsandsoda/2015/03/18/392860281/alarming-number-of-women-think-spousal-abuse-is-sometimes-ok> (accessed 25 August 2017).

Bery, S., Bosworth, B., and Panagariya, A. (2011) *India Policy Forum 2010–11*, Sage Publications India, New Delhi.

Central Bank of Kenya, KNBS, and FSD Kenya (2016) *The 2016 FinAccess Household Survey on Financial Inclusion*, Central Bank of Kenya, Kenya National Bureau of Statistics (KNBS) and FSD Kenya, Nairobi.

Cuberes, D. and Teignier, M. (2011) *Gender Inequality and Economic Growth*, World Bank, Washington DC. Available from: <https://openknowledge.worldbank.org/bitstream/handle/10986/9117/WDR2012-0019.pdf?sequence=1&isAllowed=y> (accessed 7 February 2020).

Duflo, E. (2012) 'Women empowerment and economic development', *Journal of Economic Literature* 50 (4): 1051–79 <https://doi.org/10.1257/jel.50.4.1051>.

Fotso, J.-C. et al. (2013) 'Birth spacing and child mortality: an analysis of prospective data from the Nairobi urban health and demographic surveillance system', *Journal of Biosocial Science* 45 (6): 779–98 <https://doi.org/10.1017/S0021932012000570>.

Heyer, A. and King, M. (eds) (2015) *Kenya's Financial Transformation in the 21st Century*, FSD Kenya, Nairobi. Available from: <http://fsdkenya.org/

wp-content/uploads/2015/12/Kenyas-Financial-Transformation-in-the-21st-Century.pdf>.

Irani, L., Speizer, I., and Fotso, J.-C. (2014) 'Relationship characteristics and contraceptive use among couples in urban Kenya', *Guttmacher Institute* 40 (1): 11–20 <https://doi.org/10.1363/4001114>.

Jack, W. and Suri, T. (2014) 'Risk sharing and transactions costs: evidence from Kenya's mobile money revolution', *American Economic Review* 104 (1): 183–223 <https://doi.org/10.2307/42920692>.

Johnson, S. (2015) *Capacities to Aspire and Capacities to Save: A Gendered Analysis of Motivations Liquidity Management*, FSD Kenya, Nairobi. Available from: <http://fsdkenya.org/publication/capacities-to-aspire-and-capacities-to-save-a-gendered-analysis-of-motivations-for-liquidity-management/> (accessed 7 February 2020).

KNBS et al. (2014) *Kenya Demographic and Health Survey 2014*. Kenya National Bureau of Statistics (KNBS), Nairobi and Rockville MD. Available from: <http://dhsprogram.com/publications/publication-FR308-DHS-Final-Reports.cfm> (accessed 6 February 2020).

Mace, R. and Sear, R. (1997) 'Birth interval and the sex of children in a traditional African population: an evolutionary analysis', *Journal of Biosocial Science* 29 (4): 499–507 <https://doi.org/10.1017/S0021932097004999>.

Mason, K.O. and Smith, H.L. (2000) 'Husbands' versus wives' fertility goals and use of contraception: the influence of gender context in five Asian countries', *Demography* 37 (3): 299–311 <https://doi.org/10.2307/2648043>.

McCarthy, A.S. (2015) 'His and her fertility preferences: an experimental evaluation of asymmetric information in family planning', working paper, Department of Applied Economics, University of Minnesota, p. 45. Available from: <http://ses.wsu.edu/wp-content/uploads/2016/01/His-and-Her-Fertility-Prefs_McCarthy.pdf> (accessed 10 March 2020).

Murumba, S. (2017) 'Maternal deaths double in six months', *Daily Nation*, 17 October. Available from: <http://www.nation.co.ke/news/Maternal-deaths-double-in-six-months/1056-4144270-138tikb/index.html> (accessed 5 November 2017).

Suri, T. and Jack, W. (2016) 'The long-run poverty and gender impacts of mobile money', *Science* 354 (6317): 1288–92 <https://doi.org/10.1126/science.aah5309>.

Tilahun, T., Coene, G., Temmerman, M., and Degomme, O. (2014) 'Spousal discordance on fertility preference and its effect on contraceptive practice among married couples in Jimma zone, Ethiopia', *Reproductive Health* 11 (1): 27 <https://doi.org/10.1186/1742-4755-11-27>.

Wambui, T., Ek, A.-C., and Alehagen, S. (2009) 'Perceptions of family planning among low-income men in Western Kenya', *International Nursing Review* 56 (3): 340–5 <https://doi.org/10.1111/j.1466-7657.2009.00726.x>.

World Bank (2012) *World Development Report 2012: Gender Equality and Development*, World Bank, Washington DC. Available from: <https://openknowledge.worldbank.org/handle/10986/4391> (accessed 7 February 2020).

World Bank (2017) 'World development indicators'. Data available from: <http://data.worldbank.org/country/kenya?view=chart> (accessed 16 January 2017).

Zollmann, J. (2014) *Shilingi kwa Shilingi: The Financial Lives of the Poor*, FSD Kenya, Nairobi. Available from: <http://fsdkenya.org/publication/kenya-financial-diaries-shilingi-kwa-shilingi-the-financial-lives-of-the-poor/> (accessed 7 February 2020).

Zollmann, J. and Sanford, C. (2016) *A Buck Short: What Financial Diaries Tell Us about Building Financial Services that Matter to Low-income Women*, Omidyar Network, Redwood City CA. Available from: <https://www.omidyar.com/sites/default/files/file_archive/Pdfs/16-07-01_A_Buck_Short_Report_Digital_FINAL.pdf> (accessed 7 February 2020).

CHAPTER 6

Staying alive[1]: The difficulty in financing healthcare

Abstract

Low-income Kenyans in our study face tremendous difficulty financing healthcare. While there are some bright spots where access to care is improving (HIV, for example), poverty prevents people from getting care, and the results are devastating – physically, financially, and emotionally. Even though prices for accessing primary care facilities have fallen, low-income people are subject to a substantial quality tax, with treatment costs escalating as individuals seek care from multiple providers to resolve even common illnesses. Incomplete implementation of state-led health finance schemes, such as Kenya's free maternity programme, mean that many families are unprepared to step in when state programmes fail. Given a deep understanding of how low-income people manage money, we see that traditional health insurance is unlikely to be a complete solution to the health finance challenges ordinary Kenyans face.

Keywords: healthcare, health finance, maternal mortality, health insurance, healthcare quality, traditional medicine

Sandra, a 28-year-old mother of four, lived with her husband Tim in a rural community about a 45-minute drive from Eldoret. Here, Tim's family owned a small piece of land where she stayed with three of her children and a younger sister, whom Sandra was putting through school. Sandra's other child stayed with relatives, which made managing the cost of raising children a little bit easier. Tim did casual work and moved from place to place when a new opportunity arose. When he got something steadier in Nairobi, she tried to join him, but she found the city stressful and expensive. The kids were constantly getting sick with coughs and the flu. Once the family could save up for bus fare, she took them back upcountry.

During the Diaries, every month Tim sent Sandra about $40 on M-Pesa. About half went on school fees and the rest served as the backbone of the household budget. Sandra supplemented this with milk sales from their cow and casual work when she could find it. In early 2015, Sandra was excited to find out that she was expecting her fifth child. She started going to antenatal care clinic visits. Sometime during the fourth month, she knew something was wrong as she felt completely exhausted, much more than she had with

http://dx.doi.org/10.3362/9781788531207.006

the other pregnancies. She went to the hospital, and they told her to eat more fruit to increase her 'blood level'. But a month later, there was no improvement. The doctor told her she now needed a blood transfusion. While her antenatal care visits were free, the transfusion would cost about $500.

She called Tim in Nairobi. He told her there was no money. That was the end of the discussion. After another month, her legs were swollen, and the hospital gave her some painkillers and medicines to help reduce the swelling. But in her seventh month, her water broke. She was in pain and bleeding heavily. She rushed to the hospital but it was too late. The baby had already died.

Tim hurried back from Nairobi to find his wife distraught. They would now need to operate to remove the foetus. This time, her hospital bill would be $450 – nearly as much as the transfusion – but it had to happen, and the hospital would not release her until the bill was paid. Her husband withdrew all of his savings, sold their cow, and borrowed the rest from friends. Sandra was inconsolable. Her husband stayed at home with her for a month, but – more broke than ever – he then had to return to work or risk losing the job that was keeping the family afloat.

Months later, Sandra was still recovering from her loss. She blamed herself, wondering if there was more she could have done to manage her diet. During the other pregnancies she had a little of her own money, which she had used to buy fruit. She also wished Tim would have tried harder to find the money for the transfusion. 'It was really difficult for me. He probably thought that it was not a serious issue since we were communicating by phone.' She wished she had had some money of her own. 'Maybe if I had some money, I would have admitted myself for the blood transfusion, and my husband would have been forced to look for the remaining money.' She and other women in the area replayed their miscarriages together: 'We all have questions on how it happened and if it could have been avoided. Three other women miscarried around the same time as me in the area. People get to hear about it and come to console with you.'

After the tragedy, Tim considered registering the family for the National Hospital Insurance Fund (NHIF), which, they thought, would have brought the bill from the second hospitalization down from $450 to $100. The hospital told Sandra to wait five years before trying to have a baby again. She and Tim have not talked about whether they will try again.

Sandra's loss was heart-breaking in so many ways. Most obviously, there was the trauma of losing a child so far along in a pregnancy. For Sandra, that trauma was compounded by the tragedy of knowing that an available treatment was *just* out of reach. Among our respondents, we observed time and again how the expense of health decisions involved gut-wrenching trade-offs.

Families in poverty are by definition already surviving below a threshold of acceptable living standards. The pressure to spend more on healthcare, makes them *even more poor* today for a chance (and the odds are not always good!) to be whole again tomorrow so that they can struggle to return to their baseline economic status.

What Kenyans spend on healthcare

To understand how these trade-offs happen, even for very low, out-of-pocket healthcare expenses, it is important to revisit a typical household budget. In the Kenya Financial Diaries project, 72 per cent of the project households were getting by on less than $2 per day in consumption per capita. The median household earned just KES 7,120 ($84) per month. In the median household, food accounted for 48 per cent of the household consumption budget. Once you account for other basic needs, such as housing, cooking fuel, water, school fees, and transportation, there is not much extra room for other things, even basic but irregular things like clothing. We found that households were doing the best they could to save, but much of those savings were set aside in illiquid financial devices – like savings groups – to enable bigger investments in the future, for a new roof, cooking utensils, livestock, school fees, or business stock. Those are the kinds of investments that help families make their way out of poverty. Only about 10% (the median was about KES 870 ($10.23)) of the total saved was kept in a liquid form that would enable families to respond to unexpected financial needs, such as healthcare.

And when we looked just at medical costs in an average family, at first glance spending was quite low. The typical Kenyan requires some kind of medical attention fairly frequently. The most recent Kenya Household Health Expenditure and Utilisation Survey (KHHEUS) reported an average of three outpatient visits per person per year in 2012, up from two visits per person per year in 2002 (Ministry of Health, 2014). Diaries respondents reported slightly lower rates of risk events over five years, averaging 0.9 outpatient visits per person per year. This discrepancy may be due to our study's focus on low-income people, underreporting of free visits (given the Diaries' focus on financial transactions), and challenges with respondent recall for minor outpatient visits over a five-year period.

Over the course of the study year, outpatient transactions were the most common health expense reported, but taken individually, each of these outpatient visits was not very expensive. Diaries households reported a median cost per outpatient visit of KES 400 ($4.70).[2] Among 966 medical service payments, the median individual transaction value was KES 300 ($3.53), while the mean was KES 939 ($11). We had 1,396 transactions for medicine alone, with a median value of just KES 50 ($0.60) and a mean of KES 185 ($2.20). Free care – which is becoming more common in Kenya, at least for consultations – would not necessarily show up in Diaries data, which focused more on households' monetary transactions rather than service utilization.

Estimating that a family with five members might need to come up with KES 400 – about 6 per cent of monthly income – five times throughout the year to meet their health needs, healthcare almost seems affordable. The KHHEUS provides an estimate of total health spending in a year for the average Kenyan – KES 1,609 ($18.86) – about 5 per cent of annual per capita expenditure for a household right on the $1.25/day poverty line.[3] Many families, we assumed, could manage this. However, as we listened to people's life experiences unfold, it became obvious just how off base this kind of simplified thinking can be. It completely avoids some tragic realities.

First, much larger medical expenses – beyond the average, and beyond those for simple outpatient treatment – are not uncommon. In the Diaries, 9 per cent of households spent more than a month's worth of household income on health-care costs over the course of the main study year. When we looked at a full his-togram of costs, again we saw clustering of respondent households around very low health spending. But we also saw some long tails, where a small number of people experienced very high costs during the year. The results are similar in the KHHEUS: average household out-of-pocket spending on health in a year was KES 6,937 ($82). Nearly 7 per cent of households spent more than KES 20,000 in a year, roughly three times the average out-of-pocket annual spending. According to the KHHEUS, about 6.2 per cent of households per year were pushed into poverty as a result of high healthcare expenditures.

That risk compounds over many years, suggesting that nearly everyone will be affected at some stage in their lives by exceptionally high medical costs. Among Diaries households, the probability of hospital admission was about 3 per cent per year. For a family of five, that's about a 15 per cent chance that at least one household member will be hospitalized in the course of a year, meaning that they can expect a household member to be admit-ted about once every six or seven years. Each of these instances involved significant costs: the median inpatient expenditure in the sample was KES 5,000 ($58.82) (mean KES 19,412 ($228.38)) over the previous five years. In the KHHEUS, 11.6 per cent of Kenyan households experienced at least one hospitalization in a year, and those families incurred on average KES 12,935 ($152) in out-of-pocket expenses in those years.

Much of the risk associated with high-cost inpatient care is random. At these levels of risk, the question is not *if* a household will someday have to deal with these kinds of expenses, but rather *when*, and, as we discuss later, *how*.

The other challenge with financing large expenditures associated with health-care is that funds are typically needed quickly. While Kenyans are often able to finance other large expenditures, such as school fees, by paying slowly over time or by saving up, health needs are often unexpected and urgent. While many might have KES 300 ($3.50) on hand to pay for an outpatient visit, an available KES 1,000 ($12) for an X-ray or KES 10,000 ($120) for surgery is far less com-mon. With a median salary of KES 7,120 ($84) per month, there is not enough wiggle room in household budgets to accommodate such high expenses.

For these families, coming up with large sums of money to finance urgent healthcare spending adds tremendous new stress. Some in our study were able to do it, but few without serious delays and without impinging on their already vulnerable livelihoods. Consider Ellen, whose son was suffering from ongoing abdominal pain, which doctors began to suspect was related to a problem with his appendix. They needed KES 10,000 ($118) to perform the surgery, a sum that Ellen could not pull together quickly. She saved diligently for more than a year to build up the funds needed for the surgery to remove his appendix. Frustrated at how long it was taking her, she went to an uncle, a Coca-Cola distributor, to ask for help getting a new job. He told her she would need a driving licence to work for him. In the meantime, though, he recommended a very good paediatrician where he took his own children. Ellen used her savings to pay for this doctor, who determined, after KES 3,000 ($35) in testing, that the son's problem was with his intestines, not his appendix. He would need to come back every two months for medication and an injection at a cost of KES 2,000 ($24) plus KES 200 ($2.35) in transport for each visit. Ellen's savings covered the first round. Funding the follow-up visits remained a major challenge, but she was relieved that her son responded to the treatment and that surgery wasn't necessary.

Ellen was lucky that her son could endure the delay; this was not always the case. Urgent medical needs sometimes cropped up when low-income families were least able to manage them. Matthew's mother-in-law was hospitalized with a severe and urgent illness, and the duty to finance her hospital bill of KES 10,000 ($118) fell to him. At the same time, a bank representative showed up at his home asking him to make good on his obligation as a loan guarantor. A friend for whom he had guaranteed a loan had absconded, leaving the balance of KES 12,000 ($141) unpaid. The only way in which Matthew could pay for both was to give up his tea farm. He leased it to a local businessman who provided him with KES 10,000 ($118) upfront in exchange for three months of tea revenue. The family gave up new tea income for three months – around KES 8,000–10,000 ($94–$118) per month in good months.

Those lucky enough to have insurance cover for hospitalization still had to finance outpatient care. Combining out-of-pocket outpatient costs with premiums for hospitalization substantially increased the share of income devoted to health spending. In some cases, the urgency of medical care helped people raise money from their social networks, generating funds that were needed very quickly for urgent procedures. (In some cases, even emergency care was not provided without a 'deposit' to the hospital.)

On the other hand, if a medical expenditure was not viewed as extremely urgent, it risked falling to the bottom of a family's priority list. Calvin was a 10-year-old boy in rural Western Kenya. At the start of the Diaries, he was being treated for bladder incontinence at a local hospital. The doctors suspected that he had had some kind of accident injuring his urethra and had been too ashamed to tell his parents until it grew into a more serious, embarrassing problem. Early on, his parents invested in his treatment, paying for more and more tests and scans. Eventually they were referred to a regional hospital for further investigations. They did not know how much this would cost, and, after three years, they still did not know treatment options or costs. Calvin's father, Douglas, had been fighting one of his brothers over claims to land left to them by their father. In the process, he sold all the family's cows, spending all the funds that could have been used for Calvin's treatment. Douglas's wife, Judith, was so angry at his unilateral decision to throw all of the family wealth at what she saw as a frivolous and unproductive dispute that she left Douglas multiple times, eventually returning because she could not successfully start over at her father's home. Calvin, who was once first in his class, saw his grades and confidence suffer. Concerned teachers even called Douglas and Judith to plead with them to seek treatment. The children taunted Calvin; humiliated, he wanted to leave school. But, right or wrong, his problem did not make it to the top of the household's list of investment priorities. Even after Douglas gave up on his land case and his brother gave him KES 20,000 ($235) to mend the relationship, Calvin wasn't taken to the referral hospital for follow-up.

When Judith heard that foreign doctors were visiting a local hospital and were doing free surgeries, she brought Calvin. The hospital required KES 3,000 ($35) upfront. Judith wasn't sure what exactly happened but said that the doctors put Calvin under anaesthesia and then decided it was not an operable condition. Desperate, Judith also tried herbal medicine. The herbalist demanded KES 500 ($5.88) upfront and KES 5,000 ($59) if the boy was healed.

Calvin continued to suffer. Without an urgent threat to his life, a costly procedure didn't rise to the level of a major family fundraising priority. Treating his condition was not even among the biggest financial challenges or stresses the family reported during our update visit in 2015.

Low-income people are underspending on healthcare

Just like Calvin, many participants in our study did not receive the care they needed because they could not pay, making actual out-of-pocket expenditure a poor reflection of financing needs. During the Diaries year, 38 per cent of households reported at least once that they needed a doctor or medicine but had to go without, usually because they did not have enough money to meet the current need. Other surveys identified similar levels of forgone care. The most recent Afrobarometer survey (2014–15) found that 48 per cent of Kenyan families went without care, and about 27 per cent of households reported that they did so more than just once or twice (Afrobarometer, 2015). While high, the rate is declining, from 54 per cent of any forgone care and 36 per cent of frequently forgone care in the 2011 round. The KHHEUS, which looks at individuals rather than households or families, found that 13 per cent of individuals in 2012 (down from 17 per cent in 2007) experienced an illness and did not seek treatment.

The KHHEUS also asked why respondents went without care. While the leading reason reported in all previous rounds was the 'high cost of care', the 2012 survey introduced a new response option: 'Illness not considered serious enough.' This new option became the leading explanation, followed by cost, raising new questions. How well are Kenyans assessing the severity of their medical needs? Scarce financial resources and high costs of care can skew this perception. Very low costs of care can encourage individuals to seek unnecessary care. In contrast, perceived high costs can encourage people to downplay the severity of their need, disregard the benefits of preventive services, delay necessary care, and, in some cases, worsen their condition to the point at which effective treatment is much more difficult to administer.

This is a recognized phenomenon in Kenya and around the region. Studies in Tanzania and Uganda have found that caregivers delayed care for children under five with fevers more often in low-income families, in households where parents were not the full-time caregivers (e.g. grandparents), and where distances from clinics were longer, increasing the cost of transportation. These results could be seen even when clinical services were free (Rutebemberwa et al., 2009; Kassile et al., 2014). Separate studies of tuberculosis (TB) patients in Kenya have found that 65 per cent and 80 per cent of them delayed seeking care for more than 30 days, with one study finding that the mean number of days of delayed care was 54. Here, researchers determined a main driver of delays was the perception of the quality of care at public facilities. Those suffering from TB may have been delaying care to save up for private care while their symptoms deteriorated, and they unwittingly spread the disease to loved ones (Mutinda et al., 2014; Nyatichi et al., 2016).

One of the ways in which we saw these delays come to life was through children who would avoid telling their parents when they were injured for as long as possible. They hoped that they would heal naturally, avoiding their parents' inevitable anger at having to spend significant sums of money on medical care. When we went back to see Christine in Makueni, she told us about a major struggle she had paying a medical bill for one of her sons. He had fallen from a tree and hurt himself but hid his injury for two weeks until the pain was unbearable. At that time, Christine had no money. It was in the middle of the month, when her husband who works in Nairobi couldn't find enough funds either. By the time she got her son to the hospital, he needed to be admitted for surgery to realign the broken bone; this cost the family KES 4,600 ($54), about half of their average monthly income.

Because the Kenya Financial Diaries project followed the same households for a long period, we learned more about the circumstances under which low-income people delayed and forwent care. We also observed the consequences. As the KHHEUS picked up, some of the instances of forgone care were intentional attempts to first try the lowest-cost care option for non-urgent matters: waiting.[4] If waiting did not help the illness, families would typically follow with self-treatment through the purchase of medication from a pharmacist. Seeking medical advice, typically a higher-cost option for most, would only come after those mechanisms failed. While most of the time respondents could come up with the first KES 300–500 ($3.52–$5.88) for an initial visit to a medical practitioner, they would then run out of funds for follow-up examinations, medications, and procedures.

Cutting short courses of medication, or forgoing them completely, was the most frequent example of partially forgone care, a consequence of insufficient funds. Sometimes this forgone medication was for severe and potentially life-threatening illnesses such as TB. One respondent, for example, was sick with chest pains for some time. Eventually, she decided to look for help at the government dispensary. She spent KES 50 ($0.59) on registration and a consultation but could not afford to purchase the prescribed medication. She carried on with her normal routines but continued to deteriorate. The next time we saw her, she had been hospitalized in a referral hospital because of her TB.

Although a delay in care was not always this serious, it could mean that children missed school, adults missed work, and the sick person in the household suffered while the family tried to accumulate funds to cover the costs of care. When Candy's son was sick, she took him to the dispensary near their home in a rural part of Rift Valley and was told that he had malaria. But lacking funds, Candy did not get the medicine he required. It was always difficult for her to find funds in the middle of the month; by that time, her husband's monthly salary of KES 3,900 ($46) was usually gone, spent on household basics. Candy and her husband were only occasionally able to pick up casual work mid-month, when other needs – like medical costs – arose. They postponed their son's treatment for about a week, until they could get the funds together. He eventually made a full recovery.

Forgoing prescribed treatments forced people into choices they didn't have enough information to make. One respondent told us:

> An aunt of mine sent me some money, but it could not cover the whole expense, so I had to leave some of the prescribed medication, and I took the few I could afford. My wife said that maybe I was not getting any better because I had an incomplete prescription from the hospital.

Often patients who have limited medical knowledge and not much on-site explanation of the treatments being provided cannot distinguish between urgent, medically necessary medications and palliative care. Choices that must be made among prescribed medications were difficult to optimize.

As noted above, when patients could not afford full treatment costs, we observed that most often they simply waited. For example, Rachel, who lived in rural Vihiga, fell sick in April 2013. She took KES 400 ($4.70) from her secret emergency savings in the house to pay for a consultation. Two weeks later she was still sick. She spent KES 600 ($7.05) on more consultation fees. The prescribed medicine cost KES 1,000 ($11.76), which she couldn't afford with her monthly income of KES 2,400 ($28.23). She did not buy the medicine and prayed she would recover without it. This was a tricky situation. Insurance may not have helped her in this circumstance, depending on the policy's prescription drug benefits. Throughout the study, she was never able to borrow from friends or family. She was sometimes able to borrow around KES 1,000 ($11.76) from her *chamas*, but doing so required waiting for a group meeting and not having any loan outstanding when she needed to borrow for medicine.

Both the Diaries and the KHHEUS showed that people were probably spending 5 per cent to 6 per cent of their income on healthcare. What is harder to measure is how much they should have been spending, given the many instances in which they delayed care, didn't complete a course of treatment, or skipped important medical tests.

Recognizing such practices, many public health programmes see increased utilization of health services as one of the aims of expanded health coverage and new health finance mechanisms. In Kenya, the government has been lowering user fees at public health dispensaries and making care free for certain types of health situations, like maternity care and treatment for HIV/AIDS. While facility fees have been removed for these kinds of services, other costs remain – for diagnostics, referrals, and often medication that is frequently out of stock at front-line facilities. And many Kenyans seek primary care at facilities not covered by the government-financed services. As one might expect, utilization of services related to covered situations – such as HIV – is improving, but the improvements do not necessarily extend to other conditions that also take a heavy toll on people's health.

How much is too much spending on healthcare?

For families already living below the poverty line, even $5 spent on healthcare is $5 less that can be spent on school fees, a business, livestock, or even a mobile phone. The trade-offs medical expenses and caregiving cause can lead to enormous setbacks.

For example, while playing with friends, Ruth's son fell from a tree and broke his jaw. The surgery he needed was going to cost Ruth KES 40,000 ($470), a huge sum that far exceeded her savings. To raise the money, she sold her cow and called all her friends and family. She paid the doctor in small instalments until she had deposited enough for her son to be admitted to the hospital. Ruth put her *changaa* (local alcoholic brew) business on hold, since she had diverted all of her working capital to her son's medical expenses, and survived on casual jobs working for others.

Ruth was not alone. When large, urgent medical costs had to be paid, many of our respondents made awful choices between their health and the future welfare of their families. One respondent was desperately sick. Neighbours rushed him to the hospital, which demanded a deposit before doctors would operate. His niece came to the rescue, lending him the funds for his care. To repay her, he gave her a piece of land worth much more than the cost of his care. Another man was rushed to the hospital by his employers at the flower farm where he worked. His employers paid for his care at that time, but then deducted repayments from his salary for several years, reducing his remittances to his wife and nine children to KES 1,000 ($11.76) per month. To make ends meet, his wife tried to get as much casual work as she could, hauling sand to construction sites, fetching water, and plaiting sisal ropes. When she found work, she earned only KES 150 ($1.76) per day, either in cash or in roughly the equivalent value in maize and beans.

Apart from the opportunity cost of money spent on healthcare, we also saw that prolonged episodes of poor health also entailed opportunity costs in terms of caregiver time. Mostly, those burdens were borne by women. When someone was sick, women missed days of work and sometimes lost their informal jobs. They often closed their businesses or left them in the hands of helpers who rarely maintained normal sales levels. This made household budgets even tighter at times when families most needed to spend more to pay for healthcare.

It also meant that women's livelihoods were interrupted. Jessica told us about how tough it was for her when her 23-year-old stepdaughter became very sick. The young woman never got a full diagnosis. She was first treated for an abdomen filling with fluid, then meningitis, followed by a blood clot in her brain. All of that took about three months. Not long after the surgery to remove the clot in her brain, she became very sick again, but the doctors said that there was nothing more they could do to help her:

> The doctors told us that they had done everything possible for her condition. There was nothing else they could do except manage her pain. They were going to give us some pain medicine to manage her pain from home. They told us they would give her some tuberculosis medication in case she had gotten it in her bones. They were treating her to prevent further complications. She took the medicine for three months. I nursed her for three months. I was having a really hard time. In February 2008, she passed on.

Although Jessica didn't have to spend any of her own money for her stepdaughter's treatment, she did have to put her business on hold. Even though she had been paying rent, she lost her salon space when the landlord could see that she had stopped working. She tried to get started again, doing hair from her home, but had to rebuild her client base from scratch. Since she had several loans outstanding, she had to swallow her pride and go to work at a relative's salon in another city for several months until she could clear the loans and get back on her feet.

These kinds of opportunity costs are often overlooked in policy conversations about affordable care, in spite of the potential long-term implications. Funds diverted from livelihoods and education make it more difficult for families to invest their way out of poverty. This is precisely why it is so important to minimize out-of-pocket health expenditure while optimizing health outcomes for the poor.

Bad care is an extra tax on the poor

Lydiah lived with her husband Peter, a diligent man, who supplemented the family's tea income with masonry work throughout the community. One of his projects was completing a beautiful three-room house, a jewel in the community. Peter was a perfectionist. He felt there was still a long way to go before he had a life he could be proud of.

Lydiah was the opposite. In her mind, they had already arrived! She reminisced about the early days after marrying Peter. The two had no land then and got by through picking tea on a larger plantation. Their employer provided housing, and the only assets they had were three small, non-matching stools. They sacrificed to save. When Peter received his land allocation from his father, he planted tea, knowing that it would take time to mature but that it would be an important investment in the future. Once they could afford to, they left the plantation and built a small mud and thatch house on their own land. In time, they were able to replace that house with a semi-permanent house with an iron sheet roof. During the Diaries, Lydiah was excited that they were accumulating bricks and other materials to build a permanent house. 'We are doing so well,' she told us, 'that sometimes I can even hire someone to pick the tea on my farm.'

At 27, she was full of confidence and optimism. But, health-wise, something was wrong. Ever since the birth of her last child, she had been sick, worse at some times than at others. During the Diaries, she went to the hospital at least four times, and each time she was told that she had malaria. On each visit, she would be given new medicine. With no improvement, Lydiah sought higher- and higher-level facilities looking for help, but she grew frustrated at how little help they could offer. Later, she turned to traditional medicine, hoping for some relief.

When we went back to visit the family and share our project report, we learned that Lydiah had passed away. With her condition deteriorating, she was finally admitted to the hospital, and Peter spent all the money he had been saving to build their permanent house on her care. Days before her death, the hospital realized that she had TB, already at a very late stage. Most likely she had had TB all along. Peter traced it back at least six years to 2008 when Lydiah was given a blood transfusion for anaemia following the birth of their last child. That's when she became sick. Peter thinks the blood did not 'agree' with her. No one knew for sure. Perhaps she contracted HIV around that time (most likely completely unrelated to the blood transfusion) and the TB came later, a not uncommon occurrence.

Regardless, her underlying medical problem was missed for years, despite multiple visits to health facilities, including well-equipped hospitals. Lydia's problem was not financial; TB care is free, and her family had the resources to pay for transport and diagnostics. The medical system failed her, leaving three children without a mother.

Peter, though upset, moved on quickly. Friends and neighbours raised KES 40,000 ($471) for Lydiah's funeral. Her savings clubs gave Peter his wife's savings with some extra funds to show their condolences. Peter, unable to care for the children on his own, quickly married again. About two years after Lydiah's death, he and his new wife were expecting another baby. Peter says the other children have accepted the new wife as their mother.

Poor care did not always result in death, as it did for Lydiah, but it almost always compounded the costs of care. Even if a family could finance a first visit to a healthcare provider for one illness episode, costs multiplied when repeat visits – often to higher-level facilities – were required due to a misdiagnosis or incorrect prescription during the first round. New visits often entailed new tests, new medicines, and sometimes more expensive inpatient care. The one-year-old son of tea pickers had to be rushed to the government hospital after a first-round diagnosis and treatment failed. His parents had paid KES 300 ($3.52) for a consultation and treatment, although they were not told his diagnosis. Over a few weeks, he continued to deteriorate. They rushed him to the hospital where they spent another KES 150 ($1.76) on medicine, and finally he recovered. A total treatment cost of KES 450 ($5.29) plus transportation costs may not seem like much, but the entire average monthly income for this household was just KES 5,895 ($70).

After multiple visits to the hospital, Emmah, in rural Vihiga, was finally diagnosed with brucellosis, a condition that – judging from the experiences of at least four Diaries respondents – seemed to be frequently misdiagnosed and mismanaged. Emmah believed that she acquired the bacterial infection from consuming milk that had not been boiled. The doctors told her that recovery might take quite a long time. When she experienced a flare-up, she was able to get the KES 500 ($5.88) together for tests and consultations by borrowing from funds that a church group had asked her to hold for them. But the medicine she was prescribed cost KES 6,000 ($71) – much more than her typical monthly household income of KES 4,000 ($47). She paid a deposit of KES 900 ($10.58) and hoped to make further payments over time. But the money her husband was sending was never enough; the KES 1,200 ($14.12) was earmarked for fertilizer (or her maize crop would fail), household food and ROSCA contributions. She never came up with the full KES 6,000 ($71) and would only buy partial treatment from time to time, when she felt particularly ill.

Failures to diagnose accurately and quickly were sometimes disastrous for families in our study, since they simply could not afford endless rounds of repeat visits. This was a major factor in Monicah's untimely death. She visited the hospital more than a dozen times; after many visits and admissions, countless tests and compounding expenses, she was finally diagnosed with a throat tumour. The operation was expensive – KES 23,000 ($271) – but that expense was a fraction of the huge sum spent prior to the diagnosis, estimated to have exceeded KES 50,000 ($588).[5] Her husband, Isaac, tapped their social networks and even sold rental properties to finance those earlier visits in which doctors failed to diagnose his wife's condition. By the time they finally discovered what the problem was, Isaac and Monicah's finances were completely drained. The surgery had to be postponed. Monicah died waiting.

The 2012 Kenya Public Expenditure Tracking Survey (PETS) similarly picked up on weaknesses in the diagnostic capacities of Kenyan medical facilities (Onsomu et al., 2014). Using role-play techniques, survey staff found that only 43.7 per cent of clinicians followed the Ministry of Health diagnostic guidelines. While 97 per cent of clinicians were able to correctly diagnose TB, only 35 per cent were able to correctly identify malaria with anaemia. Even when doctors – the most accurate of the medical personnel in diagnostics – achieved a correct diagnosis, they 'prescribed full treatment in only 54 per cent of treatment cases'. PETS did not reveal any large differences in diagnostic and treatment accuracy patterns across public and private facilities but did find that rural and public dispensaries – often the front-line providers of healthcare to the poor – had the lowest levels of compliance with Ministry of Health clinical guidelines.

Because of affordability concerns, especially when a health problem was serious, most families in our study opted for government-provided health services. But that also meant they had few alternative options when the government system was shut down. Frequent strikes in government health facilities during the Diaries period took a heavy toll on our respondents. For example, Gloria, a teacher in Mombasa, was pregnant and had been saving for a caesarean birth at a public hospital, which cost about KES 10,000 ($118). When it was time to deliver, the doctors were on strike, forcing her to a private facility, where the cost of the surgery increased to KES 60,000 ($706). The hospital refused to help her until she raised the full sum. Her husband scrambled, taking emergency loans from his workplace and begging relatives on both sides of the family until they had enough money. Luckily, it was in time to allow Gloria to have a healthy birth.

Felisters' 35-year-old son was not so lucky. After complaining of stomach pains and dizziness, he was referred to a major national hospital, where he was told that he had a growth that needed to be removed. But when the nurses went on strike, all care stopped. By the time the strike was over and doctors revisited his case – more than a month later – they told him it was too late. The tumour was too big. Felisters wanted at least to try to take him to another doctor, but they already owed the hospital KES 60,000 ($706) and could pay only KES 10,000 ($118). Until the bill was paid in full, he couldn't be moved. He was kept in the hospital for another four months until he died. Felisters was left with a KES 170,000 ($2,000) bill to clear before she could take her son's body and give him a proper funeral.

As we have demonstrated, poor-quality and inconsistent care exacerbated the financial burdens for Kenya's poor. Apart from accumulating costs of care, prolonged illnesses also meant longer periods away from businesses and farms. They meant lost jobs, lost time in school, increased transport costs, and opportunity costs for caregivers who put aside their own livelihoods while caring for the sick.

For several Diaries families, a health crisis triggered long-lasting downward spirals in well-being. In 2015, we went back to visit Isaac. Almost three years after his wife Monicah's passing, we wanted to know whether he had managed to get back on his feet. He had not. After Monicah's death, he knew he could not care for the children, including one small baby, on his own. Monicah's sister took the baby, and another relative the two older children. Isaac tried to get back on his feet financially. He had used everything to pay for Monicah's treatment, including selling off their rental property. Fishing was down in the area; he couldn't keep up with the rent. He found himself sleeping in the streets or on the floors of friends' homes, barely getting by. His frustrations boiled over. He got into a fight with another man and attacked him with a *panga* (bush knife/machete) and ended up in jail for three months.

When he was released, he swallowed his pride and went back to his rural home. He had cleared some family land for a *shamba* (farm) but still needed money to build a house. He slept in a makeshift shelter and called his children to come to the rural home. They would stay with his mother, their grandmother, until the new house was complete. When we saw him, he was trying to make a living from fishing, but things were not going well. He did not have his own boat or equipment, so he depended on the goodwill of others to let him come along when they went out to sea. He was trying to convince his father to sell a portion of the family land to enable him to buy a motorbike to run as a taxi in the area. He told us, 'I'm focused on starting over again after so many failures.' He said his wife had given him focus. 'She was my good luck charm.'

The persistence of traditional medicine flows from poor-quality and expensive care

By and large, our respondents did not substitute traditional medicine for modern medicine. When they could afford it – and when it worked – they had a strong preference for the latter. Over the course of the entire study year, we observed only 28 expenditures associated with traditional medicine (versus 2,362 for modern medicine), with a median value of just KES 100 ($1.20; mean KES 526 ($6.20)) per instance.

On occasion – and especially when an illness was not serious – we saw some people turn to home remedies as a first option. Respondents hoped that this might help them avoid spending money at a modern facility. For minor illnesses, this strategy sometimes worked and resulted in savings. When it did not, the family would later seek care at a modern clinic or hospital.

However, the use of traditional healers – rather than simple home remedies – was typically a strategy that families turned to when modern medicine failed. By the time healers were sought, families had already spent significant sums at clinics or hospitals and were frustrated by the lack of relief. Often they would turn to a healer because they had run out of money before a full diagnostic and treatment programme was complete. Healers' costs were more flexible. Payment terms could be negotiated.

Roxanne, in rural Western Kenya, had a problem with her menstrual cycle. She was bleeding very heavily, sometimes for a full month. Her husband was a trained community health worker attached to a local hospital, and that hospital was the first place where she sought care. Staff there could not help. She went from hospital to hospital, to no avail. Several suggested that she have an ultrasound, but the price tag of KES 3,000–4,000 ($35–$47) was just too expensive. That's when she turned to a traditional healer, whose medication seemed to help. After three days of his treatment, the bleeding stopped. Later, though, the healer asked for KES 3,000 ($35) to continue treating her. That's when she dropped him. She told us: 'If I had KES 3,000 to spare, I would have had an ultrasound!'

Low-income Kenyans did not seek traditional medicine because they were illiterate and uneducated. They did so because they were poor. Beyond that poverty, they had also been betrayed by the modern health system.

Some efforts to improve health financing are working

Some key pieces of the health system have been changing for the better. The Government of Kenya has made some important strides towards addressing the health finance challenges facing low-income people, although some of those advances took effect only after our study. At the time of writing, the Ministry of Health was revisiting the country's health finance strategy, working towards a goal of universal healthcare by 2030.

Health services at public facilities were free in postcolonial Kenya until 1988, when user fees were introduced at all public facilities as a way to generate revenue for the health system (Mwabu and Mwangi, 1986; Chuma and Maina, 2013). Since then, studies assessing the impact of user fees have shown that they pose a significant financial barrier to access, depressing healthcare utilization, especially among the poor (Moses et al., 1992; Mwabu et al., 1995).

During the 1990s, the government introduced waivers and exemptions for priority health areas, such as services for children under the age of five, maternal health services, and TB (Chuma and Maina, 2013), and made services under vertical disease programmes, such as HIV/AIDS treatment, free in public facilities. In 2004, the government adopted the 10/20 policy, whereby user charges for primary care services were capped at KES 20 and KES 10, at health centres and dispensaries respectively (Chuma et al., 2009). An early evaluation of the policy reported high adherence to the new rates on the part of health facilities and a 70 per cent increase in utilization (Ministry of Health, 2005). However, subsequent studies showed that these changes did not last. Three years after implementation of the policy, Chuma et al. (2009) found that both patients' understanding of the policy and facility adherence to it were limited.

In June 2013, the current administration announced a policy to remove all user fees at health centres and dispensaries and to abolish charges for maternal health services at all public facilities (Chuma and Maina, 2013). What set this new policy apart from the waivers, exemptions, and caps on user fees that preceded it – and gave the new policy traction – is that the national government had set aside funds to compensate facilities for the income they lost as a result of discontinuing user fees. Early evaluations of the policy to abolish user fees, using administrative data from facilities, report that outpatient services for children under five increased by 25 per cent between 2012–13 and 2013–14, while the number of deliveries at public facilities increased by 21 per cent over the same time period.

Still, the policy is far from a complete solution to the problems that our Diaries respondents faced in paying for care. First, the facilities impacted by this policy – dispensaries and health centres – accounted for only 40 per cent of outpatient visits in 2012. Many outpatient visits still took place at other facilities because of limited access, the need for care from higher-level facilities, and concerns about crowding and quality.

The policy has also shifted part of the financing burden from consultations to drugs. A 2014 study by the Health Policy Project found that 30 per cent of patients in exit interviews from covered facilities stated that drug availability had worsened following the implementation of the policy. While public facilities are supposed to provide the drugs patients require, they were frequently out of stock. If a particular drug was not available at a public health facility, the patient must spend money to purchase it from a private pharmacy. Even with the decline in user fees, total out-of-pocket expenditures per incident, and per year, for low-income families will only fall if the levels of service and treatments offered within these public primary care facilities stay constant or improve (Health Policy Project, 2014).

This is not an insignificant problem given the frequency of shortages and the high cost of drugs. The KHHEUS showed that drugs accounted for two-thirds of out-of-pocket spending for an outpatient visit. The Institute for Health Metrics and Evaluation (IHME) study found that health centres and dispensaries had about 65 per cent of the drugs on the essential medications list at the time they were surveyed. The 2012 PETS looked into the availability of 'tracer' or priority drugs from the Ministry of Health's list of essential medicines that all facilities are meant to stock, and found that 33 per cent of the public facilities sampled did not have all the drugs being tracked (Onsomu et al., 2014).

Costs also remain high if the patient is referred to higher-level facilities for additional tests or consultations. This might happen because a patient needs tests or treatment that a primary care facility is not meant to provide, such as cancer screening or treatment. Or the primary care facility might not be equipped to provide a particular service even though it is meant to do so. For example, the IHME study showed that 97 per cent of public health centres and 80 per cent of dispensaries surveyed reported offering antenatal care services to pregnant women, but only 12 per cent of facilities in the study reported having the full stock of medications, tests, and medical equipment recommended for antenatal care provision (major gaps occurred in the availability of insulin and ultrasounds). Services at secondary and tertiary care facilities still carry charges, even in the public sector, and they are not cheap.

Sandra, whose story opened this chapter, was a beneficiary of the government's free antenatal care services, but these did not cover the blood transfusion she was told would have saved her baby's life. The abolition of user fees in such circumstances is clearly only a partial solution to the larger problem of financing care. Paying for drugs and referrals for additional testing and consultation was precisely when so many of our Diaries families ran out of funds and faced the most serious hurdles to paying for care.

Special attention to TB, HIV, and diabetes care has made it possible for those with these difficult-to-manage conditions to access care. International attention to specific diseases – especially TB and HIV – has helped finance free and comprehensive care for those infected. All of our respondents who knew that they were HIV-positive were receiving free antiretroviral therapy, with the drugs being provided at regular intervals in a reliable way. Most of them also reported receiving free care for opportunistic infections at the same clinics. Similarly, we had a small number of respondents accurately diagnosed and treated for TB; their treatment and frequent follow-up visits were usually free.

Such programmes have an enormous human impact, saving the lives of working-age men and women who are then able to care for their families and prevent downstream suffering. Alice, suffering with HIV, praised the support she got from the government. She received her ARVs regularly every two months and the hospital even paid for her transport back home. She recalled how they used to give her four tablets but changed her prescription when she reacted badly to the side effects of the combination. She told us that she was deeply grateful for what the government was doing for her. If it were up to her to buy the drugs, she would not be able to afford them and said she 'would probably die'.

But in some of the more extreme poverty cases, free drugs were not enough. Pauline was an exceptionally poor mother of three in a rural area outside Eldoret. She struggled to pick up casual work washing clothes and fetching water for others. She had become very weak from poor nutrition. While she had been living in dire conditions since we first met her, when we came back to visit in 2015 we found that she had also stopped taking her ARVs. She collected them and was even given some maize flour at those collection times, but she said that the drugs made her even weaker if she was not getting enough to eat. Her daughter was scheduled to enter primary school but she did not do so since Pauline could neither clear the arrears at the child's nursery school nor gather together the admission fees for a new school. Doctors at the government clinic found that this young girl also had a lump on her lung, but they didn't have the medicine she needed in stock, and Pamela had no hope of paying for it at a private pharmacy. Her poverty was so deep that even an excellent ARV distribution project couldn't do enough to save her and enable her to be the provider that her children needed.

The country's NHIF was helpful for those who had coverage through their employers or who could afford to pay on their own. NHIF accounted for the bulk of health insurance coverage in the country, but still, according to the KHHEUS, fewer than a fifth of Kenyans had any kind of health insurance. Historically, NHIF operated as a social health insurance scheme for Kenyans employed in the formal sector and was financed through mandatory payroll contributions from formal-sector employees. It covered only hospitalization charges. For the past decade, NHIF has sought to extend its membership in the informal sector through voluntary enrolment. In 2015, NHIF expanded the benefit package to include outpatient services to all its members.

During the Diaries, monthly charges for NHIF were KES 170 ($2) per adult contributor, but they went up to KES 500 ($5.88) in 2015.[6] For informal workers – the majority of Kenya's population and workforce – that is a lot of money relative to income. It is perhaps no surprise then that our respondents who had health insurance had much higher incomes than those without – by a lot. The median household income for those with insurance was KES 16,430 ($193) versus KES 6,233 ($73) for the uninsured.

NHIF is an imperfect scheme. What exactly it *should* pay for during a covered person's hospital admission is often unclear. At times it covers an entire bill, at others just the 'bed' portion of the bill. Some payers who have moved their premium payments over time from a group to an individual plan or vice versa have found that their payment records have been lost and they are not actually covered when they go for treatment. Resolving problems with payments, registration, and tracking can be difficult, requiring personal visits to offices that are in urban centres, difficult to locate, and often crowded and confusing.

Adverse selection and outright fraud also burden the system. Our lowest-income insured respondents registered only because they had a severe chronic illness – diabetes or HIV – and were sure that they would make use of the services. With high concentrations of high-risk individuals, it is difficult to pool risk well and keep premiums low without a substantial subsidy. We also had two respondents who registered for NHIF only *after* they had incurred an enormous hospital bill. George, for example, was left with a huge bill when his wife died in the hospital. After her death, hospital staff encouraged him to register for NHIF and to pay six months of premiums in order to give his late wife backdated coverage that would dramatically reduce the sum George owed to the hospital on her behalf.

In spite of its problems, when we asked our respondents who had ever had NHIF whether they would recommend it to others, the overwhelming response was yes! Those who are able to obtain cover do believe that it is worthwhile.

When everything comes together, NHIF can be really helpful. Rosemary's husband was a police officer who worked outside their rural Makueni home, sending money back, and visiting when he could. On one visit, he started complaining of back aches, then pain all over his body. His speech started to slur and Rosemary rushed him to the nearest hospital, where they diagnosed a stroke. He was moved to a private hospital in Nairobi, but when Rosemary learned he would need a significant amount of treatment to cope with the stroke, she moved him to Kenyatta National Hospital, where her husband's NHIF cover could be used. He was admitted for two months, accruing a bill of KES 150,000 ($1,765). NHIF cleared the entire bill. Sadly, it wasn't without a fight. When he was about to be discharged, the cashiers at the hospital told her that they would need to be bribed to accept his NHIF cover. Rosemary alerted her husband's boss within the police force, and he intervened with the cashiers. When we visited in late 2015, Rosemary's husband was recovering well and undergoing physiotherapy near their rural home.

Moving ahead and beyond insurance

Insurance is no silver bullet in sorting out the health finance problems of the poor, but it seems to be the solution to which all policy discussions gravitate. Conceptually, insurance makes a lot of sense, at least for hospitalization. By pooling funds among large and diverse subscribers, those who need help this year can get the help they need. Those who don't need any help now have peace of mind and – as long as they pay regularly – they can get the help they need in the years they draw the short straw.

But a close examination of real-life experiences exposes the naivete of the assumption that insurance can solve the health finance problem.

First, premiums cost money. Just like out-of-pocket spending for acute needs, money spent on premiums is money *not* spent on food, stock for businesses, education, and other needs. How does a family assess premium affordability when it does not have enough money for other basic needs? Is it acceptable for a family to spend 10 per cent, or even 5 per cent, of its income on insurance when family members do not have enough to eat? And bear in mind that insurance products rarely cover *all* healthcare costs. For most, the premium expense is *in addition to* what is already spent on outpatient care and medications. While having health insurance may improve the use of health-care services and health outcomes, its impact on overall welfare depends on the sacrifices the family makes to pay their premiums. Policy discussions often overlook this important reality.

For insurance to work well, low-income people would need to pay premiums consistently across a number of years, a challenge for those whose incomes fluctuate. A typical Diaries household saw its income fluctuate upwards of 50 per cent from month to month, with even bigger swings from year to year. Very few are employed long term in formal jobs from which premium payments can be deducted regularly. Maintaining voluntary, user-initiated payments – month after month and year after year, in good times and bad – is almost impossible for low-income people whose circumstances are both vulnerable and volatile.

Many believed that it did not make sense to prepay into NHIF when there were so many other demands on that money. Rather than working for them, the money invested in insurance was idle. And when a truly urgent, severe health emergency occurred, the odds were that most would be able to get some help from friends and family. Seventy-seven per cent of our respondents thought that they would be able to get such help to pay a hospital bill. It is definitely a gamble; social networks are never 100 per cent reliable. But it can seem worth the risk, especially for the lowest-income families facing so many pressing needs. The relatively better-off may not have as many better-off connections to ask for help. In fact, our insured respondents and our better-off respondents were significantly less likely to expect their families and friends to help with medical expenses. For them, insurance was, in part, a substitute for a redistributive, protective social network financing mechanism.

While friends and family may come to the rescue for a large, urgent need, it was harder to turn to them for routine expenditures, like having fallen $5 behind on insurance premiums. One potentially effective way to expand the number of insured – in the absence of a more satisfying, holistic public intervention – would be to make it easier for the relatively better-off, employed helpers within the network to purchase insurance cover for their de facto dependants, those whose bills become their responsibility once a hospitalization occurs. The network may be more likely to take full responsibility for the premiums than to fill small gaps when low-income people fall behind. It's an incomplete solution, but one that providers – public and private – could offer immediately.

The beauty of social safety nets in Kenya is that they effectively transfer *new* resources to the poor. Unlike savings and credit that move money incrementally over time, they increase income, allowing a low-income family to work with a larger overall budget instead of moving resources around within the same constraints. This makes remittances and other network transfers incredibly powerful and impactful.

Figuring out how to help low-income families pay for healthcare is only part of the problem. The other is ensuring that the services offered effectively diagnose and treat health problems. No matter who is paying, five visits to properly diagnose a health problem will always be less efficient than one. Bad care not only costs more, but also leaves people sick for longer, depressing earning potential. It places real lives at risk from treatable, solvable conditions. Innovations in rapid, low-cost diagnostics, in remote personnel management, telemedicine, and electronic health record keeping could play important roles in boosting value – not just affordability – in medical care in places such as Kenya.

And yet, today, many of these innovations ignore one of the key market failures in health systems everywhere: information asymmetries. Providers don't ask and don't know what happens to their patients once they leave their doors. They rarely explain diagnoses, how they were reached, and how conditions can best be managed. Without correcting information asymmetries between providers and patients, holding providers to higher standards will never work. Ordinary people are left powerless in their efforts to manage their own health and their own lives.

Fixing healthcare in low-resource settings is tough. These stories show both how critical the need is and that the health finance solutions on the table – most often some form of insurance – may not be as promising as they seem.

Endnotes

1. Much of the content in this chapter first appeared in Zollmann and Ravishankar (2016). I am very grateful to Nirmala Ravishankar for her input into this work in particular, in contextualizing Kenya's public health history and analysing data from the Kenya Household Health Expenditure and Utilisation Survey (KHHEUS).

2. The mean value was KES 1,123 ($13.22).
3. This is based on the $1.25/day poverty line set in 2005 and adjusted for inflation up to 2015.
4. Waiting was not the most common reason, however, which is probably because of some differences in question phrasing between the Diaries and the KHHEUS. In the Diaries, we asked whether 'anyone in the household needed a doctor or medicine and went without', while the KHHEUS recorded all of those who were sick and went without care. Diaries respondents who were sick, but not feeling 'in need of care', would not have reported forgone care.
5. The expenditure we recorded during this period was about KES 15,000, but we later learned that Isaac had sold his rental property to finance an additional KES 35,000–50,000 in care that was not fully recorded at the time.
6. This contribution covers the contributor, dependent spouses, and children under age 18.

References

Afrobarometer (2015) 'Afrobarometer data, Kenya, 2015'. Data available from: <http://www.afrobarometer.org> (accessed 27 August 2017).

Chuma, J. et al. (2009) 'Reducing user fees for primary health care in Kenya: policy on paper or policy in practice?', *International Journal for Equity in Health* 8: 15 <https://doi.org/10.1186/1475-9276-8-15>.

Chuma, J. and Maina, T. (2013) *Free Maternal Care and Removal of User Fees at Primary-level Facilities in Kenya: Monitoring the Implementation and Impact Baseline Report*, Health Policy Project, Futures Group, Washington DC.

Health Policy Project (2014) 'Annual evaluation of the abolition of user fees at primary care facilities', unpublished report, Health Policy Project, Nairobi.

Kassile, T., Lokina, R., Mujinja, P., and Mmbando, B.P. (2014) 'Determinants of delay in care seeking among children under five with fever in Dodoma region, central Tanzania: a cross-sectional study', *Malaria Journal* 13 (1): 348 <http://doi.org/10.1186/1475-2875-13-348>.

Ministry of Health (2005) *RHF Unit Cost/Cost Sharing Review Study and the Impact of the 10/20 Policy*, Ministry of Health, Government of Kenya, Nairobi.

Ministry of Health (2014) *2013 Kenya Household Health Expenditure and Utilisation Survey*, Ministry of Health, Government of Kenya, Nairobi. Available from: <https://www.healthpolicyproject.com/index.cfm?id=publications&get=pubID&pubId=745> (accessed 26 August 2017).

Moses, S. et al. (1992) 'Impact of user fees on attendance at a referral centre for sexually transmitted diseases in Kenya', *The Lancet*, 340 (8817): 463–6 <https://doi.org/10.1016/0140-6736(92)91778-7>.

Mutinda, K.A., Kabiru, E.W., and Mwaniki, P.K. (2014) 'Health seeking behavior, practices of TB and access to health care among TB patients in Machakos County, Kenya. A cross-sectional study', *Journal of Biology, Agriculture and Healthcare* 4 (14): 96–106.

Mwabu, G. and Mwangi, W. (1986) 'Health care financing in Kenya: a simulation of welfare effects of user fees', *Social Science and Medicine* 22: 763–7 <https://doi.org/10.1016/0277-9536(86)90228-5>.

Mwabu, G., Mwanzia, J., and Liambila, W. (1995) 'User charges in government health facilities in Kenya: effect on attendance and revenue', *Health Policy and Planning* 10 (2): 164–70 <https://doi.org/10.1093/heapol/10.2.164>.

Nyatichi, F.O., Amimo, F.A., Nabie, B., and Ondimu, T.O. (2016) 'Factors contributing to delay in seeking treatment among pulmonary tuberculosis patients in Suneka sub-county, Kenya', *Journal of Health Education Research and Development* 4: 170 <https://doi.org/10.4172/2380-5439.1000170>.

Onsomu, E. et al. (2014) *Public Expenditure Tracking Survey in Kenya, 2012 (PETS-Plus)*, Kenya Institute for Public Policy Research and Analysis and Futures Group, Health Policy Project, Nairobi and Washington DC. Available from: <https://www.researchgate.net/publication/272509852_Public_Expenditure_Tracking_Survey_in_Kenya_2012_PETS-Plus_Washington_DC_Futures_Group_Health_Policy_Project_and_Nairobi_Kenya_Kenya_Institute_for_Public_Policy_Research_and_Analysis_Co-authored_with_> (accessed 10 February 2020).

Rutebemberwa, E., Kallander, K., Tomson, G., Peterson, S., and Pariyo, G. (2009) 'Determinants of delay in care-seeking for febrile children in eastern Uganda', *Tropical Medicine and International Health* 14 (4): 472–9 <https://doi.org/10.1111/j.1365-3156.2009.02237.x>.

Zollmann, J. and Ravishankar, N. (2016) *Struggling to Thrive: How Kenya's Low-income Families (Try to) Pay for Healthcare*, FSD Kenya, Nairobi. Available from: <http://fsdkenya.org/publication/struggling-to-thrive-how-kenyas-low-income-families-try-to-pay-for-healthcare/> (accessed 10 February 2020).

CHAPTER 7

Being a citizen: Interactions between low-income people and government

Abstract

In a clientelist state, low-income people suffer the most from shortcomings in governance. This chapter depicts the many ways in which respondents suffered from government failures and how they tried to bend a broken system to their own advantage. The chapter recalls respondents' interactions with government in the enforcement of a ban on illicit brewing, as victims and perpetrators of violence, and through attempts to access government services, protection, and justice. Ordinary people face a corruption tax to access many services necessary to build a livelihood: identity documents, electricity, healthcare, and land titles. This chapter argues that development actors must pay more attention to the ways in which structural realities – in this case governance – affect ordinary people's lives. The state can be both agent of and obstacle to development, even at the most micro-levels.

Keywords: governance, corruption, citizenship, security, justice

At 82 years old, the contours of Harriet's life have been shaped by the winds of Kenya's social history – independence, relocation, elections, and violence. The hope she had for Kenya at independence in 1963 has been tempered:

> Well, the main thing I see is that things today are expensive … At least there is freedom, though. You can buy land and rent from others. But, for us hustlers, there's not much change. I still have to wake up and struggle every day.

Harriet's father worked for the *wazungu* (white people). She is not sure what he did, but she recalls that they 'never slept hungry'. Harriet married at 20, and adulthood ushered in a range of struggles, through which the government was either absent or an obstacle: costly public education meant that she could afford to send only one of her nine children through primary school; she lost her low-cost housing in a government demolition of a squatters' camp; she lost three children to HIV/AIDS and raised three orphaned grandchildren with no external assistance.

Then came the contested presidential elections of 2007. Harriet's small grocery shop and home were razed by angry mobs in the aftermath of the vote. She and her grandchildren took shelter at a nearby police post. When we met

http://dx.doi.org/10.3362/9781788531207.007

her in 2012, we found that international donors had helped her reconstruct another small mud house on her plot, with donations of a door, a small water drum, and a sticker claiming credit for their good works. She never was able to reopen her shop, though, and barely got by on an average monthly income of just KES 2,183 ($26) during the Diaries.

As the next national election approached in 2013, Harriet – like many of our respondents – was on edge. What would happen this time? She had no particular interest in who won, but worried about how her life and the lives of her grandchildren might be disrupted.

The government that Harriet perceived was not one that concerned itself very much with citizens' welfare. It was a government they saw functioning well below capacity, where politicians and civil servants alike were interested solely in personal gain, providing minimal public services as a by-product of their positions. Those who were especially eager for their electricity to be connected, for their children to be educated, or for their homes to be safe often found themselves paying for private services or bribing government officials.

Our participants saw bribery and embezzlement all around. They personally paid off local chiefs to keep the police from shutting down their brewing operations and bribed police directly to dodge traffic fines, bail out those accused of crimes, and claim the assets of their dead. They watched the news and heard about billions looted from government coffers, even while government failure to uphold collective bargaining agreements resulted in no teachers in their children's schools and no doctors in public hospitals. They turned up for 'free' maternity care that often cost a fortune, even as more than KES 5.3 billion (about $530 million) went missing from the Ministry of Health's budget in a single fiscal year (Murumba, 2016). Even the achievements of Kenya's legendary athletes – rare sources of national pride and unity – have been marred by the theft of their prize money and other impropriety by sports officials. Olympic athletes' uniforms and plane tickets, as well as travel funds for coaches, were 'eaten' by government officials responsible for managing logistics for the Rio de Janeiro games in 2016 (Leftie and Olilo, 2016).

What the ordinary person, the common 'mwananchi', saw during our study was that the government cake was for politicians. The crumbs of public services were for the poor. Every actual public service achievement, however small – including the planting of a few trees or flowers or the completion of a long overdue road – was lauded by citizens as a small miracle.[1] As one might expect, ordinary people simply tried to adapt the rules of this unfair game, learning when and how to stay out of the way, paying to bend the will of civil servants in their favour, and playing defence against a system that all too often threatened their security and property.

Corruption and development

The stories in this chapter show a range of interactions between citizens and their government that occurred in the lives of our respondent households. Because so many of those interactions were characterized by state weakness and extraction, corruption is really the focus of this chapter. Our respondents' stories bring to life the ways in which corruption affects ordinary people in the form of small taxes, exclusion from public services, interference in their livelihoods and businesses, and threats to their security. In the context of the country's current affairs, we start to see how sometimes small, individual acts erode the basic institutions that help society function and thrive. We see how corruption exacerbates and perpetuates inequalities, extracting from and punishing the poor disproportionately.

There is some disagreement in development circles about how much of a priority tackling corruption ought to be. On the one hand, there is a fairly substantial consensus that corruption inhibits growth (Mauro, 1995; Hung Mo, 2001; Gyimah-Brempong, 2002; Campos et al., 2010). On the other, some economists and political scientists have argued that donors' concerns about corruption are out of proportion to its impact on development (Blattman, 2012) or that good governance is a consequence of growth and not the other way around (Booth, 2015). If we were to take citizens' perspectives seriously, we would need to move the issue up the development agenda. As law professor Matthew Stephenson (2014) wrote:

> As for citizens (especially poor citizens) in developing countries, if we want to know what they think about corruption, we could ask them – as indeed we have (see, for example, here (Transparency International Ghana, 2011), here (Torabi, 2012), here (Pew Research Center, 2014), here (World Bank, 2000), here (Transparency International, 2013), here (Gallup International, 2014), and here (BBC World Service, 2010)). And they consistently rank corruption as among their most significant concerns.

Of course, corruption can take many forms, and those different forms have different kinds of implications for ordinary citizens. There is high-level theft of government funds by elected officials and bureaucrats. There's the insistence by government officials (and sometimes the private sector) on kickbacks in exchange for contracts. There is the hiring and awarding of contracts to political allies. There is the theft of public land for personal benefit. And bureaucrats of all levels may extort bribes to facilitate provision of public services or to enable citizens to avoid penalties for breaking certain laws and other codes.

Considering all these forms of corruption, especially grand corruption from the government treasury, it is hard to argue simultaneously that corruption is not particularly important but that things like cash transfers and public education are. How can one possibly finance the latter when corruption is bankrupting the public treasury?

Philip Kinisu, the former head of Kenya's Ethics and Anti-Corruption Commission, reported in 2016 that direct theft of resources by government officials amounted to 30 per cent of Kenya's annual budget.[2] That would more than offset the approximately 18 per cent of the government budget filled by overseas donors (World Bank, 2015). The US government suspended education funding in 2010 (Shiundu, 2010) and health funding in 2017 (BBC, 2017) due to concerns about corruption.

Then there is 'petty' corruption, where citizens and businesses give '*kitu kidogo*' – literally, 'something small' – to access government services, evade enforcement of certain laws, win contracts with government offices, and secure government jobs.[3] This kind of corruption matters, too. It enters into daily life and is largely reflected in indices such as the Corruption Perceptions Index published by Transparency International, which, in 2016, ranked Kenya 145 out of 176 countries. A 2009 World Bank assessment of the country's business climate found bribery to be a major inhibitor to growth, increasing costs at levels 'higher than all comparator countries'. The author found that 75 per cent of Kenyan firms had made informal payments to 'get things done' (Iarossi, 2009). According to the 2014 East Africa Bribery Index, about 12 per cent of Kenyans were asked for a bribe when interacting with a government institution, although that figure was much higher when dealing with the police (Table 7.1).

In the Kenya Financial Diaries, between 14 per cent and 25 per cent of respondent households paid a bribe during the course of the study. This estimate has a wide range given the expenditure categories where different types of bribes could be recorded. Among those expenditures that were clearly demarcated as bribes, the average bribe cost KES 759 ($8.93), a median of KES 200 ($2.35) within this low-income sample.[4] We were not able to systematically record the recipients of every bribe, although the stories often were recorded in interviewers' notes, helping us recount them throughout this chapter.

And while actual corruption levels are very hard to document, Kenyans believe that things are getting worse. In the latest Afrobarometer survey in Kenya, 67 per cent of citizens felt like corruption was getting even worse, and 71 per cent believed the government was doing a poor job of addressing the

Table 7.1 Likelihood and average cost of bribery when interacting with government in Kenya.

	Probability of paying a bribe when interacting with sector	Average cost of bribe	
Police	71.7%	KES 4,821	$54.78
Tax services	31.4%	KES 6,815	$77.44
County administration	25.9%	KES 4,942	$56.16
Land services	19.4%	KES 7,219	$82.03
Registry and licensing services	19.2%	KES 1,103	$12.53
Judiciary	15.7%	KES 7,885	$89.60
Educational institutions	13.4%	KES 2,095	$23.81
Medical and health services	10.5%	KES 881	$10.01
Utilities (water and electricity)	5.7%	KES 2,121	$24.10

Source: Transparency International, 2014, p. 67.

issue (Afrobarometer, 2019). In the PWC Kenya Family Business Survey, corruption had become – and remained – the most important concern of private business owners since 2014 (PwC, 2019).

Corruption, both grand and petty, has far-reaching implications. A 2009 World Bank study estimated that corruption cost Kenyan firms 4 per cent of annual revenues (Iarossi, 2009). In 2014, 17 international Chiefs of Mission in Kenya issued a joint op-ed in the Kenyan press lamenting the ways in which corruption was handicapping the fight against terrorism. Michela Wrong pointed out that a number of suspended deals from the major Anglo Leasing scandal[5] were linked to security-related contracts, including passport security, a forensic lab, and a military surveillance system, all of which might have helped prevent terrorist attacks and find and prosecute perpetrators (Wrong, 2014). Failing to curb terrorism both perpetuates risks to ordinary people's lives and hampers economic growth, most notably through its impact on the tourism sector (Kushner, 2013). Grand corruption diverts funds that could go into high-return infrastructure investments or pro-poor government programmes, like Kenya's free maternal healthcare initiative.[6] It makes it harder to pay and keep salary agreements with key government personnel, including teachers, doctors, and nurses, all of whom went on protracted strikes between 2015 and 2017. It is the lowest-income citizens – those who cannot afford private health and education – who bear the human costs of those strikes (see Chapter 6, 'Staying alive').

Runaway corruption also sends a message to ordinary citizens: 'Power is money.' It says that you win when 'your people' are in office. It says: 'Cheat or be left behind.'

The stories in this chapter demonstrate many of the immediate, direct, micro-level consequences of different forms of rent seeking employed by government officials. Our respondents' experiences highlight just how little agency individual Kenyans feel they can exercise in their relationship with government.[7]

Corruption and livelihoods: a counterproductive crackdown on *changaa*

One of the most vibrant supply chains incorporating Kenya's low-income families is that of home-brewed alcohol, primarily *changaa* (a clear alcohol distilled from sugar or molasses and yeast), although in the communities we studied it also includes *busaa* (a traditional beer made from fermented grains, usually maize or sorghum) and *mnazi* (palm wine). Not only is there a significant, seemingly inexhaustible market for such drinks, but production and distribution can be managed in loose networks around the country in ways that allow easy entry for low-capital producers. Homemade alcohol is one of the few products with a large market that can be manufactured by poor people with limited skills, education, and capital in rural communities and informal settlements where other earning opportunities are scarce. It also offers substantial profits and a relatively stable revenue stream throughout the year.

Given the illicit status of brewing – particularly of the informal way in which most small brewers operate – it was typically not the first choice of livelihood for families in our study. But it became attractive for women who needed to work at home, for widows who lost an income from a spouse, and for those with limited capacity for hard manual labour in farm-based *vibaruas* (casual day jobs).

A quick look at the incomes of brewers in the Diaries shows why. Comparing brewing with other small businesses in rural areas, the median brewing business generated three and a half times as much in profit as the median non-brewing business over a nine-month period. In our study, the median monthly household income for brewers in rural areas was KES 6,957 ($82) versus KES 5,649 ($66) for rural non-brewers. For low-income households, an extra KES 1,300 ($15.30) per month makes an enormous difference to living standards.

Not only was brewing lucrative; it was also flexible. Those who brewed in our study produced alcohol in batches as time and capital permitted. Some took time off when other opportunities arose, when capital was short, or when they were dealing with interruptions such as funerals. The brewing world was one they could move in and out of for the most part, given that demand was relatively stable and that there were no fixed recurrent costs like rent and salaries to cover. Especially for women in rural areas, particularly widows, very few alternative livelihood paths existed that offered similar levels of income, stability, and flexibility at similar levels of investment. The median brewing business started with just KES 600 ($7.05) (mean KES 1,225 ($14.41)). Most of those who brewed in our study did not drink themselves. Brewing was strictly business. And that business has paid off.

Rebecca, who we also read about in Chapter 5, 'Being a woman', earned a living from a combination of *changaa* proceeds and remittances from her adult children. The *changaa* became central to her livelihood after her husband committed suicide and her mother-in-law refused to allocate her a plot of land to grow food. There were few ways, apart from brewing, in which a widow with no land and six children to feed could earn a living in this rural area. Brewing fed her children and put at least some of them through secondary school.

Another respondent, Clementine, told us: 'In this area, if your husband dies, you start brewing.' Clementine's husband died when her children were still small, and brewing felt like the only viable, flexible option to earn enough to pay school fees. Because she didn't want people drinking around her children, Clementine brewed exclusively for two local wholesalers.

The *changaa* business had a relatively complex supply chain with differentiated roles. There appeared to be a very large number of small brewers, like our respondents, who produced in small quantities and sold to small wholesalers who aggregated and transported the brew to retailers. Some retailers also brewed themselves, but many simply bought from these distributors as a way of better specializing and managing risk. There were also larger producers that operated semi-formally and employed staff to brew at scale. Others made a living by providing the inputs needed for brewing, especially molasses and compressed brown sugar ('*sukari nguru*'), which produced a higher-value product. These suppliers often bought their stock directly from the sugar companies in Western Kenya, joined together to share the costs of shipping to brewing communities, and individually sold inputs to brewing clients on a regular basis. The complexity and organization of this supply chain were impressive. Nothing like it existed for any other product produced in the rural areas in our study.

Of course, the production and sale of *changaa* was also illegal. The extent to which that ban was enforced has shifted over time. During our study in 2013, enforcement was moderate, as reported by our respondents, requiring only periodic bribes to keep authorities at bay. However, in July 2015, President Uhuru Kenyatta initiated a nationwide crackdown on brewing. He cited both the vice of alcoholism among youth as well as recent deaths from the consumption of adulterated brew (Mwangi and Onyango, 2005). 'When you turn the youth into addicts of illegal alcohol you are crippling the society and the whole country,' he said. Brewers, he said, were in 'the business of death'.

There were real reasons to be concerned. In one incident in 2014, 94 people were killed from methanol poisoning while consuming the brew (Muchiri and Nyawira, 2014). At other times, brews and their chemical additives caused blindness. The large number of individual brewers throughout the country made it infeasible to test and enforce the quality of home-brewed alcohol. Hence, the President opted to enforce an outright ban, just as others had attempted in previous eras.

The crackdown began with highly visible raids on brewers in Central Kenya, which then spread to our respondents' communities. But if the experiences of our respondents are any indication, the actual outcome has not been what President Kenyatta intended. Instead of shutting down the brewers, businesses have consolidated; those who employed successful evasion tactics earned more than ever before. And those meant to enforce the crackdown – police, chiefs, and assistant chiefs – experienced windfall gains via the new bribes they were able to extort.

Even before the 2015 crackdown, most of our respondents involved with the *changaa* supply chain made regular payments to their assistant chief, who then insisted that local police leave the individuals alone. Annette, who supplied molasses to brewers, for example, negotiated an agreement with the assistant chief; she paid KES 500 ($5.88) per month to 'register' her business with him and be left alone. In this area, most of the brewers (in contrast to Annette, who was a supplier) paid the assistant chief KES 500 ($5.88) twice a month to keep him from directing the police their way. During the crackdown, regular payments of KES 500 ($5.88) per month were also due directly to the local police and KES 2,000 ($23.53) to the police from the next town. But if brewers were late in paying, they would be targeted by the police and be forced to pay bribes to avoid arrest or to be released from jail.

In May 2013, Stella and Duncan's home was raided by police officers when they were late with their bribes. Stella managed to escape but Duncan was caught. The police destroyed their brewing equipment and confiscated 20 litres of the brew, worth KES 2,800 ($33). Duncan was told that he would also need to do community service, but he bribed another officer with KES 1,000 ($11.76) to drop the case. After the officers left, Stella and Duncan realized that the police had stolen KES 15,000 ($176) of Duncan's savings that had been hidden under the mattress and KES 2,000 ($23.53) stashed in Stella's purse. Duncan was hoping to use that money to buy a calf. Stella's money was earmarked as her monthly *chama* (ROSCA) contribution. Both were upset but had little recourse. They couldn't complain about the theft without confessing publicly to their illegal business and risk facing formal prosecution.

Bribes required to avoid arrest were remarkably consistent among brewers, especially in this community: KES 500 ($5.88) was a regular payment to 'register' to avoid police harassment, KES 2,000 ($23.53) after arrest but before being taken to the remand cells, and KES 5,000 ($59) to be released after being taken to the cells. Brewers also deployed a strategy for *how* to pay the bribe: even if they had the money when the police showed up, they pretended otherwise and begged for permission to circulate among the neighbours to borrow the amount they needed. Respondents believed that if they just paid up, the police would think they always had money around and would never leave them alone.

The burden of enforcement of *changaa* laws had a particularly profound impact on our poorest respondents and on women. Fatima, for example, was separated from her ex-husband and couldn't manage her five children alone. One stayed with a relative and another was taken care of by the church. Three stayed with her. She lived in a one-room house with mud walls and a dirt floor in an informal settlement in Mombasa and got by on an average of KES 6,000 ($71) per month. After her arrest for transporting her stock, Fatima was unable to pay the requested bribe to the police and was sentenced to six months of house arrest. She continued to brew. Under house arrest, what else could she do to support her kids? Her occasional work doing laundry for KES 150 ($1.76) would not feed her children.

For our respondents, the crackdown on *changaa* meant that the cost of bribery increased. Elijah, for example, told us that the extra money he spent bribing police cut into his working capital. He used to both make brew and buy it from others to sell wholesale. However, because bulk purchasing required more time on the road transporting the product and was thus one of the riskier links in the supply chain, he decided to focus on his own brewing. But with irregular capital, he couldn't ensure a consistent supply. Some of his clients began buying from more reliable sources. He reduced his brewing schedule from three times a week to two. During our 2015 update interview, he told us that he had already parted with KES 29,000 ($341) in bribes in the months following the *changaa* crackdown. He dreamed of moving into fishing to replace brewing, but he estimated that he would need around KES 300,000 ($3,529) to buy fishing equipment. Saving that much money from his average monthly income of KES 15,400 ($181) while paying his daughter's secondary school fees seemed impossible. Even with the police harassment, he decided to keep brewing. He didn't see another viable option.

Nancy told us that the crackdown, while irritating, had not really hurt her business. Instead of both brewing and selling on a retail basis, she decided to stop brewing and focus on retail sales. It was easier to hide the finished product than the brewing equipment, and with a decrease in sellers, Nancy was able to increase her client base. She paid slightly more in bribes after the crackdown began.

After the crackdown, she told us, her contacts regularly let her know about raids planned in the area, at which time she would leave. Now that her kids were growing, she wanted to move the business to another place where her children wouldn't be exposed to the behaviour of clients. She found a new location, but the assistant chief warned her that, given its proximity to the main road, he couldn't protect her there.

Clementine was one of only two respondents who had stopped brewing by late 2015 (of 18 brewing in late 2013) in response to the crackdown. Her home brewing operation was raided by police from another community, whom she had not been paying. Because she was able to come up with the standard KES 2,000 ($23.53) bribe to avoid being taken to a cell, Clementine was let go. She continued brewing, though, until she became alarmed by the violence of the police from outside the community. A neighbour's home was raided at a time when only their daughter, a high school student, was at home. She refused to give the police the key for the home and they beat her badly and slashed her face. She barely survived. The thought that this might happen to her children made Clementine stop brewing. She hoped to survive on just the vegetables that she grew, supplemented by sales of assets when necessary; for example, she was forced to sell trees from the compound to pay for school fees. Although she was anxious about making ends meet without her brewing income, Clementine decided to wait until Uhuru Kenyatta leaves office before trying brewing again.

When the police went beyond their mandate – attacking the young woman or stealing Stella and Duncan's savings, for instance – victims did not feel that they could report the incidents. After all, they were engaged in illegal activity. They accepted that vulnerability was part of the job.

Disrupting brewing livelihoods – an income source that is a lifeline for many – had an impact on the economies of entire communities. In November 2016, we visited Beauty, a woman who had been getting by on a small tailoring business. Business was terrible, she said. More women had stopped brewing, so there was much less money for families to spend in the community. And without brewing, women were all trying to sell something – kale, tomatoes, maize – from their homes. They were competing with each other, selling the same things, and none of them were making money.

Changaa may indeed be a vice. Adulterated brews have most certainly claimed a number of lives in recent years. And yet the crackdown the President mandated through the police force appeared to be failing to effectively curb consumption while potentially exacerbating corruption among police and local administrators. It transferred wealth from small, poor, mostly female producers to corrupt officials.

The *changaa* ban – whether good or ill-advised – created an opportunity for rent seeking among enforcers. Genuine enforcement of the law, however, was nearly impossible when individual police officers had so much to gain. The ultimate result was that legislation, law enforcement, and the livelihoods of the poor were all undermined. As long as there is a market, the brewing will continue. It is one of the few economic activities that is working for the rural poor. Ruth, who put all of her children through school with income from brewing, explained: '*Kuchemsha ndio shamba yetu*' – 'Brewing is our land.'

Corruption and insecurity: petty bribery and the crippling of law enforcement

Bribery and crime

On 21 September 2013, terrorists associated with al-Shabaab stormed the Westgate shopping centre in Nairobi. Seventy-one people were killed. The military remained inside for the next four days; with little information coming from the shopping centre, Kenyans remained in shock as they watched the news coverage. The country was on edge, feeling vulnerable and under siege.

A couple of weeks later, we had trouble finding one of our respondents, Charlie. Charlie had missed the previous interview, so our field supervisor made special arrangements to meet him on a Sunday. She confirmed the meeting with him on Friday. At the scheduled meeting time, Charlie didn't show. He wasn't picking up his phone. *Mteja*, unreachable. By Tuesday, though, Charlie called back. He was ready to reschedule. And, he said, he had a story.

After the Westgate attack, Charlie and two friends heard that al-Shabaab affiliates were in the market for a chemical called selenium, allegedly used in making explosives. We could find no reference to the use of selenium in explosives; the chemical is actually used as an additive to glass, for making pigments, and as a treatment for dandruff (Royal Society of Chemistry, n.d.). These three friends coordinated to steal seven kilogrammes of the substance from one of their workplaces, a university lab. They were told that the street value was KES 10,000 ($118) per gram. None of the three had any sympathy for the terrorists, but this seemed like a business opportunity they couldn't pass up. If they could find a buyer for what they (erroneously) believed was an important bomb-making ingredient, all three would be rich. One of the friends found a buyer, a student, who was apparently also misinformed about selenium's chemical properties, but who did have sympathies for the terrorist group. The father of this student learned about the plan and reported the sellers to the police. The three were promptly arrested.

One of the friends was able to get in touch with a contact who had a friend at the Directorate of Criminal Investigations who was willing to help them get released one at a time for a bribe of KES 10,000 ($118) each. A week after his arrest, Charlie was simply released, and the case disappeared.

During the arrest, Charlie couldn't report for work and lost his job as a security guard, losing both his salary and the extra income he used to make from selling small items stolen from his employer. When we saw him in 2015, he told us he was shaken by the arrest. He had stopped stealing and was trying to get by on casual construction work until he could start a business of his own.

While this situation helped Charlie make some big changes in his life, what does it mean for the nation's security when a mere KES 10,000 ($118) is sufficient to release individuals explicitly aiming to abet terrorists? How can front-line officers insist on due process when they know that taking a suspect to jail may not lead to a court appearance, much less punishment for the crime? When citizens and police both understand this reality, it creates an environment in which extrajudicial killings of 'suspects' proliferate and where the public outcry against them is dampened (Stapele, 2016).

The terrorist threat has continued to plague Kenya well after the Westgate attack. Terrorists besieged a small community, Mpeketoni, in Lamu County, killing 49 people in June 2014. In other incidents, they stopped buses and massacred non-Muslim passengers. Al-Shabaab fighters overran Garissa University in April 2015, killing 147 individuals, the overwhelming majority students, many from poor backgrounds. Those who escaped, one of our respondents among them, will be traumatized forever. It took seven hours for the military's special forces to be deployed to the scene. While the slow response has been widely criticized in public, actions to prevent attacks like this – including tracking the behaviour of people like Charlie – are mostly hidden from the public eye and undermined by corruption throughout the security forces.[8]

Charlie was not our only respondent suspected – and arrested – for serious crimes. Another respondent was arrested for murder a few days after he came home with what the police said was a stolen motorbike. The owner had been found dead, and our respondent was the prime suspect. His wife believed that he had bought the motorbike through an informal arrangement with a friend. She was angry at him for not planning the purchase with her in advance, but she didn't think he was guilty of murder. We do not know if he was guilty or innocent. What we do know is that a bribe of KES 20,000 ($235) secured his release from jail and that he never went to court.[9] Afraid that the local community members would kill him themselves, he moved away for about a year and a half until the incident had blown over.

More often, though, our respondents were victims rather than perpetrators of crimes. They sought help from the police but didn't hold high hopes for justice. In one case, amidst the tension leading up to the 2013 elections, the daughter of one of our respondents was raped in the informal settlement in Nairobi where the family lived. This family was from a minority ethnic group in this part of the community. The girl had been out collecting discarded card-board box scraps to help light the charcoal stove and heat bathwater before school when she was approached by a neighbour and raped. She said nothing to her mother, but a teacher noticed that she was distracted and walking with difficulty. She eventually coaxed the story from the girl. This teacher called the girl's mother to the school, but she was afraid to go at first, worried that the school just wanted to collect its outstanding fee balance. When the mother heard what had happened, her first reaction was to discipline her daughter for not telling her immediately. She took the girl to the nearby health centre and reported the case to the chief and the police. The police arrested the suspected rapist, who was from the majority ethnic group in the area. But the other neighbours quickly pooled together KES 5,000 ($59) to bribe the police and get the young man released. He was never tried. Our respondent, a very poor single mother, felt defeated and trapped; she could not even afford to move away from the young man who had raped her daughter and the neighbours who helped him escape the consequences.

Respondents saw first-hand the way in which bribery created impunity. One respondent, an older woman in a rural area, had five goats stolen from her home. She knew the young man who took the goats; he was a student nearing the end of his secondary school education. She reported him to the police, but the young man's parents paid a bribe for his release. Not long afterwards, the same boy was arrested for trying to rape a young girl in the community.

Another respondent, Alex, was kidnapped by armed thugs at his business in Nairobi. They came into the shop in the morning, posing as police. They said they had caught someone selling stolen gas cylinders and that the person claimed to have purchased the cylinders from his shop. The 'police' lured Alex into their car, explaining that they needed him to identify the accused thief. Once inside, the thieves drew their guns and demanded money. They took him to a number of ATMs – travelling several kilometres outside the city – to steal all of Alex's savings, a total of KES 4,000 ($47). Alex was eventually released later the same day. He never reported the kidnapping to the police, telling us that they wouldn't do anything anyway. He was probably right. In 2016, the National Economic Survey reported that the police themselves were involved in a third of all *reported* crimes in the country (KNBS, 2016).

In one very troubling account, we saw some indication of just how far police crime could extend. Kevin, the teenage son of one of our Nairobi respondents, became involved in a gang in 2015. His mother lamented his stubbornness, his refusal to help at home, and his odd hours. However, she didn't know about his gang activity until he landed in hospital with serious injuries following a clash with a rival gang. While he was in the hospital, four of his fellow gang members were killed while trying to rob an M-Pesa agent. According to our respondent, the mother of one of the slain boys had paid some police officers to kill all the other surviving gang members in revenge for getting her son caught up in the mess. Kevin was said to be on the list, and the last time we spoke with his mother she had sent him into hiding upcountry. She did not know what to do to save her son's life.

Crime – particularly theft – was rampant in respondent communities, often resulting in violence. The temptation of easy money was a strong force, particularly in the absence of effective law enforcement. Our households lived in constant fear for their own security and that of their children. On every visit, we asked our respondents whether at any time between visits they felt physically unsafe in their homes. Thirty-one per cent of our respondent households said yes at least once. About 3 per cent of households per year experienced a violent attack or mugging. Fourteen per cent of respondents in our 2015 update had experienced theft in the two years between the Diaries and the update. Violence was particularly pronounced in urban slums. One respondent reflected: 'Insecurity is the order of the day in this Mathare. We sleep not knowing what can happen tomorrow, and we wake up by the grace of God.'

While slow to act on legitimate crimes, police were persistent in their harassment of respondents for minor traffic violations and imagined offences as a means of extorting money. This went well beyond those involved in the *changaa* industry. Fifteen per cent of our households had someone arrested by the police during the Diaries study. They were arrested for walking at night, not carrying ID, buying a handkerchief from a hawker, carrying their own sewing machine without a receipt on their person, operating motorbikes after dark, and selling food on the roadside. Even if they were guilty of no crime at all, they would part with some cash (typically around $2–$5) to be released and get back to their lives.

Angry at the repeated harassment and arrest of her husband, one woman, Cindy, decided to stand her ground. The community stood with her. Our researcher wrote in her interview journal about the day:

> Today Cindy did the unbelievable and the whole community is full of praises for what a committed wife she is and how she loves her husband. Today in [the community] police were arresting all people thought to be taking or selling illicit brew, and Rafa had left the house to go and buy

---

Box 7.1 Examples of respondent statements about insecurity in Nairobi's urban slums.

- 'I really want to get out of this slum. I am not secure here, and crime is the order of the day. For my growing sons, it's not a good environment.'
- 'Yes I really feel unsafe. Did you know that last week children, eight children, were burned to death in a day care? Someone started the fire. Imagine! Mathare people don't have mercy.'
- 'This place is dangerous. Two days ago, just outside here, two guys were murdered. We found two bodies lying there in the morning, and funny enough, when they were screaming no one even opened the door.'
- 'Can you imagine? An army officer was killed down there at the petrol station. [This area] is very unsafe but we must be here to make a living.'

airtime. On his way back he met with the police, community police, and the area chief who arrested him as one of those who drink.

Cindy was in the house, and she had no idea what was happening outside. Then, one of the women who sells brew came to inform her that Rafa had been arrested. Cindy rushed to the scene and found that Rafa had truly been arrested, and he was being dragged away. When Rafa got to an electricity post, he refused to move and held it tight. That's when Cindy joined him and demanded to know why her husband was being arrested and yet he doesn't even drink alcohol. [Rafa is an observant Muslim.] The team insisted that they will talk at the police station, while Cindy insisted that they will talk there and then as no one was going to the police station since they don't have money to bribe them. One of the police tried to slap her, but she slapped him back.

Cindy decided to make a scene there while insulting them on how they like arresting people arbitrarily so that they can get bribes, but today they have touched the wrong people, and she was ready even if it meant shedding blood. The whole community joined in defending them as everyone knows that Rafa doesn't take alcohol. The police had no other choice but to release Rafa. So, today Cindy is the heroine and talk of the community of what a good wife she is. Most people are saying that they can't even think of picking a fight with her.

From their personal experiences, respondents seemed to feel that, if you want help from the police, you must bribe them. And if you want to get out of custody, you must also bribe them. It's an endless, farcical cycle. David, a respondent in a rural area, had taken in one of his teenage nephews. At some point between the Diaries and the update, the nephew was accused by another man of beating his three-month-old baby. The claim seemed a bit ridiculous, but David went with his nephew to the chief who would hear the details of the case. After some investigation, the chief determined that the case was concocted by the accuser, who hoped that David would give him some money. But, according to our respondent, the accuser instead went to the next big town and bribed the police to arrest David's nephew anyway. He was taken to the police station at night and locked in a cell. David went to the station and paid a KES 10,000 ($118) 'bond' as well as a KES 5,000 ($59) bribe, without which the police refused to help him at all. David had to borrow all of this from neighbours and still owed them KES 12,000 ($141) when we talked to him last. Feeling overwhelmed by this additional expense, David moved his children from a private to a public school.

Perhaps because of how little trust there was in the police (and the courts), when something went wrong, our respondents were much more likely to first report to the chief, instead of the police. Chiefs in Kenya are not traditional leaders; rather, their office is the most local level of the public administration, and (in theory) candidates are competitively recruited. They are not necessarily assigned to support areas that they know well or to which they have any special affiliation. When constituents approach a chief, he or she tries to sort out the testimonies of both parties and, where possible, broker some kind of agreement between them in lieu of turning the case over to the legal authorities. Most theft, rape, and domestic violence cases our respondents told us about were managed first by the chief and often resolved at that level. For example, one respondent complained to the chief that his avocados had been stolen and that he had seen the thieves selling them in the market. The two parties were called to the chief's office, where the thief was then forced to pay the respondent the value of the stolen goods.

But the chief is not an agent of law enforcement. Thus, agreements brokered by chiefs are unlikely to be legally enforced. And someone running an illegal business can still turn to the chief for assistance. This was particularly true of moneylenders,[10] who would often take delinquent debtors to the chief as a means of pressuring them to pay. This wasn't very effective, but it was one of the only tools informal moneylenders had to try to enforce repayment.

When legitimate justice systems break down, communities often fill the gap. Our respondents told us about a number of instances where communities resorted to mob justice when confronted with crime, especially theft. In one rural community on the coast, a group of boys who had been stealing from the community decided to confess and beg the forgiveness of community members. Instead, they were killed by the crowd. In one case, a respondent's 13-year-old son was caught with a stolen bicycle, and the owner wanted to kill him. This time the community talked him down, as the punishment did not fit the crime.

The police were also known to kill suspects without due process.[11] Our respondents sympathized, as they also wanted 'thugs' off the street and out of their neighbourhoods. When one respondent's good friend was killed by the police during a 'clean-up campaign', he assumed that they had done the right thing. The official word was that the police were killing terrorists, and he seemed to accept this explanation. 'I was shocked to learn that a person I know very well was involved in terrorism,' he said. 'You never know, anyone can be a criminal.'

The upside of discretion

Even with all their flaws, once in a while, we also heard about the police trying to use their flexibility and discretion within the system to do the right thing. In one rural community, for example, our respondent Magdalene was struggling with her son who had got into drugs. He was stealing from her and other households in the area to get money for his vices. Magdalene herself asked the police to arrest him, hoping that it would shake him up and instil some discipline. They arrested him and held him in the local jail for two weeks before calling Magdalene. If they were to keep him in custody, he would be transferred to a national prison. There, they told her, he was likely to continue using drugs and even become a more hardened criminal. Instead, they suggested he undergo a rehab programme and serve his sentence under house arrest. Magdalene listened. She put together the KES 30,000 ($353) for his treatment, and the last time we saw her, her son had been home and sober for a year. She was cautiously optimistic that he might recover, given this second chance.

Corruption in recruitment

Given the regular salaries and extra 'tips' that come from a job in the police or military, it's no wonder that young people from low-income communities aspire to these positions. Two of our respondents invested rather large sums as bribes to get their children jobs in the security forces, and they really paid off. One respondent, long a struggling vendor of fried potatoes, saw her chance for a better life when her son became eligible for army recruitment. She took a loan of KES 40,000 ($471) from Kenya Women's Finance Trust (a women-focused microfinance institution) and borrowed another KES 20,000 ($235) from family and friends. Her daughter chipped in KES 10,000 ($118) and her husband rounded up another KES 10,000 ($118). They pooled this all together for a bribe of KES 80,000 ($941) to have their son accepted into the army. It worked. And it changed everything. Her son sent money every month. Her stress was gone. 'Now, if I have a problem, the solution is just a phone call away,' she said. She didn't regret the bribe; it changed her life. The income her daughter earned after migrating to Dubai paled in comparison to what her son was making in the Kenyan military.

Bribes in police and military recruitment are fairly well known. Testimony appearing in the Truth, Justice, and Reconciliation Commission's report states:

> The other issue which I have followed with the authorities is the recruitment of youth into the army, police, prisons and AP [Administration Police] service. During the recruitment exercise, money changes hands. If you cannot part with KES 60,000, your son cannot be employed. We formed a committee of 40 elders from this district and went to Nairobi to complain about these malpractices, but nothing has happened so far. We have not succeeded. (TJRC, 2013: 102)

A July 2014 recruitment exercise for the National Police Service was so tainted by corruption that the Independent Police Oversight Authority went to court to have the process annulled. The court cancelled the recruitment exercise completely. Although President Uhuru Kenyatta instructed the National Police Service to ignore the ruling and train the recruits anyway, he eventually had to rescind that order (Hope, 2017).

Some argue that corruption is fuelled by low salaries.[12] However, even the lowest-level police salary, set at KES 17,000 ($200) per month (those with a university degree start at KES 36,000 ($423) a month) (Agutu, 2017), compared quite favourably with the median salary in our sample of KES 7,000 ($82) per month for the entire household. Even the formal pay of the police alone would be a substantial increase in income for most families, before considering any irregular payments.

'Taxed' for access to government services

Our respondents looked to government to provide a range of services. Government is the sole provider of essential official documents, such as birth certificates, identification cards, and passports, as well as land titles and land transfer paperwork. Such documents were essential for many government and private interactions. Children could not sit for KPCE exams (when leaving primary school) without a birth certificate, which was why many parents began to chase down these certificates when their children were approaching their last year of primary school. You could not open a bank account, register a SIM card, or (officially) transact on M-Pesa without a national ID. Lacking a land title meant that you would struggle to sell your property or you would have to sell at a lower price. Not having a title opened up room for disputes among family members and others who claimed ownership of the land. Transfers became messy and got tangled in long court battles, destroying the finances of both parties. Lacking title and other documentation on property also meant that it could not be used for collateral with most formal lenders.

Apart from these administrative functions, government was also a major provider of healthcare, education, water, and electricity. In recent years, the government has made strides to make more of these services accessible for low-income people, particularly in terms of healthcare and electricity. The government eliminated user fees in public primary care health facilities and made maternity care at public facilities free (See Chapter 6, 'Staying alive'). In 2014, the government and the World Bank started pushing for much lower-cost power connections, including free connections to beneficiaries in some very low-income areas. As a result, in two years, the government's power company added one million connections per year, claiming to cover 60 per cent of the population.

Our respondents were thrilled by these advances; every service actually delivered by government was a gift. However, when they were denied free maternity care because healthcare workers were on strike or when they could not access the benefits of their government-issued health insurance (which they have paid for), they were rarely surprised. Low-level administrators served as gatekeepers to government services. Ordinary people felt coerced into paying. Rather than outraged, they felt resigned. And, sometimes, that system also allowed them to bend the rules in their favour.

Access to electricity

Let's take the example of electricity. When we began our study in 2012, 26 per cent of our respondent households had electricity connected to their homes. The rest aspired to this luxury, not only for higher-quality lighting, but also to charge phones, light their businesses at night, enable children to study, and regularly listen to radio and watch TV, especially the nightly news. But even before the government and World Bank subsidy programme to extend connections, our respondents complained about the extra charges that the staff from the Kenya Power and Light Company (KPLC) demanded to install connections.

One rural respondent, Rosemary, was the wife of a police officer who lived and worked in the city. The two had been waiting more than a year for KPLC to install their connection. They were willing to pay the full price (which they anticipated to be around KES 50,000 ($588)), but they still could not lure KPLC staff to their home. Our respondent wanted to bribe them, knowing that was how her neighbours got their connections, but her husband refused.[13] In the end, the pair invested in a solar home system and did not connect to the power grid at all.

Once the subsidized connection programme started, many of our respondent households were able to connect. Twenty-five of them connected in a two-year period between 2013 and 2015. But the price for connections varied widely, depending on bribes negotiated between households and personnel (or contractors) working in the area. In just one slum area where a number of new connections were made, the 'price' ranged from free to about KES 4,000 ($47). One respondent was told that she didn't qualify for one of the free connections, but she paid a bribe of KES 1,000 ($11.76) – and suddenly she qualified. Another who did qualify for a free connection but who was not at home when they visited her part of the neighbourhood was told that they would come back only if she could come up with KES 2,000 ($23.53) to make it worth their time. She could not.

Bribes also served to override disconnections due to non-payment. A number of respondents paid frequent, small bribes (typically KES 500 ($5.88)) to area KPLC staff sent to disconnect those with outstanding arrears. For several, this was a perpetual habit, rather than a one-off occurrence.[14]

Identity cards and birth certificates

The process of securing or replacing basic identity documents such as birth certificates and national identification cards could be daunting for our respondents, especially in rural areas. In addition to the small official fees charged for these services, applicants paid for transportation to follow up on their applications as well as bribes solicited by government clerks to 'facilitate' or expedite processing.

Kathleen in Mombasa was going through a particularly hard time when her son started his final year of primary school. 'I have never known happiness since I've been married,' she told our researcher. Her husband had disappeared, leaving her to handle all the household finances alone, and she was incredibly stressed about all of this when she went to the government office to apply for her son's birth certificate. The clerk asked her for a bribe. She had only KES

500 ($5.88) to her name at that moment, but she handed it over. 'This is only a deposit,' he told her. 'More will be due when the certificate is ready.'

For Rachel in rural Makueni, the frequent trips to follow up on the certificate became a major burden. She had to travel from her home to the county office in Wote seven times over three months, and each trip cost her KES 400 ($4.71) and the better part of a day. After the seventh trip, she paid for the certificates even though they weren't ready and gave a clerk in the office KES 150 ($1.76) to pick up the certificates for her when they were.

Those who could afford to circumvented the normal channels to secure needed documents. Greta, from one of the richest households in our study, lost her ID. She couldn't remember her number and didn't have a copy of her birth certificate. Knowing the local ID office would not be helpful, she paid a 'friend' KES 2,000 ($23.53) to search for her name and get a new ID processed within a week. It worked. Others, especially those without means or connections, simply went without, sometimes with dire consequences. In one rural household, for example, the husband paid for National Health Insurance Fund (NHIF) cover, but his wife could not make use of it because she had no ID. Apparently, avoiding the headache of securing an ID was more valuable than the substantial benefits of having one. Many delayed for years before replacing lost and stolen IDs, given the financial and opportunity costs involved.

Both the hassles of securing key documents and the frustration of managing without them were 'normal'. In the latest Afrobarometer survey, 39 per cent of those who needed a new permit or government document had to pay a bribe to get it (Afrobarometer, 2019). By and large, for low-income Kenyans, the system functions exactly as they expect it to – as a system of private favours paid for by bribes.[15]

Healthcare

The same respondent who had refused to pay a bribe for a rural electricity connection had a stroke the year before our update interview. Luckily, his wife quickly got him to the hospital and he was transferred to the top referral hospital in the country. As a police officer, he was covered by NHIF, government health insurance for which he had been paying for many years. But when his wife went to settle his hospital bill, the cashiers demanded a bribe in order to accept the insurance. Distraught and outraged, his wife went to the superior police officers and requested their help in convincing the cashiers to accept the insurance, which eventually they did.

Cashiers at health facilities had substantial leverage, given the massive bills that families accumulated when someone was seriously injured or sick. When Kevin, the gang member, was badly beaten and stabbed in a clash with a rival gang, he was admitted to a government hospital for three months and accumulated a bill of KES 150,000 ($1,764), an impossible sum for his mother to pay. Then she learned about a scheme in which hospital staff would, for a fee, smuggle out patients unable to pay their bills. Initially, she was told that the price for this 'service' was KES 30,000 ($353), but they negotiated down to KES 20,000 ($235), half paid upfront and half upon successful escape. To pay, our respondent borrowed money from three different friends. Her welfare group of 60 members then contributed KES 300 ($3.52) each to help her pay back those loans.

In other cases, hospital staff colluded with patients to help them register and pay backdated NHIF premiums *after* a bill had accumulated. Corruption within health facilities undermines government health financing strategies. Even if some low-income people ultimately benefit, it is impossible to determine how much cheaper above-board treatment could be for everyone if the system had less leakage.

Land titles and transfers

Nina was a single woman who worked as a caretaker at a local Nairobi school, taking care of the students who boarded there. During the Diaries, she earned KES 8,000 ($94) per month; out of that amount, she diligently saved KES 2,000 ($23.53) in a commitment savings account. Towards the end of the study, Nina's pastor told her about a group of squatters who were coming together to buy a piece of land. Once they purchased the larger parcel, they would subdivide it into individual plots, a common practice for land on the outskirts of urban areas in Kenya. Nina was thrilled. For KES 20,000 ($235), she would get a plot on which she dreamed of building rental units to supplement her salary. She withdrew money from her commitment savings, bought her plot, and began constructing a perimeter wall there. When we closed the Diaries, she was waiting for an allotment letter confirming her ownership of the plot. She told us that making this purchase was the proudest accomplishment of her life.

When we came back two years later, Nina was crushed. She had spent another KES 70,000 ($823) to finish the perimeter wall around her new plot. One day she went to visit the plot with her sister to discuss exactly how they would develop the land. While there, she found a group of people also eyeing the plot. She asked what they were doing and learned that they were members of the group of squatters that had 'sold' her the land. One of them told her that they were planning to bring down the wall she had built, since the land did not belong to her. The land, they said, belonged to a politician, and there was an open case in court to determine its ownership. Nina protested, explaining that she had already paid for the land, but the others laughed, saying, 'How can you buy a plot of land in Nairobi at KES 20,000?' The land was reclaimed, and Nina never heard about it again. She lost her KES 20,000 ($235) and the KES 70,000 ($823) spent on the perimeter wall. Deflated, she said that she would not even consider buying another piece of land again.

Sadly, Nina's story was not unique. Obtaining legal documentation for land purchases was no easy task. Corruption among land brokers and sellers, and within government land offices, made proving ownership before and after a purchase fraught with risk. Even without any particular complications, obtaining a title could easily take several years and improprieties could take decades to come to light. These challenges were layered on top of complicated registry systems prone to manipulation, large swaths of historically untitled or improperly titled land, complex and heated family disputes over land ownership and transfer, and gender norms about ownership that sometimes conflicted with legal processes. All of this risk was embedded into assets that were incredibly important – and high value – especially for low-income people.

Inspired by the work of Hernando de Soto, many economists and governments recognize the importance of protecting property rights as a means to allow people to use their land as collateral. In Kenya at the time of our study, titling for the purpose of reducing fraud was a much more urgent concern.[16] Land was the most important source of wealth for our respondents. It was also aspirational: the most important and most expensive purchase many would ever make. But many, like Nina, were infrequent buyers, without experience or adequate information about such transactions, and they were particularly susceptible to scams or their own misunderstanding about legal processes and risks. One bad deal could cost them many years of saving and investment.

Even very savvy buyers have run into conflicts over improper titling. In 2016, local newspapers covered a story in which former President Moi allegedly sold the same plot of land to three separate buyers, all individuals and institutions of significant means and sophistication, including a university and the head of one of the country's largest banks. An ordinary person is left wondering if it is possible for anyone to do an honest land deal.

When Felisters bought a piece of land, it was a major accomplishment. She had gotten up the courage to leave her husband after he had come home with a second wife without her consent. He had expected the two women to happily share one home. After struggling to put her children through school, Felisters eventually saved enough to buy a plot worth KES 100,000 ($1,176) on her own. The owner assured her that he would transfer the official title to her when it was ready. Years later, he finally confessed that he had no title. To obtain one, Felisters would need another KES 10,000 ($118) to bribe the land office to help with her case. When we last saw her, there was still no resolution. She was incredibly stressed about finding the money she needed and anxious about the security of the huge investment she had made.

Some of the land disputes our respondents faced stretched over years through inefficient court processes. That they were often family matters added a layer of discomfort and tension. All lived in uncertainty while the costly court procedures played out.

One example was Kombo, who retired to his rural home several years before the study, even though the family land was in dispute. He told us that he lived as a squatter since his own land was inhabited by others. His great-grandfather had told some friends that they could graze on his land, since he wasn't using it. But, when the great-grandfather died, those who had been using the land went to court, claiming the land as their own. The dispute had been passed down through the generations. When the survey was completed, another name – not Kombo's – was assigned to the farm. Still, he thought he would get a title for the place where he was staying when residents in the area more generally received their titles. If not, he said, he would resist eviction through the courts. There was one thing he was sure of: the land dispute that had been around for generations would take many more years to ever conclude through the courts.

Denied justice

The justice system is supposed to be something that protects the poor and marginalized, by resolving disputes and ensuring accountability for wrongdoing. But getting a justice system right is difficult even in resource-rich settings. The complications are tremendous in resource-poor settings, where there is not enough money for proper investigations and legal representation, where the courts are overburdened with caseloads and by inefficient management. Corruption disrupts the process even more, increasing the power differential between rich and poor.

Our respondents were willing to use the courts for high-stakes disputes – often around land – but at a substantial cost, knowing that the outcome would either be bought through bribery or be left to a high-stakes gamble. There was little hope of a truly 'just' outcome. For many other legal issues, however, our respondents expected in advance that the pursuit of justice would be so slow and so costly as to make it silly to even try to right wrongs (although Kombo saw this reality as an advantage).

Some found themselves involved in court cases anyway, and they paid the price. Patrick, an artisan in Nairobi, was accused of purchasing stolen metals for his *jiko*-making (charcoal cookstove-making) business. He had spent just KES 3,500 ($41) on the metals. But, forced to defend himself, he hired a lawyer and spent more than KES 50,000 ($588) to resolve the case. He was eventually absolved of the accusations and told that he could go and collect the metals. But he was exhausted and didn't want to throw good money after bad. 'I have already spent so much money,' he told us, 'I have to think about my responsibilities.' Another respondent had been the victim of a car accident in Mombasa, where her legal case was pending for more than five years. She periodically had to travel for hearings in Mombasa at great expense, with no end in sight.

Knowing the costs of pursuing justice makes many, like Nina, give up without even trying to right the wrongs against them. Several of our respondents were approached by a local organization calling itself 'Move On Development'. The agency promised to give them loans if they started saving with them. The women saved hefty sums and paid additional sums in the form of 'fees' and 'insurance' just to apply for their loans. They were told that the savings were being collected by Move On's representative and deposited in a bank on their behalf. But the women got nervous when they never received their promised loans. When they asked for their savings back, they were told the money was not available. The women went to Move On Development's office to seek help. There, they were told that the agency's collector had stolen their money and had bought land. The organization did not offer to help them get their money back, and instead just sent them away.

Outraged on their behalf, we reported the case to the Central Bank. After all, unlicensed institutions are not allowed to accept deposits. Nothing happened. Two years later, our respondents all gave up, not one seeking any kind of judgment against Move On for stealing their savings. When asked why, the response was nearly universal: 'We have already lost so much, we cannot afford to lose any more.' They couldn't come up with the extra money to visit the police, to hire lawyers, to go to court, to follow up for years on end. They were trying to cut their losses. Meanwhile, Move On continues to operate, taking savings, and – purportedly – making loans through rural women's groups.

Fixing what's broken

Kenya's 2013 constitution sets out a powerful vision of equality and rights for its citizens. But today that vision is aspirational, and the depth of the governance problems that prevail in this vibrant and capable society undermine that vision and, along with it, national unity.

The challenges faced by our respondents show the nature of the problem and the impacts on ordinary people. They are not as good at pointing towards solutions.

Widespread corruption is hard to beat back. According to the theoretical model developed by Murphy, Shleifer, and Vishny, corruption has a snowball effect. Rent seeking by some invites rent seeking by others. Rent seeking looks more attractive than productive activities, crowding out growth. After reaching a tipping point where returns on rent seeking are equal to productive activities, rent seekers crowd in, pushing down productive activities and resulting in an economy stuck with both low growth and large numbers of rent seekers. Escape from this 'bad equilibrium' requires massive overhauls that eliminate large numbers of rent seekers, which is a huge challenge from a policy perspective (Murphy et al., 1993).

If Kenya is not yet in this 'bad equilibrium', helpful policy responses include increasing returns to private enterprise/productive activities and decreasing returns to rent seeking (through, for example, more stringent enforcement and the removal of opportunities for rent seeking). If Kenya is already at the 'bad equilibrium' stage, all of that must be complemented with a massive effort aimed at removing rent seekers from the system, getting them out of their rent-seeking roles and into productive activities (or into jail).

New technologies offer the possibility to reduce some forms of corruption. Well-functioning e-government systems, for example, can make it easier and faster to access government services such as IDs and birth certificates. A major initiative called eCitizen seeks to automate government administration and payments and has shown some early promise in improving efficiency in some services.[17] Electronic databases, GPS, and blockchain technologies could improve the reliability of land and vehicle registries. Case management software and electronic arbitration could improve the efficiency and fairness of some legal decisions and law enforcement practices. But for such systems to work, they must be backed by officials and institutions with a genuine will to make them reliable, efficient, transparent, and robust. These are not easy benchmarks to reach.

At its heart, widespread corruption is not a technical problem – although there can be partial technical solutions. Ultimately, it is a problem of norms and incentives. Dan Ariely, who has studied the behavioural elements of dishonesty, says: 'Corruption is when you know something is wrong and you don't care … And "everybody else is doing it" is a good method for getting people to not care' (Clark, 2013). Truly tackling corruption in Kenya will mean reaching a new equilibrium where rent seeking is seen as a serious moral failing. Those who are tempted to steal need to feel profound and deep shame at the idea of exploiting others. And, at least today, there is no app for that.

Endnotes

1. For examples, see the comments in this newspaper article (Mwanzia, 2016).
2. See Reuters (2016). Kinisu was later forced to resign over his own alleged role in the National Youth Service scandal.
3. Another major type of corruption that we don't have space to cover here, but that is important to Kenyans, is the improper and possibly illegal acquisition of land by government officials. The legality or illegality of many of these acquisitions has not been fully determined, although supposed land grabs are a source of deep historical resentment and a cause of some protests, including one in which schoolchildren were tear-gassed during a protest against a 'land grab' of their playground by a hotel allegedly owned by Deputy President William Ruto (see <http://www.cnn.com/2015/01/20/africa/kenya-playground-children-tear-gassed/index.html>; <http://www.the-star.co.ke/news/2015/01/22/weston-hotel-owner-and-dp-ruto-have-been-friends-since-yk-92_c1071315>; <http://www.the-star.co.ke/news/2016/01/11/i-built-weston-hotel-ruto-admits_c1273316> (all accessed 25 August 2017).
4. There are multiple categories of expenditure that could be considered bribes, one very explicit, the others embedded in things such as 'fines' and 'penalties'. We provide a range that covers the explicit to the possible, but look at costs only for explicit bribes, which may be an underestimation of overall bribe value.
5. The Anglo Leasing scandal refers to an extensive set of fraudulent contracts made by the Kenyan government in the late 1990s and early 2000s for services never delivered or massively overpriced. One of these contracts

was for about $33 million through a fictitious company, Anglo Leasing, for the supply of new, high-tech passports.

6. See Gaffey (2017). The 2016 Afya House scandal was linked to the disappearance of funds earmarked for free maternity care.

7. The experiences of our respondents – as told to us – are inherently one-sided. We know only as much as the respondents tell us. In their totality, the stories tell us not about the absolute truth of any given case or incident but some more general truths about low-income Kenyans' experience of their interactions with government.

8. The Kenya Defence Forces (KDF) are accused of colluding with al-Shabaab in lucrative smuggling operations. The KDF is also accused of extensive rights violations during deployments. Auditor General reports cite suspected theft and procurement irregularities, and the recruitment of KDF soldiers is often rife with corruption, with recruits paying bribes for entry. In December 2016, the President signed into law a new act that limits civilian oversight of military spending, further weakening corruption controls in the defence forces (Journalists for Justice, 2015; Mutahi, 2015; Kasami, 2015; Ombati, 2015).

9. When we followed up in November 2016 to confirm the details of this case, the respondent told us that the KES 20,000 was for 'bail' and that they were given a receipt. I find this hard to believe, since this is a huge sum that they then never followed up on for a refund. Our respondent says that the man who sold him the motorbike went to court and is now in jail. We are unable to confirm whether or not this is true.

10. Microfinance institutions also historically have used chiefs to track and attempt to force payment from delinquent borrowers.

11. Extrajudicial killings of young men in Mathare have now been documented more rigorously by the Mathare Social Justice Centre (2017).

12. However, there is some empirical evidence suggesting that higher salaries do not alone reduce bribery (Foltz and Opoku-Agyemang, 2015).

13. We do not know if he was an all-round honest policeman. Households in our study are composed of those who live together and share resources. So in situations like this, we measure the income to Rebecca's household, which includes her husband's income only when it reaches Rebecca via remittances.

14. Median electricity payments in our sample were KES 400 ($ 4.70), but this includes prepaid meters and informal connections. We did not distinguish among those possibilities in the recording of cash flows.

15. In late 2013, the government began introducing Huduma Centres in all counties to help citizens navigate these services. Our study is not helpful in assessing whether these centres have had an impact on these processes. The core of our study was finished before the centres opened, and, given the relative infrequency of these needs, it is not something that came up often in the follow-up interviews in 2015.

16. In fact, using land titles as loan collateral is a relatively new practice. Formal banks have historically been too distant, both geographically and culturally, for rural Kenyans to use. But even as banking has spread, using titles as collateral has grown. The practice is complicated by fraudulent

titles and the need to have the consent of the extended family, who typically own familial land together.
17. However, it also proved to be a channel for extracting rents for high-level government officials via an unauthorized fee collected by an unauthorized company leading up to the 2017 elections (Wasuna, 2017).

References

Afrobarometer (2019) 'Kenya, Round 7, 2018'. Data available from: <http://www.afrobarometer.org> (accessed 15 December 2019).

Agutu, N. (2017) 'Police service reviews salaries, lowest paid cops to get 19% raise', *The Star*, 28 July. Available from: <https://www.the-star.co.ke/news/2017/07/28/police-service-reviews-salaries-lowest-paid-cops-to-get-19-raise_c1606298> (accessed 25 August 2017).

BBC (2017) 'US cuts Kenya health aid money over corruption allegations', *BBC News*, 9 May. Available from: <http://www.bbc.com/news/world-africa-39857470> (accessed 25 August 2017).

BBC World Service (2010) 'Global poll: corruption is world's most talked about problem', BBC, 9 December. Available from: <http://www.bbc.co.uk/pressoffice/pressreleases/stories/2010/12_december/09/corruption.shtml> (accessed 25 August 2017).

Blattman, C. (2012) 'Corruption and development: not what you think?', 5 November. Available from: <https://chrisblattman.com/2012/11/05/corruption-and-development-not-what-you-think/> (accessed 24 August 2017).

Booth, D. (2015) 'Five myths about governance and development', ODI, 16 February. Available from: <https://www.odi.org/comment/9274-five-myths-about-governance-and-development> (accessed 24 August 2017).

Campos, N.F., Dimova, R.D., and Saleh, A. (2010) 'Whither corruption? A quantitative survey of the literature on corruption and growth', SSRN Scholarly Paper 1718935, Social Science Research Network (SSRN), Rochester NY. Available from: <https://papers.ssrn.com/abstract=1718935> (accessed 25 August 2017).

Clark, D. (2013) 'Dan Ariely on why we're all a little dishonest – and what to do about it', *Forbes*, 29 October. Available from: <https://www.forbes.com/sites/dorieclark/2013/10/29/dan-ariely-on-why-were-all-a-little-dishonest-and-what-to-do-about-it/> (accessed 25 August 2017).

Foltz, J. and Opoku-Agyemang, K.A. (2015) 'Do higher salaries lower petty corruption? A policy experiment on West Africa's highways', Working Paper, International Growth Centre, London. Available from: <https://assets.publishing.service.gov.uk/media/57a08986e5274a27b2000111/89108_IGC_Foltz-Opoku-Agyemang-2016-Working-paper.pdf> (accessed 10 February 2020).

Gaffey, C. (2017) 'Why the US suspended $21 million in health aid to Kenya', *Newsweek*, 10 May. Available from: <http://www.newsweek.com/kenya-health-ministry-corruption-us-foreign-aid-606624> (accessed 23 August 2017).

Gallup International (2014) *Corruption Tops the List as the World's Most Important Problem According to WIN/Gallup International's Annual Poll*, Gallup International, Sofia. Available from: <http://www.gallup-international. bg/en/Publications/71-Publications/181-Corruption-Tops-the-List-as-the-World%E2%80%99s-Most-Important-Problem-According-to-WIN-Gallup-International%E2%80%99s-Annual-Poll> (accessed 25 August 2017).

Gyimah-Brempong, K. (2002) 'Corruption, economic growth, and income inequality in Africa', *Economics of Governance* 3 (3): 183–209 <https://doi. org/10.1007/s101010200045>.

Hope, K.R. (2017) 'Corruption in Kenya', in K.R. Hope, *Corruption and Governance in Africa*, pp. 61–123, Palgrave Macmillan, Cham.

Hung Mo, P. (2001) 'Corruption and economic growth', *Journal of Comparative Economics* 29 (1): 66–79 <https://doi.org/10.1006/jcec.2000.1703>.

Iarossi, G. (2009) *An Assessment of the Investment Climate in Kenya*, World Bank, Washington DC. Available from: <https://openknowledge.worldbank.org/ handle/10986/2603> (accessed 10 February 2020).

Journalists for Justice (2015) *Black and White: Kenya's Criminal Racket in Somalia*, Journalists for Justice, Nairobi. Available from: <https://jfjustice. net/wp-content/uploads/2020/01/Black-and-White-web.pdf> (accessed 10 February 2020).

Kasami, D. (2015) 'KDF soldiers looted KSh 74 million through fake tours, audit', Tuko.co.ke. Available from: <https://www.tuko.co.ke/25331-kdf-officers-looted-ksh-74-million-through-fake-tours-audit.html> (accessed 25 August 2017).

KNBS (2016) *Economic Survey 2016*, Kenya National Bureau of Statistics (KNBS), Nairobi. Available from: <https://www.ke.undp.org/content/dam/kenya/ docs/IEG/Economic%20Survey%202016.pdf> (accessed 10 February 2020).

Kushner, J. (2013) 'Mall attack to cost Kenya $200 million in tourism', *USA Today*, 1 October. Available from: <https://www.usatoday.com/story/news/ world/2013/10/01/kenya-mall-attack-tourism/2903005/> (accessed 24 August 2017).

Leftie, P. and Olilo, C. (2016) 'Betrayal in Rio: how mismanagement has left our heroes fuming', *Daily Nation*, 14 August. Available from: <http://www. nation.co.ke/news/The-scandal-of-Kenya-s-Rio-Olympics/1056-3343980-kvao27z/index.html> (accessed 10 February 2020).

Mathare Social Justice Centre (2017) 'Who is next? A participatory action research report against the normalization of extrajudicial executions in Mathare', Mathare Social Justice Centre, Nairobi.

Mauro, P. (1995) 'Corruption and growth', *Quarterly Journal of Economics* 110 (3): 681–712 <https://doi.org/10.2307/2946696>.

Muchiri, J. and Nyawira, L. (2014) 'Death toll of killer brew rises to 94', *The Standard*, 11 May. Available from: <https://www.standardmedia.co.ke/article/2000119687/death-toll-of-killer-brew-rises-to-94> (accessed 25 August 2017).

Murphy, K.M., Shleifer, A., and Vishny, R.W. (1993) 'Why is rent-seeking so costly to growth?', *American Economic Review* 83 (2): 409–14 <https://doi. org/10.2307/2117699>.

Murumba, S. (2016) 'Revealed: taxpayers lose Sh5bn in NYS-style Afya House theft', *Business Daily*, 26 October. Available from: <https://www.

businessdailyafrica.com/news/Revealed--Taxpayers-lose-Sh5bn-in-NYS-style-Afya-House-theft/539546-3430494-cufcplz/index.html> (accessed 29 December 2019).

Mutahi, P. (2015) 'Just when Kenya's military needs more civilian oversight, a proposed bill calls for less', *African Arguments*, 1 October. Available from: <http://africanarguments.org/2015/10/01/just-when-kenyas-military-needs-more-civilian-oversight-a-proposed-bill-calls-for-less/> (accessed 25 August 2017).

Mwangi, A. and Onyango, S. (2005) 'Uhuru orders GSU to lead war on illicit alcohol in Central', Mediamax Network, 2 July. Available from: <http://www.mediamaxnetwork.co.ke/people-daily/152956/uhuru-orders-gsu-to-lead-war-on-illicit-alcohol-in-central/> (accessed 25 August 2017).

Mwanzia, M. (2016) 'Machakos is a pothole-free zone, says Mutua as he launches reporting hotline', *The Star*, 7 October. Available from: <https://www.the-star.co.ke/news/2016/10/07/machakos-is-a-pothole-free-zone-says-mutua-as-he-launches-reporting_c1433385> (accessed 10 September 2017).

Ombati, C. (2015) 'Audit report: Kenya's military bought 32 faulty vehicles', *The Standard*, 29 July. Available from: <https://www.standardmedia.co.ke/article/2000170767/audit-report-kenya-s-military-bought-32-faulty-vehicles> (accessed 25 August 2017).

Pew Research Center (2014) *Indians Reflect on their Country and the World*, Pew Research Center, Washington DC. Available from: <http://www.pewglobal.org/2014/03/31/indians-reflect-on-their-country-the-world/> (accessed 25 August 2017).

PwC (2019) *Family Business Survey 2018: The Values Effect*, PricewaterhouseCoopers (PwC) Kenya, Nairobi. Available from: <https://www.pwc.com/ke/en/publications/family-business-survey.html> (accessed 29 December 2019).

Reuters (2016) 'Sh608 billion of Kenya budget lost to corruption every year – EACC chairman Kinisu', *The Star*, 10 March. Available from: <http://www.the-star.co.ke/news/2016/03/10/sh608-billion-of-kenya-budget-lost-to-corruption-every-year-eacc_c1310903> (accessed 24 August 2017).

Royal Society of Chemistry (n.d.) 'Selenium: element information, properties and uses. Periodic table'. Available from: <http://www.rsc.org/periodic-table/element/34/selenium> (accessed 10 September 2017).

Shiundu, A. (2010) 'US suspends Kenya education cash', *Daily Nation*, 26 January. Available from: <http://www.nation.co.ke/News/-/1056/849984/-/vpg3t6/-/index.html> (accessed 25 August 2017).

Stapele, N. van (2016) '"We are not Kenyans": extra-judicial killings, manhood and citizenship in Mathare, a Nairobi ghetto', *Conflict, Security and Development* 16 (4): 301–25 <https://doi.org/10.1080/14678802.2016.1200313>.

Stephenson, M. (2014) 'Yes, corruption is bad for development. No, corruption is not a Western obsession', Global Anticorruption Blog, 29 April. Available from: <https://globalanticorruptionblog.com/2014/04/29/yes-corruption-is-bad-for-development-no-corruption-is-not-a-western-obsession-2/> (accessed 25 August 2017).

TJRC (2013) *TJRC Final Report: Volume IIB (22 May 2013 Version)*, Truth, Justice and Reconciliation Commission, Nairobi. Available from: <http://digitalcommons.law.seattleu.edu/tjrc/3/> (accessed 23 August 2017).

Torabi, Y. (2012) 'The growing challenge of corruption in Afghanistan: reflections on a survey of the Afghan people. Part 3 of 4', Occasional Paper 15, Asia Foundation, San Francisco. Available from: <http://asiafoundation. org/resources/pdfs/FNLcorruptionchapterOccasionalPaperJuly30.pdf> (accessed 25 August 2017).

TransparencyInternational(2013)*GlobalCorruptionBarometer2013*,Transparency International, Berlin. Available from: <https://www.transparency. org/gcb2013/report> (accessed 10 February 2020).

Transparency International (2014) *The East African Bribery Index 2014*, Transparency International, Berlin. Available from: <http://tikenya. org/wp-content/uploads/2017/06/east-african-bribery-index-2014.pdf> (accessed 23 August 2017).

Transparency International Ghana (2011) 'Release of report of the Voice of the People 2011', Transparency.org, 9 December. Available from: <https://www. transparency.org/news/pressrelease/20111209_votp_report> (accessed 25 August 2017).

Wasuna, B. (2017) 'Treasury now disowns eCitizen platform company', *Business Daily*, 13 November. Available from: <http://www.businessdailyafrica. com/news/Treasury-now-disowns-eCitizen-platform-company/539546- 4185702-15ly2cq/index.html> (accessed 16 December 2017).

World Bank (2000) *Poverty: Listen to the Voices, Voices of the Poor*. Available from: <http://web.worldbank.org/WBSITE/EXTERNAL/TOPICS/ EXTPOVERTY/0,,contentMDK:20612465~menuPK:336998~pagePK: 148956~piPK:216618~theSitePK:336992~isCURL:Y,00.html#4> (accessed 25 August 2017).

World Bank (2015) 'Net ODA received (% of central government expense), World Development Indicators'. Data available from: <http://data.world-bank.org/indicator/DT.ODA.ODAT.XP.ZS> (accessed 25 August 2017).

Wrong, M. (2014) 'Everyone is corrupt in Kenya, even grandmothers', *Foreign Policy*, 6 May. Available from: <https://foreignpolicy.com/2014/05/06/ everyone-is-corrupt-in-kenya-even-grandmothers/> (accessed 25 August 2017).

CHAPTER 8

Living the dream: Hopeful stories of achievement and aspiration

Abstract

While Kenya Financial Diaries participants believed their lives were on an upward trajectory in 2015, there is reason to believe that this might be changing in Kenya at large. New evidence suggests increasing divergence between macro-level economic growth and the feelings of economic welfare among ordinary Kenyans. As of 2015, many study participants aspired to and succeeded in building new homes, educating their children, affirming their social status, having fun, and staying sane. Their narratives of achievement and aspiration demonstrate important links between material and emotional well-being. They believed that their own development was in their hands and that life would keep on improving through hard work and disciplined saving. We ask whether such feelings are warranted in light of the structural constraints we observe in people's lives throughout the book.

Keywords: aspirations, economic divergence, hope, achievement, structure and agency

In late 2015, I went to visit Nancy, a respondent we met in Chapter 7, 'Being a citizen', with Catherine Wanjala, one of our project researchers. Nancy was a popular *changaa* brewer and seller in one of our research sites in Western Kenya. I had been to her home a number of times before. We had arrived for an early interview, at around 8am during the growing season. As we walked to her home, neighbors shouted their greetings from their plots, bent over weeding. In Nancy's sitting room, three early morning drinkers were dressed up like they were heading to town, sitting quietly and sipping from small glasses, playing with their phones while the stereo blasted dance tunes and the sun poured in through the open front door, filling the cheerful room.

Nancy sent her patrons to take their drinks on the road so that we could talk. She seemed to look forward to these visits with Catherine. She would update her on the latest happenings of her life, the struggles and the achievements, with full-hearted humour. I remember one long story that started with a lament about her unfaithful husband that somehow turned into a comedic re-enactment, with her satirizing her husband's imagined pick-up lines: 'You know, he has no money to give them, just the contents of the shop, which

http://dx.doi.org/10.3362/9781788531207.008

I stocked! He is probably like, "Hey girl, let me help you out with some free sanitary pads."'

On this visit, her husband was again the butt of her jokes as she told us about what felt to her like a pressing need: paying her parents some dowry. She and her husband – like many couples – were not formally married before they had their first child. In fact, it was a bit of a scandal. At that time, her husband was in a seminary, studying to become a Catholic priest. Nancy herself was on track to go to college. When their first son was born, Nancy's parents raised him for the first four years of his life so that Nancy could study, and she was extremely grateful for that support. Now that this first son was 11 years old, she felt that the debt to her parents had become more urgent than any other spending she and her husband might do. She was frustrated that her husband still had made no attempt to settle this debt – one that was squarely his, she added – after all these years. I tried to confirm, wondering if he has made some small contributions, 'So he hasn't paid anything at all yet?'

'Nothing! Not. Even. A. Cat!' she exclaimed, throwing up her hands and bursting into laughter.

A whole-life view

Naomi was one of many respondents whose lives were full, not just of struggle but also of humour, community, ambition, and achievement. Participants in the Financial Diaries had difficult lives. Our research tools – tracking the ins and outs of money flowing around households when there was so little to actually track – shined a spotlight on the most difficult parts of those lives. But it would be misleading to say that their lives were characterized only by the resources they lacked. For the most part, our respondents were not miserable, and few would even call themselves 'poor'. Instead, alongside struggle dwelled honour and achievement, boredom and entertainment. There were celebrations and lamentations, mirth and monotony. There was the simple ordinariness of ordinary life.

Apart from not having enough money, most respondents felt pretty good about other dimensions of their lives. What's more, they expressed earnest optimism about their economic futures. The overwhelming majority shared the hope that an improvement in material circumstance was just around the corner. Their economic dreams were mostly modest and achievable, focused on comfort rather than accumulation. Even more than personal success, pride and comfort came from caring for one's family, helping children, siblings, and parents build a house, finish school, and escape the worst of times when a health shock struck.

Our respondents believed that their economic lives were set to improve, that even within five years they would see an end to the stress of scarcity and replace it with the pride of securing a comfortable life. Indeed, many in our sample felt that they had already achieved that basic level of comfort, even if few deemed themselves 'financially successful.' Working together, they were already bringing forth their own *maendeleo* (development), and they believed that their children would have even better lives, so long as they cultivated the personal virtue of hard work. It is an inspiring, if not altogether realistic, world view.

Scarcity in context

Throughout this book, we have explored the many ways in which scarcity shaped different, sometimes unexpected, realms of people's lives. One example was relationships. We demonstrated the ways in which money was exchanged among networks, helping people move towards collective goals, but also about how money altered relationships of power within the household. What we have not seen are the ways in which respondents themselves judged their own well-being.

On each biweekly visit, our team asked all adult members of the household four simple questions to assess their perceived well-being: economic well-being, happiness, relationships, and confidence. Respondents answered, giving each dimension a score of 1 for very poor to 5 for very good. These questions often served as a starting point for a conversation about what was currently going on in their lives, stories documented throughout this book.

The scores themselves also tell an interesting story. In Figure 8.1, you see histograms of respondents' average individual scores in each category. A quick glance shows that a significant number regularly feel uneasy about their economic situation. However, average happiness, relationships, and confidence scores are much higher, only rarely dipping below a 3, the neutral score.

The only statistically significant difference in average scores across men and women was in the area of confidence, with men slightly more likely to report higher levels of confidence on a regular basis. However, women were more likely to report a lower minimum score at some point throughout the study in all four dimensions of well-being.

The relationship between our measures of well-being and poverty were more complicated. Respondents in households living below the $2 per day poverty line (72 per cent of our sample) were more likely to report lower average scores across most dimensions of well-being (excluding confidence). However, individual incomes had no statistically significant relationship to well-being in terms of happiness or relationships.

All this suggests that, yes, scarcity can make everything in life more challenging, but it does not necessarily preclude well-being in a broader sense, especially once a person has escaped some threshold of absolute poverty. It does not force people to become downtrodden and defeated. It does not stop a large number of people from living what they feel are good lives. It does not stop them from desiring more or from constantly driving themselves forward for their own sakes and for their children.

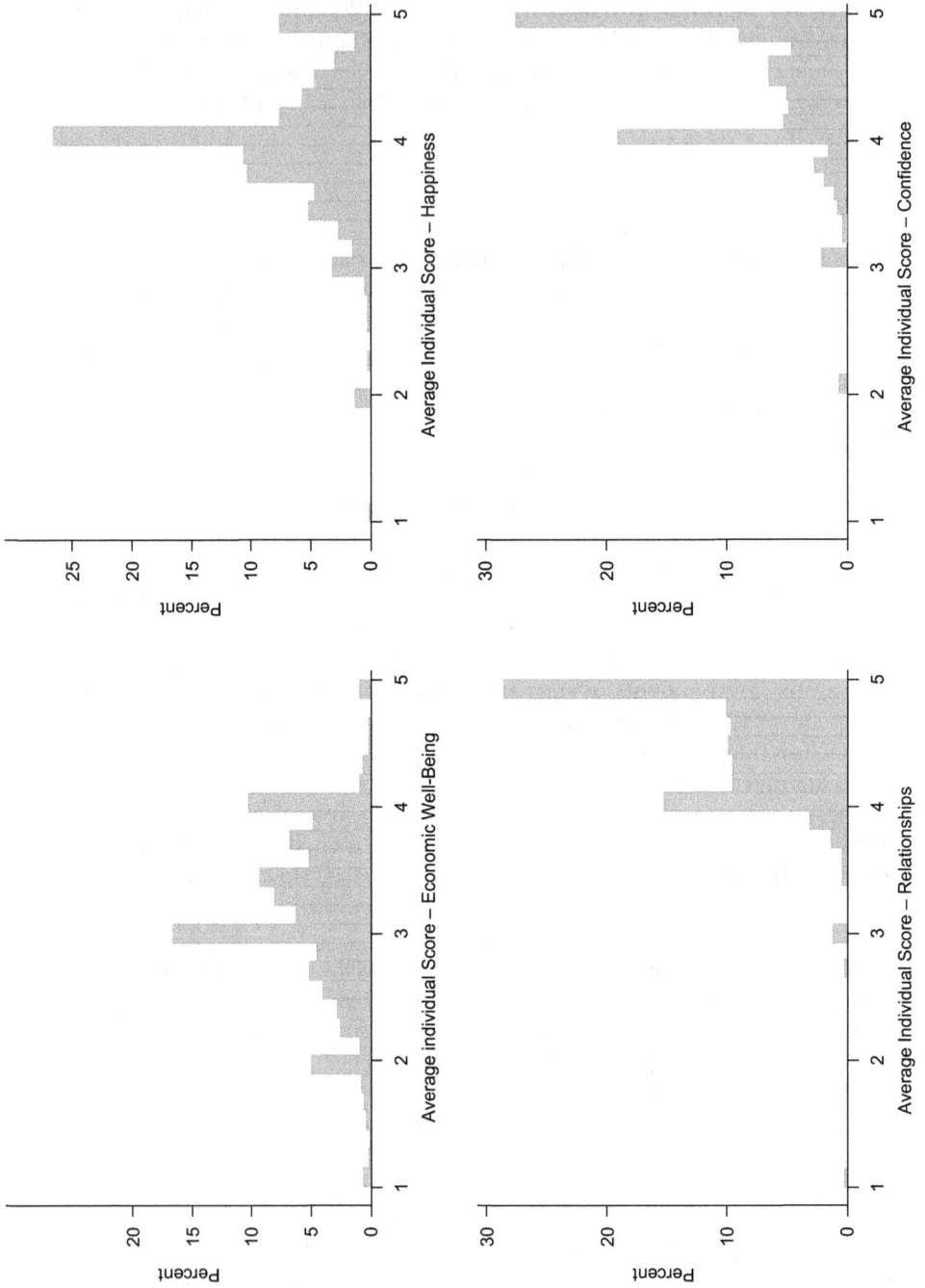

Figure 8.1 Average individual scores across four dimensions of well-being.

Aspiration and achievement

We have also seen throughout this book that the drive for personal and familial economic advancement, the commitment to *maendeleo*, is strong and enduring. It is about constant improvement, not just reaching some threshold of satisfaction. Although only a modest share of respondents – 22% – believed that they were already financially successful at the end of the Diaries study in 2013, nearly all had accomplished important life goals that served as a source of personal pride. Among the most common sources of pride were having children, raising them with strong values, and sending them through school. Many respondents were proud of starting and running businesses, acquiring land, and building homes. Also very high up on the list was being able to help others: to build a home for a parent, pay a medical bill for an extended family member, or send younger siblings to school.

Setting and accomplishing financial goals was a habit. At any given moment, we could ask respondents about their 'projects' – those forward-looking investments they were planning to make – and get a clear response and plan to achieve them. We documented these at the close of the Diaries in 2013 and asked about how those plans had gone during our update in 2015. Overwhelmingly, respondents had accomplished at least some of these goals, foremost among them paying substantial sums in school fees.

Respondents tended to have very similar financial goals for their families. They wanted to educate their children in the best possible schools to the high-est possible levels, have good relationships with their relatives, build perma-nent homes, open and expand businesses, and acquire small pieces of land both to farm and to pass on to their children. The vision is there, and most were taking incremental steps every year towards those goals.

By and large, those investments were paying off. When we visited respon-dents for the 2015 update, we found that median monthly household income had risen from about KES 7,955[1] ($80) to KES 10,541 ($105). The median house-hold had experienced about a 31 per cent increase in real per capita income, which translated into about KES 614 ($6) per month per capita, a substantial if not transformative increase. Poverty, as measured by income[2] per capita falling below $2/day, had decreased from 67 per cent to 55 per cent of households. Subjectively, 49 per cent of households in the update reported that their eco-nomic situation had improved since the Diaries period. (Eighteen per cent reported that things were more or less the same, and 33 per cent reported that things were worse.) Respondents' investments – primarily in business – were the main drivers of improving conditions.

Not only did many households experience real improvements in economic well-being between 2013 and 2015, the overwhelming majority – 82 per cent – expected things to get even better in five years. For many, this was an opti-mism grounded in real changing conditions in their lives. Many had children finishing school or training programmes. They expected them to soon begin working and remitting money home to their parents, our respondents. They were making investments in livestock, rental houses, and fruit trees, and within a few years they expected those investments to generate returns. Others were expanding their businesses or had recently made lifestyle changes they thought would put them on a better track. All of these justifications represented not just hope, but agency, what Lybbert and Wydick (2018) called 'aspirational optimism'. A smaller share simply had hope; they hoped that positive trends in their lives would continue or that 'God will provide'.

Similarly, many expect their children's lives to be better than their own. About 68 per cent of respondents with children expect that their children will be financially successful, although 25 per cent were not sure and 6 per cent were worried that their children would not enjoy much success. What was the source of this optimism? Overwhelmingly, without prompting, parents told us, 'Because I am working hard to pay school fees.' They fully expect that educational investments will bring bountiful returns. And, they told us, children will be successful if they are hard-working. '*Bila kutafuta juu chini, utarudi mkono tupu,*' remarked one respondent. 'Without hustling up and down, you will come back empty.' Success depends on everyone's hard work. What they did not say is that their children will be successful if Kenya keeps growing, if the country creates more jobs, if politics remain stable, or if structural barriers to the advancement of ordinary people fall.

The life stories of respondents are collages of all that is inspiring and tragic about living on little in Kenya. In spite of all the struggle, ordinary people lean towards hope. They can see around them examples of people who made it, who invested their way into better, more stable lives. They look around and see people like Christopher, who grew up in what he considered debilitating poverty in a large family in Mumias, a sugar-producing region of Kenya. As a child, he would work in the sugar farms to earn money for his educational expenses. When he finished primary school, there was no way his parents could afford for him to continue. He moved to a small city, where his brother-in-law gave him a place to stay and food to eat in exchange for helping out in his spice business. Christopher came with almost nothing, only the clothes on his back. 'I only had one shoe, *akala*, which is made up of used automobile tyres.'

Once he was ready to start a family of his own, his brother-in-law lent him some spice stock to help him get started. Slowly, he grew that business, keeping expenses low, with his wife living in a rural area. Over about 10 years, he built a home for his family. In 2008 he took another big leap, borrowing from a bank to expand his business. That paid off, and he took out two other loans to buy motorbikes and further increase the family income. He was able to buy land, which he hopes to develop into apartments one day. 'I am successful,' he told us. 'I am going to be somebody's landlord one day.'

A cruel kind of hope?

In an influential 2004 essay, Arjun Appadurai argued that the cultural 'capacity to aspire' was something development practitioners ought to recognize and work to cultivate among the poor. He argued that the poor were 'invariably' deprived of this capacity, which he described as the skill or 'navigational capacity' to pursue their socio-economic goals. Appadurai wrote:

> In strengthening the capacity to aspire, conceived as a cultural capacity, especially among the poor, the future-oriented logic of development could find a natural ally, and the poor could find the resources required to contest and alter the conditions of their own poverty. (Appadurai, 2004)

Other researchers have explored this idea as well: the idea that a sense of optimism and agency can – at least marginally – make low-income people try things, take risks, and make investments that help improve their situation (Ray, 2006; Duflo, 2012; Dalton et al., 2016; Galiani et al., 2018).

While this may be true in a marginal sense, our Kenyan respondents seemed to have the capacity to aspire – individually and socially – in abundance. They demonstrated both hope and agency, albeit not at all times nor in equal measures. They pursued good lives and often found them. They were fully dedicated to the project of *maendeleo* and upliftment. They were devoted savers and planners. They could articulate clearly their past achievements, they worked themselves into better living conditions, and they could describe for us how they got there. They expected that their children would be even more successful – provided, of course, that they work hard, stay in school, and stay focused. The success of their families, they believed, was completely up to them. They have bought into the *harambee* (community self-help) narrative, which goes back to Jomo Kenyatta, that hard work and entrepreneurial hustle will deliver results for families, communities, and the nation.

But in some ways it is a cruel form of optimism, one in which poor people swallow the blame for their own poverty in a country where only 16 per cent of workers have formal jobs and where ordinary people lack access to affordable healthcare and education, while newspaper headlines proclaiming the latest public theft of resources constantly remind people of the public goods that might have been. Between the poor and their aspirations sit a predatory state, restrictive gender norms, an oligopolistic, unpredictable economy, threats of violence and theft, and the forces of globalization further concentrating wealth and power.

In our 2015 update study, our participants were optimistic about the future despite all that. They believed things were mostly getting better, and that Kenya still afforded them the space and freedom they needed to make their own futures even brighter. However, there are reasons to believe that the space may be shrinking. In the 2019 FinAccess study, only 24 per cent of Kenyans felt that their economic situation was improving; 51 per cent felt it was getting worse. The percentage of the population that is considered financially healthy dropped from 39 per cent to 22 per cent between 2016 and 2019, despite real GDP growth over the period of between 5 per cent and 6 per cent per year.

This divergence between macro-growth and the declining well-being of ordinary people ought to give us pause. All that individual agency, the hope, the ambition, the dedicated saving and investing we observe among our respondents only matters in as much as structures make space for such virtues to pay off. It calls us to care about both micro-level decisions and behaviours and how those interact with social, political, and market systems. It demands that we listen differently and more expansively in our research and that we look for possibilities for change beyond the so-called 'low-hanging fruit' solutions.

Towards knowing better

The Kenya Financial Diaries allowed us an opportunity to take what David Roodman called 'a good long stare' at poverty (Roodman, 2009). Through that long stare, we started to see some known realities in new ways. We saw the improvised livelihoods of ordinary people come to life and saw just how elastic incomes could be – both up and down. We could see in greater depth the ways in which families grew together, particularly through the importance of remittances as both an income source and a risk mitigation strategy. We gained a new appreciation of the importance of small enterprises, recognizing the serious impediments to their growth, which were just as much about limited markets as about limited capital. A close look at money management highlighted just how much energy ordinary people were putting into investing in their own development, in spite of the barrage of demands on their meagre incomes. To protect those savings and that hope in the future, respondents held a huge share of their savings in illiquid form, which made dealing with small shocks often stressful. Healthcare was one of those key areas in which the lack of even small sums meant that people went without important care and where 'cheap' services were often quite expensive, as inaccurate diagnoses and incomplete treatment compounded the costs of care and too often ended in long illnesses, lost work, and premature death.

Listening to the stories of our participants added new depth to our understanding of how social roles shape the experience of poverty. We gained a deeper understanding of what it is like to transition into adulthood, navigating all the challenges of growing up while also facing immediate pressures to earn money and – for girls – have children. We saw in sharp relief the ways in which gender roles have an impact on life trajectories and livelihoods. We observed that the nature of cash flows of different family members – not just their total incomes – can affect who gets to decide the family's future investments and which types of development goals become prioritized. And, finally, we ventured into the territory of the state, seeing the ways in which government agents shaped the fairness of the playing field, exacerbating inequality and jeopardizing people's basic security.

Our respondents have given us a fuller view of what it is like to live on little, both the challenges and the hope, that promise of *maendeleo*. The broad picture they painted suggests new directions for development practitioners, particularly in the ways in which we carry out micro-interventions while keeping wider structures and systems in mind. If we are able to do that well, we might move from just knowing better to doing better, easing the painful trade-offs low-income people make today while helping them build more prosperous tomorrows.

Endnotes

1. This accounts for inflation and excludes households who did not participate in the update.
2. Due to time constraints, we did not measure consumption in the update. At the time of the Diaries, 72% of the 298 households completing the study fell below the $2/day poverty line on a consumption basis.

References

Appadurai, A. (2004) 'The capacity to aspire: culture and the terms of recognition', in V. Rao and M. Walton (eds), *Culture and Public Action*, pp. 59–84, World Bank, Washington DC.

Dalton, P.S., Ghosal, S., and Mani, A. (2016) 'Poverty and aspirations failure', *Economic Journal* 126 (590): 165–88 <https://doi.org/10.1111/ecoj.12210>.

Duflo, E. (2012) 'Human values and the design of the fight against poverty', Tanner Lectures, Mahindra Humanities Center and Office of the President, Harvard University, Cambridge MA. Available from: <http://mahindrahumanities.fas.harvard.edu/content/lecture-1-esther-duflo-human-values-and-design-fight-against-poverty> (accessed 17 August 2018).

Galiani, S., Gertler, P., and Undurraga, R. (2018) 'The audacity of hope: poverty and aspirations', *Voxdev*, 24 April. Available from: <https://voxdev.org/topic/public-economics/audacity-hope-poverty-and-aspirations> (accessed 17 August 2018).

Lybbert, T.J. and Wydick, B. (2018) 'Poverty, aspirations, and the economics of hope', *Economic Development and Cultural Change* 66 (4): 709–53 <https://doi.org/10.1086/696968>.

Ray, D. (2006) 'Aspirations, poverty, and economic change', in A.V. Banerjee, Benabou, R., and Mookherjee, D. (eds), *Understanding Poverty*, pp. 409–22, Oxford University Press, New York.

Roodman, D. (2009) 'Review of portfolios of the poor: how the world's poor live on $2 a day', Center for Global Development, 23 May. Available from: <https://www.cgdev.org/blog/review-portfolios-poor-how-worlds-poor-live-2-day> (accessed 31 December 2019).

APPENDIX
Methodological note

Origins of this project

The data in this book were derived from the Kenya Financial Diaries project, which was funded jointly by the Bill & Melinda Gates Foundation's Gateway Financial Innovations for Savings (GAFIS) project[1] and Financial Sector Deepening (FSD) Kenya with the aim of understanding in depth low-income Kenyans' financial lives. Bankable Frontier Associates (BFA) led the project in Kenya in partnership with Digital Divide Data (DDD).

By the time the project was starting, M-Pesa had already been widely adopted. One of the largest banks in the country, Equity Bank, was in the process of rolling out an expansive agent network as well. The infrastructure enabling outreach of financial services to remote areas and underserved communities was developing rapidly. Our partners hoped that this research would help shape the next generation of services enabled by that infrastructure.

As the project was getting under way, BFA was also involved in a number of other Financial Diaries studies in other countries, both as part of the GAFIS project and with the start-up of the US Financial Diaries.[2] As much as possible, the project teams tried to harmonize tools and protocols to enable easier cross-country comparisons. Such comparisons appear in one paper looking at cash and cashless payments and another that analysed gender and financial management (Zollmann and Cojocaru, 2015; Zollmann and Sanford, 2016).

Sampling

Sampling in a Financial Diaries study is always a challenge. Often, the hope is to represent the behaviours and experiences of a broad population of interest. However, statistically representative sampling would be very expensive and logistically challenging, since interviewers must visit the same sample of households every two weeks for an extended period. It is also important that families mostly see the same interviewer over time, building a relationship of trust and understanding, which improves data quality and depth.

Our focus in the study was on Kenya's low-income households. We knew that our sample would skew to higher levels of poverty compared with nationally representative surveys. However, within that broad universe of low-income households, we hoped to capture as much of Kenya's diversity as possible, reflecting key features of the wider population in somewhat similar proportions. We knew that the most recent census found a 70 per cent to

30 per cent rural–urban split in the country, so that became our first target. We then asked an advisory group composed of local academics, development practitioners, and central bank researchers for their input on which parts of the country to include. Our hope was to capture a sample of 300 households with 10 researchers (each covering 30 households). We chose to pair those researchers regionally, so that they could support one another. That meant selecting five regions of focus. After much discussion, our advisory group agreed on the areas for the research, because they represented a large share of the various ethnic and livelihood zones in the country:

- Nairobi, the country's capital, full of diverse forms of urban livelihoods;
- Makueni, a dry, food-insecure, rural area east of Nairobi;
- Mombasa, where we could access both a second urban site connected to the port and a rural site in a region with high levels of rural poverty;
- Eldoret, where we could include a small number of urban residents and a larger number of rural families producing both cash crops (tea) and food crops (maize); and
- Vihiga, where we would observe smallholder families in the densely populated western part of the country, and where we might also pick up some families participating in savings groups supported by CARE, a grantee of FSD Kenya.

Based on this guidance, our team visited dozens of communities in these areas to select specific groups of focus by meeting local officials and talking with local businesspeople, teachers, and others about the region in general and each community in particular. We wanted to make sure that they reflected the interests of the advisory group and to receive confirmation from local authorities that our team would be welcome.

After recruiting and training field staff, each member was assigned to a particular site, based largely on language fit. Researchers would live in or near their research sites for the duration of the study. Once placed, researchers were given some time to simply settle in, get to know their communities, and introduce themselves to local government officials, community health workers, teachers, and village elders. Typically, area chiefs would introduce them to the community at large in a public meeting (called *barazas*), easing their way into interviewing families for screening. Village elders and community health workers then introduced the researchers to a wide range of families, and researchers made appointments to go and visit in private later. During that session, researchers informed families about the demands of the research and talked about initial levels of interest. Those who were interested completed a short screening interview, which researchers captured on tablets and submitted to the office daily.

Unlike other kinds of representative research, one of our screening questions was about families' interest and their willingness to commit to such a long-term, time-consuming research process. We were concerned that high levels of attrition would undermine the value of the study. This also meant, however, that we likely underrepresent households that were most severely affected by addiction and mental illness.

The team had a set of household characteristic targets in mind for a sample that would largely reflect the Kenyan population, in terms of things such as a rural–urban split, education levels of household heads, and self-reported main livelihoods. This helped guide the screening process, which took about two months. Families selected by the office were then visited again so that researchers could walk them through the informed consent process and answer questions. All adult members of the household had to consent for a household to be included. This often took multiple visits to be sure that respondents fully understood their commitment and so that researchers could answer potential respondents' questions. Those who chose not to participate were replaced with a pre-screened substitute household.

In total, researchers screened 647 households, and we started the research with an initial sample of about 350. The research took place during an election year – the first election under a new constitution and the first following the violent 2007 elections. We decided to oversample to protect the study in the event of election-related displacement that might push respondents out of our reach. In reality, only a small number of respondents ever voluntarily dropped out or relocated beyond where we could reach them. However, we had to release about 10 families when one area we were working in became too dangerous for our researcher to visit. We dropped another three or four households because we felt that they were consistently misleading researchers, and we were unable to gain enough of their trust to get clear and consistent data. Others were dropped after the elections to help researchers manage overwhelming workloads. We present quantitative data only on households that were part of the study for the entire period.

The 2015 update included all the families that we could relocate and visit for a follow-up interview. Our retention rate was quite high: 94 per cent of households that completed the Diaries study participated in the update.

Since our sample was not statistically representative, to what extent is it similar or different from Kenya as a whole? In Table A.1 below, we compare the Diaries sample with several recent, nationally representative surveys. The Diaries sample is slightly more rural than more recent studies. Diaries households are larger as well, perhaps because they are more rural and perhaps because, over time, researchers elicit a more comprehensive household roster.

Diaries households were less likely to be headed by men, which may be a function of how we defined a household. We did not consider individuals to be part of the household if they spent more than four nights per week away. As a consequence, men working in the city and visiting only at the weekend or a few times per year were not considered part of the household. We had no way to track their financial behaviours, even if they had significant power over the decision making of our respondents. Instead, we tracked their contributions as remittances to the households we studied.

Table A.1 Comparing the Kenya Diaries sample with recent nationally representative surveys.

	Kenya Financial Diaries 2013, 2015	Kenya Integrated Household Budget Survey (KIHBS) 2015–16	National Census 2009	Demographic and Health Survey (DHS) 2014	FinAccess 2016
Urban	31%	43.6%	32%	40.8% women; 43.9% men	37%
Rural	69%	56.4%	68%	59.2% women; 56.1% men	63%
Household size	5.2 (Diaries); 5.0 (update)	4.0	4.4	3.9	4.2
Male-headed households	54.7%	67.6%	68%	67.8%	74%
Cook primarily with firewood	62%	55%	65%	56%	63%
Main dwelling has an earth floor	52%	30%	57%	47%	57% (2009)[4]
Age of household head	47.7	44.6			
Years of education of household head[1]	8.3	8.1			
Household head with no education	5%	13.7%			
Per capita monthly consumption (KES)	3,595 (mean); 2,673 (median)[2]	7,811 (mean); 5,830 (median)[3]			
Share of consumption on food items	56.8%	54.3%			
Sample	298 households	21,773 households	38 million individuals; 8.78 million households	40,300 households	8,665 adults

Notes
[1]This was calculated using a shared methodology across the two surveys, based on raw data.
[2]This consumption figure includes consumer durables in order to equate with KIHBS' measure. It inflates 2013 figures up to 2015 using the consumer price index to adjust for inflation.
[3]The KIHBS consumption aggregate is based on different methodology, extrapolating from recall over seven days for food, 30 for non-food, and 365 for durables. KIHBS also equalizes prices across locations. The Diaries use respondent-reported expenditure figures and estimated values of food consumed from household production, taking the household average over the course of the study.
[4]There was a problem in the coding of this variable in the 2016 and 2013 FinAccess surveys.

Distribution of per capita monthly consumption (inflation adjusted) by survey

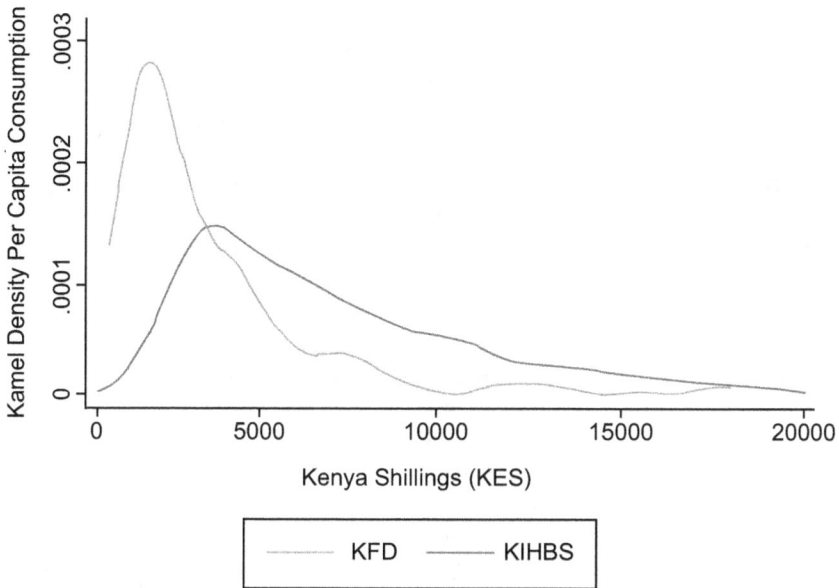

Figure A.1 Kernel density estimation for per capita monthly expenditure in the Kenya Financial Diaries and the KIHBS of 2015.

It is important to note that the Diaries sample tends to be poorer than the country as a whole. This is by design, given our focus. We attempt to gauge where the Diaries sample fits into the national picture by comparing means in Table A.1 and by comparing kernel distributions in Figure A.1. However, these measures of per capita consumption are not entirely equivalent across studies. While the Kenya Financial Diaries estimates consumption based on averages in reported actual, nominal household expenditures and consumption from household production over a long period, the KIHBS produces estimates from shorter periods of recall and by equalizing prices by region.

Data collection

Tools

Researchers often ask if they may have a copy of our research instrument. This is quite tricky since the Financial Diaries do not have just one research tool used week in and week out. Instead, our team used a custom-built tablet application that generates specific data-entry forms for each household on each visit. This application and the back-end database were developed based on one used in the South Africa Financial Diaries. Inside the application, there are specific set-up questionnaires (whose fields may always be updated), but the cash flow categories are customized by household, and completing the interview involves a complex form of interviewing around eliciting and balancing a comprehensive set of sources and uses of funds. It is very different from filling in a questionnaire from top to bottom.

Following the informed consent process, researchers guided households through the set of enrolment interviews, usually over about four sessions. These interviews captured information on household member demographics, housing conditions, a baseline registry of physical assets, income sources and histories, and a financial device inventory. Each financial device type (a bank account or M-Pesa wallet, for instance) had a separate questionnaire capturing important information: for example, when it was opened, its primary use, and other key features. Things such as income sources, financial devices, housing, and household members could be added, removed, opened, or closed at any interview in the future, but the set of enrolment interviews established these, while also giving researchers time to get to know families prior to asking very many detailed questions about their money.

When the Diaries visits began, each household had a unique data input area which reminded researchers of their personalized income sources, financial devices, and all of the household members. These regular Diaries interviews captured some non-financial information first: how are household members doing? Have there been any big events? Have there been needs that could not be met because of money (like medical care forgone)? From there, researchers moved through a process of accounting for all inflows and outflows in an iterative discussion. The application constantly balanced these, flagging when sources were greater than uses and vice versa.

Researchers also made handwritten notes about their interaction with the household during the visit. Following each interview, the researcher added these notes to the 'journal' section of the interview. These notes told the story of what was happening in households from visit to visit. They helped explain the patterns we saw in the cash flow data and were the source of many of the stories in this book.

Alongside this core data collection we also introduced a few special 'modules' on topics we wanted to understand more deeply. One of these – on risk – was administered to every household. But others, on things such as gender, financial management rules of thumb and savings groups were conducted with a smaller subset of respondents. All of these data were attached to the ongoing file on each family.

Team and training

This is a complex form of research, requiring both patient and skilled researchers and significant levels of training. Our team consisted of myself, a full-time research manager, field supervisor, data analyst, and 10 full-time field researchers. We later added a full-time driver and an additional researcher to help fill in for staff who needed a vacation and to help conduct modules and other supplementary data collection.

We staggered training sessions in intervals, first covering relationship building and recruitment, then covering enrolment interviews, and later Diaries interviewing. There were ongoing sessions on note writing and special topics. Training was provided on staff retreats and through one-on-one coaching in the field. A supervisor spoke with every researcher by phone every day to troubleshoot problems and the team had weekly calls to discuss difficult parts of the data collection process, and to share their insights with one another. We believe that this was important for improving the level of detail captured in qualitative journal entries.

Strategy

The aim of this research was to capture cash flows every two weeks. However, it was not always possible to see respondents at these exact intervals. Each interview would capture the time between visits, regardless of the exact day count. Some respondents chose to record many of their transactions on paper, although we did not require this. There were also some periods when we knew that we would need to take a break from fieldwork, including both during the elections and over the Christmas holidays. We provided respondents with worksheets during these periods, hoping that they could keep some notes on their transactions. During the elections, we also did one phone interview to check in on respondents' welfare and movements.

The depth of this research is primarily the result of strong relationships built between researchers and respondents over time. Respondents told us that they looked forward to their interviews with researchers. Even now, years after our last visits, respondents call researchers to update them on important life events. After the study finished, we went to visit each family and took a copy of our report and personalized reports for each family. We asked respondents if they would participate again, knowing now how much time it would take. Overwhelmingly, they said yes. They appreciated a chance to tell their story. Someone was listening and paying attention to their lives. Many liked the company. They could share things with the researcher that they couldn't share with neighbours or, sometimes, even spouses. As researchers, we cannot assume that this will always happen or that we are always welcome. I believe that our team, under the excellent leadership of our field supervisor in particular, put relationships first, and I believe that made a world of difference.

We also provided respondents with gifts. We did not talk about these gifts during recruitment, hoping that families would feel freer to turn down our invitation to participate in such a demanding study. When the gifts began, they came in surprise values and at surprise times to minimize their impact on respondents' financial plans. All of these gifts are documented in the cash flow data and were typically small, even relative to respondents' low incomes. Gifts were distributed on M-Pesa wherever families had an account and in cash otherwise (or where spouses disputed the funds). We also occasionally provided branded in-kind gifts from DDD (such as umbrellas). Exchanging resources is key to maintaining relationships in Kenya (Kusimba et al., 2016) and these small tokens seemed to strengthen those bonds.

Limitations

We are often asked, 'Don't people just lie?' Financial Diaries – like any kind of research that relies on interviews – is not perfect. There are bound to be things that respondents forgot or chose not to share. We have no particular way to judge the scale of those gaps. However, based on the stories respondents *did* share, I suspect that pervasive and extensive misleading reporting on expenditures and incomes is unlikely. We heard about sensitive criminal charges. We heard about gifts to mistresses and fights with spouses. For every family, the picture that emerged over time became increasingly clear, but there is simply no way that any kind of recall data can be a perfect reflection of reality.

Other researchers also ask whether the study itself produces a treatment effect in the way in which people behave. In this particular study, we have no way of knowing that for certain. It is possible that we made some participants more aware of their financial choices, potentially increasing their savings, for example. We did not have a good way of measuring this treatment effect in our study. However, one study in Uganda attempted to test the validity of self-administered Diaries among microcredit users, and found no impact on numeracy, consumption, income, or loan repayment. While Diaries participants did have slightly higher savings compared with others, this was less than the value of the incentives they received for their participation in the Diaries themselves (Smits and Günther, 2018).

The other important limitation of this research is that it is not statistically representative. It is something different from a big survey or randomized control trial. Its depth provided our team with the opportunity to have flashes of insight around experiences sometimes shared by only a few households at first. When put together, the stories gave us a chance to sit with the dissonance between existing theories and our own observations. They offered our team an opportunity to imagine new theoretical possibilities, which I hope this book has also done. I hope that other researchers will find some of these possibilities interesting enough to test in other ways.

Additional materials

Cash flow data from the Diaries study, along with case studies and a wide range of study-related reports and blog posts, can be found on the FSD Kenya website at <http://fsdkenya.org/financial-diaries/>.

Endnotes

1. See <https://bfaglobal.com/project/the-gateway-to-financial-innovations-for-savings-gafis/> (accessed 26 February 2020).
2. See <https://www.usfinancialdiaries.org/>.

References

Kusimba, S., Yang, Y., and Chawla, N. (2016) 'Hearthholds of mobile money in Western Kenya', *Economic Anthropology* 3 (2): 266–79 <https://doi.org/10.1002/sea2.12055>.

Smits, J. and Günther, I. (2018) 'Do Financial Diaries affect financial outcomes? Evidence from a randomized experiment in Uganda', *Development Engineering* 3: 72–82 <https://doi.org/10.1016/j.deveng.2018.02.001>.

Zollmann, J. and Cojocaru, L. (2015) *Cashlite Report: Are We There Yet? Rethinking the Evolution of Electronic Payments in Kenya*, FSD Kenya, Nairobi. Available from: <http://fsdkenya.org/publication/cashlite-report-are-we-there-yet-rethinking-the-evolution-of-electronic-payments-in-kenya-based-on-evidence-in-the-kenyan-and-south-african-financial-diaries/> (accessed 5 August 2018).

Zollmann, J. and Sanford, C. (2016) *A Buck Short: What Financial Diaries Tell Us about Building Financial Services that Matter to Low-Income Women*, Omidyar Network, Redwood City CA. Available from: <https://www.omidyar.com/sites/default/files/file_archive/Pdfs/16-07-01_A_Buck_Short_Report_Digital_FINAL.pdf> (accessed 7 February 2020).

Index

Page numbers in *italics* refer to figures and tables.

accumulating savings and credit association (ASCA) 40, 43
active money, necessity of 59–61
Afrobarometer surveys 128, 148–9, 163
agriculture 20, 22–4
  gender differences 101
al-Shabaab terrorists 154, 155
alcohol brewing (*changaa*), counterproductive crackdown on 149–54
alcoholism and mental health 80–2
apprenticeships 87
aspiration
  and achievement 179–80
  'capacity to aspire' 180–1

Bankable Frontier Associates (BFA) 185
Bill & Melinda Gates Foundation 3
  GAFIS project 185
birth certificates 162–3
borrowing *see* credit sources; M-Shwari; savings and credit associations (SCAs/ SACCO); social networks
bribery *see* corruption; police
budget stretching vs income growth 55–9
businesses 28–34
  youth-owned 86, 87

'capacity to aspire' 180–1
cash transfers ('non-employment income') 24
casual work (*vibarua*) 28
chiefs 158–9
children 71–4
  delayed healthcare 129
  of early partnerships 82
  family size 110–11
  future lives 180
  see also women
children and young people 69–70
  alcoholism and mental health 80–2
  lure of crime 79–80
  partnerships 82–4
  pressure to earn 77–9
  and success of family 70–1
  towards independence 84–6
  youth transitions 81, 86–7
  see also education/schools
church/religious teachings on gender roles 108, 114–15

confidence, as dimension of well-being 177, *178*
corruption
  and access to government services 161–6
  counterproductive crackdown on *changaa* 149–54
  and denial of justice 166–7
  and development 146–9
  impact and reduction 167–8
  and insecurity 154–61
credit sources 56–8
  see also savings and credit associations (SCAs/SACCOs); social networks
crime
  and bribery 154–9
  and young men 79–80

delayed and forgone healthcare 129–31
development
  and corruption 146–9
  and gender inequality 92–5
  maendeleo 22, 26, 28, 70, 74, 177, 181, 182–3
Digital Data Divide (DDD) 185
digital financial services 43–4, 64–5
  see also M-Pesa; M-Shwari
digital technologies reducing corruption 167–8
distributed networks *see* social networks
domestic violence/beatings 93, 109, 110, 159
dowries 104, 105, 108, 116–17

e-government systems/eCitizen 167–8
early childhood 71
East African Bribery Index 148
economic growth 19
  and declining optimism 181–2
  poverty and inequality 1–2, 6–7
economic improvement 176–7, 179–80
economic well-being 177, *178*
education/schools 74–7
  fees 39, 40, 73, 75, 76–7
  funding and policies 86–7
  national examination 77–8
  premature leaving 73–4, 78–9, 82
  primary 73, 74–5
  secondary 75–8, 87
  universities and training colleges 77

electricity, access to 161–2
entrepreneurship 29
Ethics and Anti-Corruption
    Commission 147–8
extended family as primary carers 72–3

FinAccess surveys 29, 45, 101, 181
financial health concept 45
financial inclusion 44–5, 64–5
financial management 39–43
    challenges 46–64
    and financial inclusion 44–5, 64–5
Financial Sector Deepening (FSD) Kenya 2, 185
financial tools *41*, 43–4, 64–5
    see also specific types
fulfilling businesses 33–4
fungibility in money management 59–61

gangs 80, 156–7, 163–4
gender *see* women
gifts 24–7
girls' education 73
government 6, 145–6
    colonial era and independence 5–6
    e-government systems 167–8
    effective healthcare policies 137–40
    see also corruption
grandparents as primary carers 72–3

happiness, as dimension of well-being
    177, *178*
health insurance 127
    limitations of 141–2
    National Hospital Insurance Fund (NHIF)
        124, 139–40, 141
Health Policy Project 138
healthcare and corruption 163–4
healthcare financing 123–4
    costs and spending 125–8
    effective government policies 137–40
    excessive spending 131–2
    persistence of traditional medicine 136–7
    poor quality care 132–6
    underspending 128–31
Higher Education Loans Board (HELB) 77
HIV 72, 82, 98–9
    free care 131, 138–9
home ownership 95–6
hopeful stories 175–6
    aspiration and achievement 179–80
    and cruel optimism 180–2
    scarcity in context 177, *178*
    towards knowing better 182–3
    whole life view 176–7
hospital admission/inpatient care 126–7

identity cards 162–3
income generation sources 15–19
    agriculture 22–4
    businesses 28–34

cash transfers ('non-employment
    income') 24
casual work 28
gender differences 100–4
inefficiency and opportunity 34–5
livelihood patterns 19–21
'regular' employment 27
remittances and gifts ('resources
    received') 24–7
see also specific sources
income growth vs budget stretching 55–9
inefficiency and opportunity in
    businesses 34–5
inequality 1–2, 7
    gender 92–5
infertility 113–14
infidelity 105–8, 111, 112
informal businesses 30
information asymmetries in healthcare 142
inheritance practices 98
Institute of Health Metrics and Evaluation
    (IHME) 138
insurance 61
    see also health insurance

justice
    denial of 166–7
    mob 159

Kenya (overview) 1–2, 5–7
Kenya Financial Diaries 3–5
    comparison with nationally representative
        surveys *9*, *188*
    data collection 189–92
    limitations 192
    origins of project 185
    pseudonym index vii–xiv
    sample 7–10, 185–9
Kenya Household Health and Expenditure
    Survey (KHHEUS) 125–6, 128–9,
        130–1, 138, 139
Kenya shillings (KES)-US dollar ($) exchange
    rates xiv
kidnapping 156

land titles and transfers 164–6
livelihoods *see* income generation sources
loans *see* credit sources; M-Shwari; savings
    and credit associations (SCAs/
    SACCOs); social networks
low growth businesses 32–3
low investment, low revenue
    businesses 29–30
low tech businesses 31–2

M-Pesa 1, 25, 42–3, 59, 60, 102
    and agent banking 3
M-Shwari 44, 58, 59, 60
managing money *see* financial
    management

marriage
  building a future together 115–17
  expectations and realities 104–9
  and informal partnerships 82–4
maternal healthcare 112–13
maternal mortality 93
mental health 81–2
methodology *see* Kenya Financial Diaries
military recruitment, corruption in 160
mob justice 159
mobile money *see* M-Pesa; M-Shwari
money guard 43

National Hospital Insurance Fund (NHIF)
  124, 139–40, 141
National Youth Service 86
non-parental caregiving 72–3

Okoa Jahazi 44
opportunity and inefficiency in
  businesses 34–5
outpatient visits 125, 127

partnerships 82–4
  see also marriage
police
  bribes 146, 151–2, 153, 154–9
  corruption in recruitment 160–1
  flexibility and discretion 159–60
  killings 159
Portfolios of the Poor 44, 50–1
poverty
  and inequality 1–2, 6–7
  and trade-offs among expenditure
    choices 50–9
poverty reduction 6–7, 23–4
primary schools 73, 74–5
Public Expenditure Tracking Survey (PETS)
  134–5, 138
PWC Kenya Family Business Survey 149

rape 155–6, 159
recruitment, corruption in 160–1
'regular' employment 27
relationships, as dimension of well-being
  177, *178*
religious/church teachings on gender roles
  108, 114–15
remittances 20
  gender differences 102–4
  and gifts 24–7
  M-Pesa 25, 42–3, 102
risk management 25–6, 61–4
rotating savings and credit association
  (ROSCA) 40, 43, 60

savings
  liquid and illiquid 55–6, 59–61
  M-Shwari 58, 59, 60
  and risk management 63
  separate and secret, within
    marriage 116–17
savings clubs (*chamas*) 96
savings and credit associations (SCAs/
  SACCOs) 43, 60
  ASCA/ROSCA 40, 43, 60
  'Move On Development' corruption 166–7
scholarships 77, 87
secondary schools 75–8, 87
security and terrorism 149, 154–9
Shilingi kwa Shilingi report 52
shocks and responses *see* risk management
small businesses *see* businesses
social networks
  and risk management 25–6, 63–4
  vs health insurance 11–12
structure and agency 181–2

TB 129–30, 133, 138–9
temporary businesses 31
terrorism and security 149, 154–9
theft 157, 159
trade-offs among expenditure choices 50–9
traditional medicine 136–7
Transparency International: Corruption
  Perceptions Index 148
Truth, Justice and Reconciliation
  Commission 160

undifferentiated businesses 31
universities and training colleges 77
unpredictable incomes and expenses 46–50
urgent medical needs 127

welfare groups 43
well-being, four dimensions of 177, *178*
whole life view 176–7
women 91–2
  gender inequality and development 92–5
  gendered family roles and their
    enforcement 109–15
  independent livelihoods 100–4
  life experiences 95–7
  life journeys 97–100
  see also marriage; partnerships
World Bank 1, 2, 24, 75, 147, 148, 149,
  161, 162

young people *see* children and young people
youth bulge 71
youth transitions 81, 86–7

www.ingramcontent.com/pod-product-compliance
Lightning Source LLC
Chambersburg PA
CBHW070925030426
42336CB00014BA/2547